The
FOREST
and the
TREES

A Guide to
Excellent Forestry

Gordon Robinson

Foreword by Michael McCloskey
Chairman, Sierra Club

ISLAND PRESS

Washington, D.C. □ *Covelo, California*

ABOUT ISLAND PRESS

Island Press, a nonprofit organization, publishes, markets, and distributes the most advanced thinking on the conservation of our natural resources—books about soil, land, water, forests, wildlife, and hazardous and toxic wastes. These books are practical tools used by public officials, business and industry leaders, natural resource managers, and concerned citizens working to solve both local and global resource problems.

Founded in 1978, Island Press reorganized in 1984 to meet the increasing demand for substantive books on all resource-related issues. Island Press publishes and distributes under its own imprint and offers these services to other nonprofit organizations.

Funding to support Island Press is provided by The Ford Foundation, The George Gund Foundation, The William and Flora Hewlett Foundation, The Joyce Foundation, The Andrew W. Mellon Foundation, Northwest Area Foundation, Jessie Smith Noyes Foundation, Rockefeller Brothers Fund, and The Tides Foundation.

For additional information about Island Press publishing services and a catalog of current and forthcoming titles, contact Island Press, P.O. Box 7, Covelo, California 95428.

© 1988 Gordon Robinson

Library of Congress Cataloging in Publication Data

```
Robinson, Gordon.
   The forest and the trees : a guide to excellent forestry / Gordon
Robinson ; foreword by Michael McCloskey.
      p.   cm.
   Includes indexes.
   ISBN 0-933280-41-6 : $24.95.   ISBN 0-933280-40-8 (pbk.) : $17.95
   1. Forest reserves--United States--Management.  2. Forest
conservation--United States.  3. Forest policy--United States.
4. Timber--United States.  5. United States. Forest Service.
I. Title.
SD42.R63 1988
333.75'15'0973--dc19                                        88-9011
                                                                CIP
```

ISBN   0-933280-41-6
ISBN   0-933280-40-8 (pbk.)

10 9 8 7 6 5 4 3 2

Contents

Part Four
Supporting Research and Informed Opinions

Foreword

Environmentalists feel a massive sense of betrayal with respect to America's national forests. They were supposed to be the people's forests. Instead, they have come to be managed almost as if they were the timber industry's forests. They were supposed to stand in contrast to the industry's own ravaged lands but instead have become adjuncts of their lands—their reserve source of supply.

As recreationists and local activists saw this change taking place in the decade from the mid-1950s to the mid-1960s, they reacted with consternation and outrage. Lands that were supposed to serve the broad public were being managed to make up for the depletion of industry lands. How could this happen? Who authorized it? How do you fight it?

At first, those fighting on different fronts weren't sure whether there was a general pattern or whether they were merely dealing with a local anomaly. But two gathering forces were moving toward a head-on collision: the timber industry, trying to co-opt the national forests for its own ends, and a burgeoning movement of public interest activists looking to the national forests as a source of more wilderness, recreation, and environmental quality. By the late 1960s the pattern had become evident, and a public policy war had clearly broken out.

Over the past two decades the Forest Service has tried to control this conflict by desperate efforts to cast it in terms of the technicalities of forestry. This maximized its own authority and tended to keep the irate public at bay, leaving them feeling ill-equipped and inadequate in the debate with both Forest Service and timber industry officials. What volunteer knew much about "mean annual increments," "allowable cut effects," and Scribner rules?

A profound change occurred in the character of the debate in 1966 when the critics hired their first professional forester. Gordon Robinson was hired by the Sierra Club and started addressing these questions. He brought with him 27 years of credibility as the chief forester of the Southern Pacific Land Company. He was no green graduate just out of forestry school. He had successfully managed timber on one of the largest blocks of industrial timberland in the country. He had dealt with the Forest Service for years; he was privy to what the timber industry thought and its ambitions. He had seen what had worked and what had not worked, and backed it up with a good education. And he could express himself clearly and demystify seemingly complex subjects.

We no longer had to try to decode the jargon by ourselves. We had our own expert who could tell us what it was all about, and most importantly, he confirmed our suspicions that something terribly wrong was taking place. More than any single factor, Gordon enabled the environmental movement to become competitive in this field during the period 1966–1979. He enabled us to penetrate the veil of professional expertise. He evened the scales in the debates.

Gordon traveled all over the country counseling local activists and lawyers—in Alaska, Arkansas, Texas, West Virginia, Colorado, Wyoming, Montana, and up and down the West Coast. He played pivotal roles in the battles over the National Timber Supply Act, the Monongahela suit, the National Forest Management Act of 1976, The Tongass National Forest suit, the creation of the Redwood National Park and its expansion, and the California Forest Practices Act. He became the friend and inspiration for a network of forest activists across the country. Through his counseling, they became confident in dealing with the concepts and vocabulary of forestry, and, most importantly, they began to make a difference.

And while winning individual campaigns was important, something even more important began to happen. Almost single-handedly Gordon revived the tradition of idealism and courage in forestry—the tradition of Gifford Pinchot, Aldo Leopold, and Bob Marshall; the tradition that had made foresters important in conservation in the decades earlier in this century. He saw foresters as professionals having a mission apart from businessmen. He saw forestry as concerned with maintaining forests, not removing them for profit. He saw forestry concerned as much with soil, water, wildlife, and ecosystems as with timbering. His was a singular vision when so many in the profession seemed to have "sold out" or become totally cowed.

And today that vision—his vision of excellent forestry—looks more and more relevant. The pretense of the intervening decades is now threadbare: most of the industry lands in the West are cut out, and the few good old-line companies have been taken over by corporate raiders to be gutted. Even the Forest Service is admitting that things have gone too far. Many of their studies now call for reducing the allowable cuts to protect multiple-use values. And with their planning process mired in trench-warfare-like stalemates all over the country, they are beginning to admit that their efforts to stay in control as professionals are not working. They are seeing themselves more as facilitators in debates over public policy.

In *The Forest and the Trees,* Gordon tells us how we got into this imbroglio and what it will take to get out, and he supplies the activist with the information needed to help this to happen. All who read this book will be grateful to Gordon that he has at last put his insights and research into an accessible form. And we all hope that this book will build a demand for excellent forestry that will not be denied.

Michael McCloskey
Chairman, Sierra Club

Preface

Anyone can identify destructive forest practices. You don't have to be a professional forester to recognize bad forestry any more than you need to be a doctor to recognize ill health. If logging looks bad, it is bad. If a forest appears to be mismanaged, it is mismanaged. But a certain level of expertise is needed if you are going to be effective in doing something about it.

The purpose of this book is to give concerned citizens who are not foresters the technical information they need, along with summaries of relevant research, to enable them to compete with the "experts" when commenting on the plans that will determine how our national forests are to be managed. In addition, I hope that this book will be of practical help to the professional foresters who are working to change current management policies. Finally, forest owners, forestry students, and people involved with environmental impact statements should also find this work useful.

In this book I am deliberately offering a polemic in support of a return to uneven-aged management of our national forests—management in which stands of trees within a forest are small and irregular in size and shape, trees are of a variety of ages and species and are allowed to grow to maturity before being logged, and logging is done selectively and with care. This type of management safeguards the rich variety of trees and vegetation within a forest. It also protects all the forest's uses simultaneously and in perpetuity: the soil, watershed, fish and wildlife, and aesthetic beauty, and thus its value for outdoor recreation as well as its ability to supply a sustained yield of high-quality timber.

I say "a return to" deliberately, for this is how our national forests were intended to be managed when they were established early in this century. However, in the 1950s and 1960s, the private timber industry, having overcut its own lands, began to look to the public's forests for more and more of its timber supply. Industry has since become alarmingly successful in persuading the Forest Service to lose sight of its own guiding principles, to the point where "multiple use" and uneven-aged management have been replaced by "dominant use" and even-aged management of the nation's commercial forestlands.

In recent years I have been disturbed to learn that many forestry students and good conservationists who work on forestry problems do not realize how far and why the Forest Service has strayed from its purpose. Disturbed, but not surprised, because as the Forest Service and its plans and practices have become increasingly dominated by industry's view, even our great forestry schools have gone along with the changing attitude. There are some signs now that the schools may be changing again, however, to a new appreciation of the original practice of multiple-use forestry. These are signs I greet with enthusiasm.

It seems to me that one of the great difficulties with our educational institutions is that many teachers have fallen into the habit of showing both sides of controversial matters in their field without sharing their own opinions with the students. I recall, years ago, hearing instructors advising us to take stands but not doing so themselves, arguing that in their position they were obliged to be neutral. Unfortunately, we teach more by what we do than by what we say. Students tend to imitate their instructors, finding their example in this case a convenient model for keeping themselves out of trouble. Consequently, our qualified experts, those who should be leading society in their special fields, are reneging on their public responsibilities and instead leaving leadership to those who are the most concerned but who usually are less skilled.

In this book I do not intend to follow the tradition of offering a "balanced" view. Spokesmen for the timber industry and officials of the USDA Forest Service—indeed professional foresters in general—have been successfully presenting industry's point of view for many years.

As a child in the Pacific Northwest, I was shocked to see woodsmen cutting down the trees where I used to play. I argued with them that it might be all right to cut down some trees, but cutting them all and destroying the forest was wrong. A fine old Swedish lumberjack explained to me with considerable compassion that it bothered him too, but that the trees would grow back. It remained heartbreaking to me to see the forest destroyed. The woodpeckers disappeared. I no longer heard the eerie squeals of trees rubbing against each other in the wind and the hoots of owls in the twilight.

During the Depression years I worked my way through college. First I attended Marin Junior College in Kentfield, California. In those days, a statement was posted on the bulletin board at the start of each semester rating various professions by job opportunity. Every semester we changed our majors accordingly. One day, when I was complaining about my problem of choosing a profession, one of my teachers suggested I simply forget the whole thing and go to school to improve the enjoyment of life. That took an immense load off my mind, as I realized that was what I was actually doing anyhow. Consequently, I spent another year at the junior college and enrolled in a batch of courses to satisfy my curiosity: art history, philosophy, psychology, and several others.

Then I transferred to Berkeley, entering the University of California as a junior. As I enrolled, the clerk asked what I was majoring in. "I don't have a major," I answered. "Well, we can't accept your enrollment without a major," came the reply. That put me back in the dilemma I thought I had escaped from. So, I dug out the results of the *Strong Professional Aptitude Test* I had taken some years earlier. The test showed that I would very likely be happy as a doctor, chemist, physicist, farmer, minister, engineer, and something else I can't recall. Minister was scratched immediately because I didn't believe in God. (I hadn't yet heard of the Unitarians!) I systematically scratched those majors I didn't have prerequisites for, eliminated those with high lab fees, and looked to see which of the remainder had the best job opportunities. That somehow led me to foreign trade. I made out my schedule accordingly and enrolled.

That evening my phone rang. It was old Ed Griffith, a buddy of mine from Marin who had somehow managed to locate me. He wanted to visit. I was delighted because I didn't know a soul in Berkeley and was feeling very much alone. Right off he wanted to know what I was majoring in. So I told him this long story. "What's *your* major?" I asked. "Forestry." That was a new one. It wasn't on my list, and I hadn't heard of it. "What are the job opportunities?" "I don't know," he said. "Why are you taking it?" "I just want to keep them from pulling up all the trees." That sounded pretty good to me.

Ed said, "Let me see your record." I showed it to him and he made out a schedule for me in forestry. Well, I didn't have the prerequisites— it would take an extra year. The whole thing was silly.

He went home and I went to bed. Then I began tossing around and couldn't go to sleep. What shall I do tomorrow morning? I asked myself. At eight o'clock there's the class in foreign trade I had planned to take in Old South Hall, and at the same time there's one in forestry in Giannini Hall. Finally, in order to get to sleep I decided that if tomorrow turned out to be a socked-in, foggy day, as we often have in Berkeley, I'd take the foreign trade course; if it was a bright, clear day and the birds were all hollering and yelling, I'd go take the forestry course. With that I dozed off. When I awoke it was a beautiful day!

When I graduated in 1937, nobody was hiring foresters. As I recall, about 2,500 graduates took the Junior Forester Examination, which was conducted annually by the U.S. Civil Service, and about 1,800 passed. Seven were employed! I succeeded in finding temporary employment, mostly in forestry, for the next two years. Then, in 1939, I received three offers. One was with Tidewater Associated Oil Company in the southern states, having something to do with management of timber on the lands where they had their oil wells. In those days, black people were treated there much as they are today in South Africa, and my sympathies were with them. Not being an aggressive sort, I knew I could not endure the situation. Another offer was with the Forest Service as an assistant ranger in the Klamath National Forest. By then I'd had sufficient experience with the Forest Service to realize that their foresters could not make decisions on their own; they had to refer to a manual of instructions or get advice from the boss for everything they did. I did not want to spend my life that way.

Finally, there was the offer from the Southern Pacific Railroad, which I accepted. I had learned that they owned more timberland in California than anyone else and were doing nothing with it, simply selling land to lumber companies who cut the timber and disposed of the property. They offered me a position as field agent, which meant I would be cruising and appraising timberlands in preparation for their sale. Fortunately, I had gained considerable experience doing that kind of work for the Forest Service during summer vacations and in temporary employment after graduation.

When I became acquainted with Southern Pacific's holdings, I recommended that they withdraw their timberlands from sale and let me manage them for sustained yield, selling timber only at a rate consistent with growth. I pointed out that if they were serious about remaining in the transportation business, they should be concerned about the resources their customers need for their own survival. The proposal succeeded. I wrote the new policy, obtained approval of the board of directors, and proceeded to hire a staff and initiate sales of timber under the selection system of management I had learned from the Forest Service. Subsequently, Southern Pacific became known for having the best timber management system in the state of California.

In 1966 I left that position to become staff forester for the Sierra Club. My work there began with the Redwood National Park project. The club needed someone to help them determine the impact the proposed park would have on the timber industry and on employment in the area, and questions had been raised about the intentions of the affected lumber companies. They needed to know whether the companies were really practicing sustained yield or merely liquidating their timber resources, as industry had generally done in the past. I later represented the Sierra Club before congressional committees in connection with proposed legislation concerning forestry matters, particularly the national forests. I also helped local groups with their forestry problems and wilderness proposals, wrote articles for the *Sierra Club Bulletin,* and served as witness in litigation for conservation groups.

Throughout my career I have collected reports of research that tended to support good forest practices. Usually, when I found something of the sort, I would summarize it on a card, give it a title, and document it. One day Mike McCloskey, executive director of the Sierra Club, suggested that I might publish the material on those cards as an annotated bibliography for use by conservationists. When I retired in 1979, I planned to write a book on multiple-use forestry and to include that bibliography. But somehow I kept getting interrupted. When I'd return to work on the manuscript, I would hate what I had written and would make a fresh start. After half a dozen attempts, I concluded that I simply did not have whatever is required to write a book. I gave my files to the Bancroft Library and turned to other interests. However, I did occasionally accept invitations to speak to students and to conduct seminars for people interested in forestry.

About two years ago, I received an invitation to conduct a seminar at the College of the Siskiyous in Weed, California. I accepted, on the condition that someone would record my presentation and provide me with a transcript, which was to become the start of one last attempt to put my thoughts and findings in writing. Kathy Hall and Kenoli (Ken O'Leary), of Black Bear Ranch at Forks of Salmon in Siskiyou County, responded. Later that year they came to see me with a partial transcript, wanting to know how serious I was and what my plans were. A few weeks later, they returned and told me they had received a grant to help me write the book. They needed the book because they were factors in CATS (Citizens Against Toxic Sprays). In their fight against chemical forestry, they had come to the conclusion that they were attacking the wrong thing. They had decided to fight the methods of forest management that require toxic sprays rather than the use of the sprays themselves, and they were convinced that the practice of multiple-use forestry would eliminate the need for poisons. So those two beautiful people came home with me and got me organized. We developed an outline for the book, then they made a folder for each chapter, went through my collection of works, and inserted things I had written that were pertinent to each. They went back to the ranch and returned in six months to see what I'd accomplished. During their second visit, we rented a computer.

Shortly before the third visit, my wife asked me to go out and buy a word processor to have on hand when they returned. That did it. Once I learned how to use the computer and had a reasonable outline to follow, I was able to work effectively. So now I offer my heartfelt thanks to Kathy and Kenoli for their most constructive assistance. I hope this book will make it possible for people who care about the forests but have no formal forestry education to compete with the experts when they comment on the Forest Service's plans for the national forests and to apply themselves wherever the timbered wilderness needs help.

One further thought before we get on with our task. It may be helpful to readers to recognize the distinction between the role of advocate and that of administrator or public official. The advocate's role is to describe the ideal, all the while realizing that it probably never can be fully achieved. The role of the administrator, perhaps too often to the contrary, is to make the compromises that seem necessary to keep society functioning. So I offer here a description of ideal forest management as I perceive it, and all the information I have been able to assemble, to help you concerned people—professional and nonprofessional alike—to argue effectively for the protection of the forests we all love.

Gordon Robinson

Introduction

Where excellent forestry is practiced, the land usually offers a satisfactory aesthetic experience to the visitor. Excellent forestry consists of limiting the cutting of timber to that which can be removed annually in perpetuity. It consists of growing timber on long rotations, generally from one to two hundred years, depending on the species of trees and the quality of soil, but in any case allowing trees to reach full maturity before being cut. It consists of practicing a selection system of cutting wherever this is consistent with the biological requirements of the species involved and, except in emergency situations, keeping the openings no larger than is necessary to meet those requirements. It consists of retaining whatever growth is needed for the comfort and prosperity of all the native plants and animals. Finally, it consists of taking extreme precautions to protect the soil, our all-important basic resource.

This is true multiple-use forestry. It is what foresters had in mind when they first offered "multiple use" as a slogan to describe the policies and practices of the USDA Forest Service. In recent years, however, the term has been turned around so that it means quite the opposite of what I have described. Throughout this book, when I use the term "multiple-use forestry," I mean it in its original sense. Here "multiple-use forestry" and "excellent forestry" both imply uneven-aged management of timber for sustained yield (see Chapter 4). There is no question whatsoever about this definition of excellent forestry. The advantages of such management are overwhelming and cannot be refuted.

It takes timber to grow timber. It is not enough to have orderly fields of young trees, varying in age from patch to patch. In looking at a well-managed forest, one will observe that it is fully stocked with trees of all sizes and ages. It will be obvious in most forest types that the land is growing all the timber it can and that most of the growth consists of high-quality, highly valuable material in the lower portions of the large, older trees. It will be evident that little if any erosion is taking place. The soil will be intact; the forest floor will be covered with leaf litter and other vegetative matter in various stages of growth and decomposition. This absorbent layer holds rain and melting snow, allowing it to soak into the ground through pores such as worm holes, channels dug by ants, and tracks left by the decaying roots of past generations of vegetation. In this way the forest becomes a vast reservoir of water, which gradually seeps down through the land and comes out in clear, cool springs. This is how the forest stabilizes stream flow, and this is what is referred to when one reads of the forest serving to protect our watersheds. In the well-managed forest one also observes that there are frequent minor openings stocked with herbs and browse, which serve as food and shelter for wildlife. Finally, one observes that such a forest maintains its beauty and continues to serve the recreational needs of most people as long as it is so managed. This description of a well-managed forest is no mere pipe dream; it describes the way the Forest Service tried to manage the national forests from its beginning until the 1960s. Unfortunately, it is not the way our national forests are being managed today.

When I was a forestry student in the 1930s, my class was taken into the Plumas National Forest in northern California by Dave Rogers, who was the forest supervisor, and two of his staff assistants to see multiple-use forestry in practice. We saw a forest that was substantially intact. Three years before, the overmature and defective trees had been removed, and the men had to point out stumps to convince us that the area had actually been logged. Dave also explained that there are privately owned lands within the national forest boundaries and that without determining the ownership of the land, we must not blame the Forest Service for the clearcutting we sometimes find.

I had a similar experience in the 1950s with Bill Fisher, supervisor of the Six Rivers National Forest. He showed me areas of Douglas-fir that had been selectively logged under his supervision and pointed out the seedlings and saplings that had been protected during logging or had become established since. And it was in 1950 that the Forest Service and the California State Division of Forestry jointly published *These Green Hills*, which describes good forest practices and contains photographs of cutover forest that looks virgin.

Gifford Pinchot, who is generally regarded as the father of the Forest Service and who was its first chief, brought the word "conservation" into popular usage in application to natural resources.* It was also largely because of Pinchot's influence that Congress directed the Forest Service to sell only mature timber and required that timber to be sold must be

---

*Michael Frome, *The Forest Service*, 2d ed. (Boulder, CO: Westview Press, 1984), 12.

marked and designated as well as cut and removed.* This was what Pinchot called "conservation through use," in contrast with "preservation."† Ferdinand A. Silcox, chief of the Forest Service in 1939, supported federal legislation that would have outlawed clearcutting on private land as well as in the national forests.

Unfortunately, this kind of forestry—which protects the watershed, wildlife, soils, and beauty of the forest and restricts timber cutting to levels that are matched by growth—has rarely been practiced on the millions of acres of private land owned by the timber industry.

The lumber industry in this country has been transient from its inception. When a firm exhausted its available timber resources, it simply abandoned the land and moved on to a new location, leaving the workers behind. When timber became scarce on private land, companies turned to the national forests, arguing that they must have timber to sustain their operations until industry "tree farms" developed growth of sufficient quantity and maturity to permit a return for another cycle of logging.

THE PUBLIC FORESTER AND THE PRIVATE BUSINESSMAN

Good forestry is not a lucrative business. It never was and never will be, because it takes longer than a lifetime to grow high-quality timber, longer than anyone can wait for a return on investment. It takes 75 to 150 years to grow timber in sizes useful for lumber and plywood; it takes twice that long to grow high-quality wood for fine furniture and musical instruments. The large spruce trees in Alaska that are being cut and shipped to Japan for piano sounding boards, guitars, and exquisite residential paneling are often as much as 1,000 years old.

Trees growing on our better lands become marketable for pulp in as short a period as 25 years. Trees can be mass-produced for pulp, rough lumber, and construction-grade plywood under sustained yield in 50 to 75 years. However, since it takes much longer to grow high-quality wood, a forest being managed for this purpose will seem uneconomical because it will always contain a large inventory of low-quality timber that could be sold. The higher the quality of wood one wants, the higher the inventory will be; it takes a lot of low-quality marketable timber to

---

*Harold K. Steen, *The U.S. Forest Service: A History* (Seattle, WA: University of Washington Press, 1976), 36.
†Michael Frome, *Whose Woods These Are: The Story of the National Forests* (Garden City, NY: Doubleday & Company, 1962), 180.

grow high-quality wood. Consequently, the value of the amount of timber that can be sold annually under a high level of sustained yield will never represent a high percentage of the *total* value of the forest because as the price of lumber rises, the value of one's entire inventory rises with it. Generally, the value of the sustained yield or the annual income of a well-managed forest will range from 1 to 2 percent of the cash value of the entire forest inventory. Likewise, a 1960 survey determined that the annual return on investment in commercial timberland in the United States was only 2.5 to 3.5 percent, far less than the 10 to 15 percent for other industries.* The percentages are likely to be the same today. A well-managed forest, therefore, will always seem to be inefficiently managed in the short run and consequently will always be in danger of being exploited by the timber industry.

Owners of timberland, confronted with the choice between a high income for themselves and an even higher income for their heirs, will nearly always choose the former. Few of us can afford to be philanthropists. Firms with large investments will generally do what they must to obtain the highest possible rate of return, and in the case of timber companies, this too often means growing low-quality timber and cutting trees as soon as they become marketable instead of letting them grow to achieve high quality.

The forester, on the other hand, if he loves the forest and has not confused his role with that of the businessman, will resist the temptation to maximize income and will be more concerned with a wide range of environmental factors. He will want to restrict the cutting of timber to those trees whose removal will improve the health and vigor of the forest. He will want to keep trees growing until they reach their highest value, and he will recognize that maintaining a high inventory of marketable trees is an absolute necessity if the forest is to be managed for recreation, watershed, and wildlife as well as for raw material for industry.

For these reasons we require a clear separation of responsibility between the forester and the businessman. The forester alone should have responsibility for the forest. It is quite properly the role of the businessman to make what profit he can from the timber the forester makes available. But the businessman should not be allowed to set policy or production goals for the forester. When this occurs, forestry cannot be properly practiced.

---

*William L. Moise, "Factors Which Attract Equity and Borrowed Capital to Timberlands—The Investor's Viewpoint" (paper presented at the Thirteenth Industrial Forestry Seminar, New Haven, CT, January 1960), in *Financial Management of Large Forest Ownerships*, Yale School of Forestry Bulletin no. 66 (New Haven, CT: Yale University Press, 1960), 46.

HOW TO USE THIS BOOK

Part One is a brief outline of the history of forestry and the timber industry in the United States. It explains how clearcutting and "tree farming" came to replace multiple-use forestry and traces the development of national forest policy. It is written from the point of view of a forester who loves the forest and would prefer to see no trees cut, yet who has had the practical experience of successfully managing the largest industrial timber holdings in the state of California using the principles of "excellent forestry."

Part Two describes excellent forestry and explains what is good about it. It also explains what is wrong with tree farming and dwells on the nature and importance of soils and the need for soil conservation.

Part Three is an introduction to the mathematics of forestry, which serious critics of contemporary forestry should understand in order to deal effectively with forest plans. It also provides a few valuable suggestions for responding to forest plans.

Part Four is a collection of nearly four hundred summaries of research and informed opinion supporting multiple-use forestry that I have collected over the past fifty years. Readers will find this section useful for building solid cases in opposition to tree farming and for offering constructive criticism of forest plans.

PART ONE

A BRIEF OUTLINE OF HISTORY

A brief sketch of the history of forest conservation in the United States will give those people who are trying to influence current policy some background on how clearcutting came to be and, perhaps, a sense of confidence that their instincts about forestry are trustworthy. This is an anecdotal account by one who was there during the period of most rapid change in national forest policy, when decisions were made, put into practice, and contested.

My purpose is to demonstrate that our national forest policy began with a philosophy of management aimed at preserving the aesthetic values of the commercial forest even as it was being used as a source of lumber for housing and industry.

CHAPTER ONE

Early History of Forestry in the United States

The great revival of interest in the quality of our environment that began with Earth Day on April 22, 1970, largely ignored the condition of our forestlands until the public began to object to clearcutting late in the decade. However, concern for our forests marked the beginning of American conservation at the turn of the century, and this is not surprising. Forests are the source of the bulk of our water, the home of our wildlife, the scene of most of our recreation, and the resource base of one of our largest and oldest industries. Yet the forests of America have been relentlessly plundered ever since Europeans invaded the Western Hemisphere five hundred years ago. Despite public efforts to halt clearcutting and to enforce better management of our national forests, the destruction of both public and private forestland continues today at a rate that is clearly cause for serious concern.

As I mentioned previously, it takes longer to grow trees than most people are either willing or able to wait for a return on their investment in planting and cultivating them. Also, it takes far less time to develop a new way of using existing materials or species or sizes of trees than it does to grow timber that will meet the requirements of an existing technology. For these reasons, few people in the building trades have ever been deeply concerned with the survival of the lumber industry as we know it. When we run out of one species, we turn to another. As good-quality timber becomes scarce on one continent, we move to another. When large trees suitable for manufacturing high-quality lumber become scarce, we develop a technology for making two-by-fours, plywood, and various composition boards from very small trees. Should we ever run out of these, we may ultimately turn to use of brick, stone, and concrete for home construction.

As evidence of its increasing scarcity, the price of lumber, adjusted for inflation, has risen remarkably smoothly from 1800 to the present while the production of softwood and hardwood lumber in the United States has been almost constant, within the range of 30 to 40 billion board feet per year, since 1900. (Peak production was in 1909, with 44 billion board feet.) We seem to have achieved a sustained yield in terms of lumber produced. Unfortunately, this production has not been matched with growth or even with the continuation of the quality we used to take for granted. Major changes in attitude toward ownership and management of forest property must occur soon if the United States and Canada are to escape the disasters that followed deforestation of China, North Africa, and southern Europe.

EUROPEAN EXPERIENCE

The practice of forestry and silviculture is only about two hundred years old. It developed in Europe in response to an alarming shortage of wood caused by conversion of forest to farmland and grazing land. Scientific forestry began in Germany in the 1780s with the work of Heinrich Cotta and G. L. Hartig. A short time later, Bernard Lorentz and Adolphe Prade started its practice in France. Thus the age of modern silviculture is roughly equivalent to only three or four generations of forest trees.

The forests of eighteenth-century western Europe had been exploited since at least the Middle Ages. In most cases either the best trees had been removed, leaving undesirable specimens to regenerate the forest, or the forest had been clearcut. What remained was damaged by cattle grazing, overpopulation of game, the practice of collecting fallen limbs and snags for fuel, and the raking up of leaf litter to bed down farm animals. By the end of the century it was obvious that drastic measures would be required to rehabilitate the forests. Good trees had been removed and defective ones left for so long that selection management had become impractical. To remedy that situation, Cotta recommended clearcutting, and replanting if necessary, but insisted that his proposal was for one time only and must not become standard practice because of the hazards of monoculture.

Nevertheless, clearcutting did become standard practice. Landowners, more interested in profit than in the environment, cultivated even-aged stands of spruce and pine because those were the best commercial species available to them. From then on, those species were grown on short rotations for low quality lumber and pulp. Deciduous hardwoods and true fir became nearly extinct. But by the time of the First World War it had become clearly apparent that something was very wrong. Trees were stunted; many died before they even approached the size of the original forest trees. Soils had become impoverished, and trees suffered increasingly from storms, insects, and diseases.

Bill Fisher, supervisor of the Six Rivers National Forest, taught silviculture at the University of Edinburgh in Scotland after his retirement. He told me that clearcutting has lost favor in most European countries. Many foresters are returning to reliance on natural regeneration, constant preservation of the forest canopy, and flexible cutting methods. Allowable cuts are being reduced and rotations lengthened. Hardwood species are being interplanted with the more commercially desirable species in a second round of drastic measures to restore the productivity of the forests. Yet with all these efforts and Europe's head start on the United States, European forests today produce only a fraction of the growth experienced in those of the Pacific Northwest. Dietrich Muelder and several other German foresters have told me that they are appalled to find American foresters making the same mistakes their predecessors made across the Atlantic.

DEVELOPMENT OF THE AMERICAN LUMBER INDUSTRY

The American lumber industry as we know it today began in the mid-1850s, got its greatest boost with the post–Civil War building boom, and advanced further about the time of the Chicago fire in 1871. (I would like to blame it all on Mrs. O'Leary's cow.) Prior to that time, building with wood was a complicated craft, practiced by skilled laborers. Frame structures were held together with mortise and tenon. Nails were of wrought iron, were made by blacksmiths, and were very expensive.

In the 1880s, J. M. Van Osdel wrote an article for a Chicago monthly titled "The History of Chicago Architecture" in which he described a remarkable invention, "the 'balloon frame' method of constructing wooden buildings, which in this city [has] completely superceded the old style of framing with posts, girts, beams and braces." The principle of the balloon frame involves the substitution of thin plates and studs, running the entire height of the building and held together only by nails, for the ancient and expensive method of construction with mortised and tenoned joints. To put a house together like a box, using only nails, must have seemed utterly revolutionary to carpenters.

The advent of the balloon frame method marked the point at which industrialization began to penetrate housing. Sawmills were established to cut lumber of standard dimensions to correspond with standard structural designs. Along with this development, others were inventing machines for cutting and heading nails from wire. When the manufacture of cut nails was first undertaken, wrought nails cost 25 cents a pound, which made their use for housing prohibitive. All this changed with the introduction of machinery. The price of nails was suddenly reduced: in 1833 the price dropped to 5 cents a pound; in 1842, to 3 cents. So the invention of the balloon frame coincided with the improvement of sawmill machinery as well as with the mass production of nails. With this new method of construction, after the rebuilding of Chicago, the housing industry, having been geared up, went on to build the new cities of the West. The balloon frame played an important role in the conquest of the West, from Chicago to the Pacific Coast.

ORIGIN AND CONSEQUENCES OF CLEARCUTTING

The original forests of the United States comprised approximately 822 million acres, according to a 1923 Forest Service study.* Today this area has been reduced to 500 million acres. The lumber industry started out, in part at least, as a means of using material otherwise wasted in the clearing of land for agriculture. Under the circumstances, there was no reason to protect young or vigorous trees; cleared land usually reverted to forest unless preventive measures, such as plowing and removal of hardwood stumps, were taken. So by the time the industry moved west and lumbering itself became the principal motivation for logging, clearcutting was standard practice, and it is doubtful that people in the industry seriously considered anything else.

When the lumber industry became large and coupled with the home-building industry, whole states were largely stripped of their timber. On a tour of the forests of Wisconsin in 1955, Calvin Stott of the Forest Service told me that all of the merchantable virgin timber of Minnesota had been cut by 1890 and that only 80 acres of virgin forest remained in the state of Wisconsin. That was left only because someone had made a mistake in land description and it did not pay to have the loggers return for the small quantity remaining after the error was discovered. This tremendous devastation of forest had complex and far-reaching effects on water resources. The loss of forest cover contributed substantially to floods, including the disaster of Johnstown, Pennsylvania, on May 31, 1889, in which 2,200 people drowned. This, coupled with concern about the future supplies of wood, led to formation of the national forests and gave great impetus to the conservation movement.

*Raphael Zon and H. L. Schantz, "The Physical Basis for Agriculture," Part I of *Natural Vegetation Atlas of American Agriculture* (Department of Agriculture, Forest Service, 1923).

BIRTH OF THE NATIONAL FOREST SYSTEM

During the closing decades of the nineteenth century, intimations of a timber famine were heard throughout the land. On March 3, 1891, Congress enacted the Forest Reserve Act, authorizing the president to withdraw forestlands from the public domain so they could not be disposed of under the various public land laws. Congress thus created the National Forest System and, in 1905, put the protection and management of the reserves under the jurisdiction of the Bureau of Forestry in the Department of Agriculture. Forestry schools were established, and under the leadership of Gifford Pinchot, the first chief of the Forest Service, efforts were made to persuade lumber companies to practice forestry.

At first, the main purpose of the reserves was to protect the watersheds; the reserves were merely closed areas, as no plan of operation applied to them. But through the influence of Pinchot, Congress passed the Organic Act of 1897, which permitted the sale of dead, mature, and large-growth trees but required that trees to be sold must be marked, designated, and removed. The act gave the forester in charge of timber sales the authority to require removal of diseased or other undesirable trees and to protect and save the healthy and desirable ones to improve the productivity of the land. This was sustained-yield timber management under the principles of multiple-use forestry, and the Forest Service proudly and consistently managed the national forests in conformity with this law until timber became scarce in the private forestlands.

ATTEMPTS TO REFORM PRIVATE INDUSTRY

Conservation leaders in the United States have recognized the need for public regulation of private forestry since the turn of the century. Yet every major effort to achieve this objective has failed. Pinchot thought at first that he could persuade timber industry entrepreneurs to practice forestry by demonstrating its feasibility through the example of the national forests. However, he soon found that this would not work and concluded that public regulation of private forest management was needed to avoid a timber famine. The first serious proposal for such regulation was launched by the Society of American Foresters in an article appearing in the December 1919 issue of the *Journal of Forestry*. In response to that article, Senator Arthur Capper of Kansas introduced a bill in 1920 that would have authorized the Forest Service to control cutting practices on private forestlands. The bill called for regulation by the states, set a time schedule for the adoption of satisfactory minimum standards, and specified that if a state failed to act, the federal government would step in. The bill did not pass.

The courts, not Congress, blocked the next attempt at public regulation. Under the National Industrial Recovery Act of June 1933, the secretary of agriculture required that all timber operators on "lands under their ownership or control" practice "conservation and sustained production of forest resources." A series of conferences, attended by both the forest products industry and the general public, was held to draw up forest-practice regulations for the various forest regions. Unfortunately, the Supreme Court struck down the National Industrial Recovery Act before the new regulations were put into effect.

A National Forest Practice Act was subsequently introduced by Senator Walter M. Pierce of Oregon in 1941, again by Senator Frank Eugene Hook of Michigan in 1947, and finally by New Mexico's Senator Clinton Anderson in 1949—all without success. Each of these bills would have created a federal forestry board, which, through the states, would require the establishment of administrative areas to govern private forest practices. For each area, a forest-practice committee would have issued rules to protect forests from fire, insects, and disease; to provide for reforestation; to prevent cutting of immature timber; to preserve vigorous trees as growing stock to keep lands productive; to control logging methods to protect young growth and the soil; and to regulate grazing. Clearcutting would have been prohibited.

In 1971, Senator Lee Metcalf of Montana introduced yet another bill to control forestry on private lands. Metcalf's bill required the states to license foresters and forbade logging except under state supervision. It also required owners to file timber management plans prepared by licensed foresters. The stated purpose of the bill was to "create and maintain an effective and comprehensive system of regulation and use of all forest lands in the nation so as to ensure that (1) the environmental quality and productivity of forest lands are restored, enhanced, and maintained; (2) multiple-use values are effectively taken into account with respect to the management of such lands; and (3) the goal of maximum sustained yield of high quality timber products is achieved consistent with such multiple-use values." The bill was never voted out of committee.

The foresight of those conservationists and foresters who supported legislative proposals like Metcalf's is now evident, for the long-predicted timber shortage on private land is now here and will be with us for many years to come. The need for legislation has become obvious and acute, yet we still do not have anything like adequate public regulation of private forestry. A 1973 survey by Brian R. Wall of the Forest Service indicates that we can expect a 73 percent decline in the output of softwood timber products from forest industry lands in western Oregon between that year and the year 2000 because of excessive cutting and careless management practices. Likewise, redwood lumbering in California is drawing to a close because this uniquely valuable species has been relentlessly exploited without provision for perpetuating a supply of trees large enough to continue the industry once the virgin timber is gone. There is not enough old-growth redwood to last much beyond another decade at the 1970 rate of cut. Similar disasters lie ahead for other species of trees in other forest regions throughout the West.

After the Second World War there was a lot of optimism about forestry in the South. Natural regeneration on abandoned farmland brought about an important recovery of the southern forests. As one forester put it, "I'd hate to have to stamp out pine trees in the South." During the depression years, the Forest Service purchased a considerable acreage of abandoned plantations. By the early 1970s, the southern national forests contained large numbers of pines that were 80 or more years old. These woods were beginning to resemble old-growth forests when private timber companies, having liquidated their timber in the West, started moving south, investing millions in acquiring young forests and building integrated mills for producing a variety of wood products, including plywood, lumber, and pulp. As this trend began, owners of small holdings enthusiastically planted forest trees. But the big companies were encouraging even-aged management, which meant that farmers had no market for their trees for many years after planting. When farmers did sell, the big companies paid them poorly. Today, despite the continued growth of the forest products industry in the South as measured by mill activities, farmers are discouraged by low prices and only intermittent opportunies to sell their wood. Worst of all, surveys show a decline in growth rates in the southern forests, the cause of which is unknown. If present trends continue, these young southern pine forests will be liquidated before they are old enough to yield a sustained supply of timber, much less a continuing supply of trees of optimum size for high-quality lumber and plywood. Furthermore, lumber manufactured from such southern pine as is now large enough to log fails to meet building code specifications.

Efforts by the Forest Service

Over the years, the Forest Service tried to improve the conduct of forestry on private land through information and persuasion. In the 1920s and early 1930s, the Forest Service published a series of bulletins dealing with the twelve principal forest regions of the United States. These publications proposed two general groups of measures that could be taken to protect forestland. The first group outlined the minimum safeguards, based on local physical conditions, needed to prevent timber-bearing land from becoming barren. These consisted mainly of providing fire protection and adjusting forest taxation to the business of timber growing.

The second group of measures described supplementary procedures that the Forest Service hoped would be adopted by firms interested in practicing forestry as a business. In the Douglas-fir region, for example, the Forest Service recommended that a forest survey be conducted to determine the quantity of timber present and its potential rate of growth so that adjustments could be made in either the rate of cut or the size of the holdings in order to ensure a permanent enterprise. The bulletin also called for leaving seed trees, planting areas that did not reseed naturally after clearcutting, and establishing firebreaks and fire trails. However, the Forest Service generally did not go so far as to recommend uneven-aged management or multiple-use forestry, as was being practiced in most of the national forests, until after the depression years.

During the 1930s, the Forest Service did recommend selection management to industry. Typical of Forest Service publications of that era was *Selective Timber Management in the Douglas Fir Region*, written in 1936 by Burt P. Kirkland and Axel J. F. Brandstrom. In that work the authors thoroughly explored the whole range of techniques and types of equipment required and the economics involved. A few quotations are instructive:

66. Contrast between forestry starting with bare land and selective sustained yield management of existing timber. Timber growing in this region has been and is still being thought of very largely in terms of conventional "bareland" forestry. In its purest form, this contemplates that the timber-growing enterprise would start with an investment in logged-off lands and a further investment in planting, and thereafter continue for perhaps 60, 80, or 100 years with annual expenses for administration, protection, and taxes. Compound interest, at rates sufficiently high to cover the extraordinary risks that are here involved, will commonly run the total accumulated investment to large amounts. The prospective timber grower, under such circumstances, is confronted with the problem of building up a forest from "scratch." He finds that there are many uncertainties involved as to costs and returns. He logically reasons that he is spending money in the present for uncertain returns in the long-deferred future; that he is tackling a job that will not be finished during his lifetime; that he is attempting to work against the devastating effect which compound interest has on an enterprise in which for many long decades money will constantly be going out with nothing coming in.

Intensive selective management as applied to a forest with a long-time timber supply will create an entirely different basis for the timber-growing end of the business. Timber growing will begin with orderly selective liquidation and intensive management control of the existing timber, and the forest will be gradually brought to a high state of productivity by eliminating the declining or least productive growing stock and by putting the land to work at its maximum productive capacity. This, as has been shown, may be accomplished very largely by taking money out of the forest, not by putting money into it. Such timber growing "costs" as the owner may find it advisable to assume in order to obtain increased productivity can be charged off currently like any other item of current production costs. This will avoid the stumpage depletion costs that would have to be charged against the annual cut in case the productivity (i.e., the capital value) of the forest were not to be maintained on a permanent basis. The current costs of forest management should seldom amount to more than a very small fraction of such depletion charges.*

The publication closed with the following paragraph:

Although this report deals only with commercial timber production, the values in recreation and other forest uses should not be overlooked. As selective management retains a heavy forest cover, broken here and there only by small openings, beauty of the forest and its values for wildlife are fully preserved.†

This typified the attitude of professional foresters in the United States at that time. A variety of similar publications were published relating to other forest regions. The leading forestry schools emphasized selection management, although they also provided students with an understanding of the full range of alternatives theoretically applicable to forest management.

Another strategy begun by the Forest Service in the 1930s was to place restrictions on logging of private lands that lumber companies wished to exchange for cutting rights in the national forests. Congress had authorized the Forest Service to acquire private land within and adjoining the

---

*Burt P. Kirkland and Axel J. F. Brandstrom, *Selective Timber Management in the Douglas Fir Region* (Department of Agriculture, Forest Service, 1936), 117, 118.
†Ibid., 152.

national forests through exchange for timber of equal value. The restrictions consisted of requiring applicants to leave the healthy young trees undamaged and to remove defective trees that might be a source of danger to the residual forest. While the requirements could not be regarded as practice of uneven-aged silviculture, they often did result in leaving as much as 10 to 20 percent of the original timber volume standing in the western pine forests. Besides, mill operators had a chance to discover for themselves that they could make more money concentrating on the larger trees and leaving behind those that cost more to log and manufacture than the value of the lumber they produced.

In the western pine region, east of the Cascades and throughout the Rocky Mountains and most of California, the smaller lumber companies generally accepted the constraints placed on them when they logged in the national forests. But in the Pacific Northwest, where the bulk of our lumber was being produced, nearly all of the timber companies rejected the Forest Service's restrictions. They were accustomed to clearcutting and took for granted that selective logging was an unnecessary nuisance and would involve excessive costs. (They were mistaken on this last point. It costs no more to selectively log than to clearcut, and even if this were not so, the cost of logging was allowed for in the appraisal of national forest timber to be sold.)   Consequently, comparatively little timber from the national forests in the Pacific Northwest was actually sold until after the Second World War. The prevailing attitude was that the forest would come back by itself if left alone. In fact, this often is the case, particularly on the very best timberlands, which were the first to be logged. However, the best lands in western Oregon and Washington have largely been diverted to other use, principally agriculture, and much of the forest being logged today is very difficult to reforest and does not respond well to clearcutting and planting.

Industry's attitude toward sustained-yield forestry is well illustrated by the following story. In 1955, while working as a forester for the Southern Pacific Land Company, I was out in the woods with Jude White of International Paper Company, who was vice president in charge of their Long-Bell Division. He was negotiating for purchase of all of Southern Pacific's timber in the Trinity River drainage area of northern California, to be liquidated over a 20-year period. That region constituted about one-third of my company's entire timber resources. I refused to consider the proposal because it violated our policy of sustained yield. Jude said, "Hell, Robbie. We're on sustained yield. When we clean up the timber in the West, we'll return to New England, where the industry began." Clearcutting was practiced by most lumber companies simply because they had no intention of returning for another "crop" of trees. From 1939 into 1966 I had something to do with every application for purchase of timber the Southern Pacific Land Company received, as I was their principal forester. During those 27 years we received hundreds of applications for purchase of timber from firms that had liquidated their timber resources in the Northwest or the South and were looking for an opportunity to start over in new territory. The sad fact is that none of these companies, not one, was willing to enter into any sort of sustained-yield agreement. All they wanted was a 10-year supply of timber, sufficient to write off their investment in manufacturing facilities. One or two firms were willing to consider a 20-year liquidation plan, but that was the best I could get out of them. Those applicants included several of the most prominent and well-known lumber companies in the United States.

From time to time, exponents of the timber industry resolved to practice sustained-yield forestry, to take the steps necessary to ensure themselves a continuing timber supply. Unfortunately, very few maintained their policies for long. When times were good, they cut heavily, reasoning that they had to make money while they had the opportunity. When times were bad, they thought they could not afford to invest in forestry.

COMPANIES PRACTICING SUSTAINED YIELD

Nevertheless, during the 1940s and 1950s a few lumber companies decided that they were in permanent business. Boothe-Kelley Lumber Company was the principal industry of Eugene, Oregon, and was much admired for its conservative policies. Diamond Match Company, headquartered at Chico, California, was proud of its sustained-yield forestry. The same was true of Michigan-California Lumber Company of Camino, California, and the Pacific Lumber Company at Scotia, California. There must have been a dozen or two such firms in the pine region covering the Rocky Mountains, the Cascades, and the Sierra Nevada, and in the Douglas-fir and redwood regions of the Pacific Coast. Certainly there were a number of such enterprises in the northeastern hardwood forests and in the southern pine region.

Collins Pine Company, which logs land it owns in Plumas County, California, continues to practice multiple-use forestry. The company has set aside reserves as controls that are not to be logged in order to assess its efforts at maintaining healthy uneven-aged stands on the cutover portions of its land. Collins Pine allows recreation and hunting on its lands and charges local residents less per cord for gathering firewood than does the Forest Service on land allocated for that purpose.

Wilmon Timberlands in Vredenburgh, Alabama, has been practicing sustained yield since the company was established in 1912. It manages forests for a number of other owners along with its own. The company's *Land Management—Policy Statement* reads as follows:

Wilmon Timberlands, Inc., believes in a forestry management system called selective management, which is intensive forestry at its best.

Selective management is practical forestry based on the judgments of men in the woods working with existing stands of timber, and requires unusual perception and silvicultural understanding to make on the ground judgments. It is an art in which the forester will use his professional knowledge to make decisions in the field, since no amount of description can completely explain the applications.

Some of the techniques, methods, practices, systems, and alternatives will include:

1. The use of thinnings, improvements, liberation, salvage, and sanitation cuts to improve the timber stands.
2. The encouragement of natural regeneration through seed tree, shelterwood, or selection cuts.
3. Managing existing stands whether they are even-aged, uneven-aged or all-aged.
4. Planting open areas which will not re-seed naturally.
5. Leaving game food trees and plants for wildlife.
6. Other proper choices from the complete range of forestry practices.

These techniques and skills will be used to tailor management practices for the various private landowners' needs and objectives.

Many industries in the South use the clear-cut and plant method to put their lands into timber production. Except for areas which have no seed source and for areas on which trees' seed will not germinate, Wilmon Timberlands, Inc., feels that the clear-cut and plant method is not in the best interest of the private non-industrial landowner. The reasons are as follows:

1. High initial cost.
2. No income possibility for 15 years—the average private forest landowner's age being 57 and average tenure about 20 years.
3. Risk of loss from fire, insects, and disease is high.
4. Loss of flexibility in ownership objectives.
5. Danger of soil erosion, thus lowering production capacity of soil.

6. Danger of destroying the ecological system of the land.
7. Danger of destroying the game habitat.

Wilmon Timberlands, Inc., recognizes the multiple use concept in forest management and feels that the selective management system is the best method to facilitate such a concept, while at the same time, making the forest esthetically pleasing to the eye.*

Another excellent manager of its timberlands is the Southern Pacific Land Company, which holds more than 700,000 acres of forested remnants of railroad land-grant lands. This company has been profitably practicing multiple-use forestry since 1952. The following are some extracts from Southern Pacific's *Environmental Guide*:

. . . We harvest our timber upon a tree selection basis, carefully removing only those trees which are ready for cutting. . . .
   All timber to be cut must be examined and marked in advance on a selective basis by trained foresters in a manner that will maintain or enhance resulting tree growth. . . .
   . . . Our District Foresters mark for cutting those defective and overmature trees which are not producing any new growth themselves, and are a high financial risk because of their susceptibility to insects, diseases, windthrow and other hazards. They are leaving the healthy, rapidly growing trees, and whatever overmature trees are considered safe risks which are needed for seed and shelter to establish reproduction. This involves marking more heavily in some areas than in others, but our experience to date shows that about 50% of the volume in virgin forest is being removed in the first cut. Further refinement of data gathered in our inventory is expected to give us information that may make it possible for us to safely reduce the proportion of timber removed in the first cut, thus permitting us to cover our holdings more rapidly, placing the lands in a productive condition sooner and possibly increasing the allowable cut. . . .
   We are not concerned as to when we will return to any specific lands for the second cut. Instead, we are gearing sales to the allowable cut, and so long as we are continuously involved in the process of inventorying our timber, keeping our records up to date as to growth and other information pertinent to our annual sales programs, we will be returning to specific areas when the forestry staff in preparing its timber sale program finds that conditions are such that another cut should be made.†

Land Management—Policy Statement (Vredenburgh, AL: Wilmon Timberlands, Inc., n.d.).
†*Environmental Guide* (San Francisco, CA: Southern Pacific Land Company, 1952).

Implementing this policy requires a high level of skill and care, which is central to the practice of multiple-use forestry. It requires the kind of encouragement, supervision, and incentive that I practiced during my tenure as forester for Southern Pacific. I made sure that my staff understood the philosophy; I encouraged them to become the best-informed foresters in their areas, the philosophers and sages of their communities; and I tried to see that they were rewarded accordingly. I wanted them to be the true masters of their domains, professionals who knew best how to manage the forest and who would pass their wisdom on.

THE IMPACT OF THE CAPITAL GAINS TAX

Unfortunately, Diamond Match, The Pacific Lumber Company, and the few other firms like them remained a minority in the 1940s. Most people in the timber industry continued to cut and run. As timber became scarce on private land, industry lobbyists sought favors from Congress that would allow their firms to enhance their incomes and would provide ways to extract more timber from the national forests. One particularly subtle measure was to persuade Congress to extend the capital gains provision of the federal income tax to include timber under Title 117K. Congress passed this act over the veto of Franklin D. Roosevelt in 1943. Ostensibly, the measure was supposed to encourage investment in forest management and encourage people to keep and manage their land. But the impact was quite otherwise. Georgia Pacific Corporation seized this as an opportunity to acquire smaller companies that owned large reserves of old-growth timber. It absorbed these companies while maintaining the book value of their timber resources. This enabled Georgia Pacific to claim capital gains on the difference between the nominal price the original owners had paid for the timber, ranging from $2 to $5 per thousand board feet, and its value as of the first Monday in March of the year Georgia Pacific cut it, which ranged from $20 to $250 per thousand board feet, depending on the date of cut. The bulk of that corporation's income, therefore, was taxable at the very favorable rate of 25 percent rather than the standard corporate rate of 50 percent. This money management strategy was copied by a number of firms that were in the process of becoming giant international corporations. They accelerated the rate of cutting, hastily liquidating timber that the acquired companies had been maintaining to provide a sustained yield. As a result, most industry-owned forests were converted to mere tree farms, devoted primarily to production of small trees for pulp and low-quality forest products, if not outright abandoned.

Estate taxes were another factor that often discouraged sustained-yield management. When an owner of private timberland died, the heirs had to raise large sums to pay inheritance and estate taxes as well as capital gains tax. This contributed to the destruction of most of the private sustained-yield operations that had been initiated prior to the Second World War because the only way the heirs could raise this money was to clearcut their land. Thus the practice of clearcutting on private lands was accelerated when the capital gains provision was extended to timber, and also to some extent by the necessity of raising estate and inheritance taxes. These two forces combined to destroy the possibility of true multiple-use forestry on most private land for the next century or more.

"TREE FARMS" AND "KEEP GREEN"

Some leading foresters, discouraged with efforts to obtain public regulation on private lands and seeing the failure of lumber companies to respond to the need for private forestry, launched a campaign to implement the strategy the Forest Service had started with their pamphlets in the 1920s and 1930s. About 1942, the Weyerhaeuser Company took the lead in this effort and helped to develop a three-point forestry program for the timber industry. One component of the program, called "Tree Farms," was designed to persuade owners to dedicate their lands to the continuous production of timber. The second part of the campaign, called "Keep Green," was a valuable and necessary effort to win public support for fire prevention and publicly financed protection from epidemics of insects and diseases. The third aim of the program was to lobby for no or low taxes on forest property. This was proposed because counties often taxed standing timber as real estate, forcing owners to pay annual taxes on property from which there is not likely to be more than one income in the owner's lifetime.

This three-point program was supposed to bring about conditions under which timber would eventually grow to merchantable size on most of the cutover land, until some enterprising person would discover it and make arrangements to cut it. The cycle would then repeat itself. This was how the free enterprise philosophy was applied to forest management during the 1940s.

The program was largely ineffective, however. Some owners of large holdings cut all of their own timber and as much more as they were able to buy in their area, then closed their mills. Some sold their land to developers. Owners of small holdings, such as farm woodlots, were often discouraged from dedicating their land to the continuous production of timber by foresters representing timber buyers. These industry foresters often advised owners of small holdings to sell their timber to be clearcut and then gave them assistance in reforestation in exchange for first right of refusal of the new timber when it became large enough to cut. This arrangement largely destroyed the owners' opportunity to earn income from other uses of the land for very long periods of time. It also made the owners dependent on the company for sale of their timber while it was barely large enough to cut, and it left them vulnerable to low offers.

As mentioned before, the existing tax structure also encouraged owners of small forest holdings to sell their timber to lumber companies for clearcutting. Conservationists in the early postwar period lobbied to charge a yield tax on timber rather than tax it as real estate, an ad valorem tax that would apply only to the timber cut during any given year. The timber industry resisted this proposal, largely because it would take the pressure off owners of woodlots and small holdings to sell their timber to get relief from county taxes. Industry continued to oppose a yield tax until most of those small holdings had been logged. In California, for example, industry changed its position around 1970 and succeeded in getting the state legislature to enact a yield tax. By that time, of course, the yield tax favored owners of large holdings by greatly reducing their county taxes.

CHAPTER TWO

The Raid on the National Forests

At the end of the Second World War, the allowable cut in the national forests was much less than it is today. It was based on the best opinions of the competent foresters who were then managing our public forestlands. In 1949 the annual allowable cut in the total National Forest System stood at 5.6 billion board feet.

However, sales that year were only 2.6 billion board feet, and in 1950 the actual cut was only 3.5 billion board feet. Many lumber companies didn't bid on public timber at that time—mainly, I believe, because they were confident that they could buy it later when they needed it and because they had to pay taxes on whatever timber they owned. Many didn't buy national forest timber because of the rigid standards imposed by the timber sale officers, such as cutting only the trees foresters had marked and avoiding damage to patches of seedlings and saplings and large trees left to grow. Lumber companies particularly disliked having to cut and remove low-value trees that the foresters had marked for cutting in order to improve the forest.

After 1950, however, changes came rapidly. The postwar housing boom created a market for large quantities of lumber. Timber by then had become scarce on private land, and alternative materials were being developed for home construction, such as concrete slabs with asphalt tile flooring, cement block walls, stucco exteriors, metal window sash, and composition roofing. Lumbermen responded to this competition by forming a coalition with the National Association of Home Builders whereby they engaged architects to develop plans for using more wood at reduced expense. This resulted in the substitution of plywood for lumber, the use of shake roofs, and the return of wood flooring and siding—all the structural features of today's expensive and highly inflammable new homes. Lumber companies and manufacturers of logging equipment also researched the cheapest ways of logging and manufacturing. Then the timber industry went after the national forests in a big way. By 1955, the allowable cut in the national forests was 8.6 billion board feet. By 1970 the allowable cut had skyrocketed, averaging 11.5 billion board feet for sawlogs alone and 13.6 billion board feet when posts, poles, and pulp logs were included. That is about where it stands today, in the mid-1980s, and the timber industry continues to want more.

Many good professional foresters were caught off guard during the 1960s when the Forest Service increased the allowable cut under intense pressure from the timber industry. Ben Hughes, chief of timber management for the California region and a good friend of mine, was one who was surprised. He was dedicated to the multiple-use forestry that until then had been practiced in the national forests. Around 1960, I saw him severely criticized at a public meeting for insisting on limiting the cut to adhere to what were then called the standard marking rules and for offering timber for sale at competitive prices. The rules required that only the dead, mature, and defective trees be marked for cutting—the high-risk timber that stood a poor chance of surviving the 30-year cutting cycle then being practiced. Ben tried to disarm his critics with a witty remark, saying that purchasers had no complaint about stumpage prices as long as loaded logging trucks were frequently seen passing each other on the highways in opposite directions. He was soon transferred "upstairs," to a position with little power in the Washington office, and replaced by Bernard Payne.

Before I knew Bernie Payne very well, I went to him for advice as to the validity of my proposal that my company, the Southern Pacific Land Company, invest in acquisition and reforestation of some good-quality cutover land. I thought we should evaluate the investment opportunity by estimating the present value of the increase in our current sustained yield that would result from the investment instead of guessing at the present value of the anticipated yield many years in the future. This approach had been recommended by Kirkland and Brandstrom in a 1936 Forest Service publication titled *Selective Timber Management in the Douglas Fir Region*.

To illustrate this formula, suppose we have 1,000 acres of good forestland that has been denuded by a forest fire. It would cost $100 per acre to replant it. The land has the capacity of producing 900 board feet of timber per acre per year in 80 years. We are presently selling timber for $125 per thousand board feet. Let us assume too that interest rates will remain at 8 percent for the forseeable future. Traditionally, we would anticipate a yield of 900 board feet per acre times 80 years and estimate a yield of 72 million board feet when the plantation would be ready for logging. At $125 per thousand board feet, those 1,000 acres would be worth $9,000,000. But discounted at 8 percent compound interest for the 80 years, the present value is only about $20,000. Obviously, the investment would be foolish if viewed that way. No one in his right mind would invest $100,000 on a project requiring 80 years to mature and having a present value of only $20,000.

The problem with this approach is that none of the variable factors can be known. What will timber be worth 80 years from now? What interest rates will prevail over the next 80 years? What are the chances of fire, insect epidemic, or other hazards upsetting our plans?

I proposed to use only present and knowable information. Cost of the proposal is $100,000 (1,000 acres times $100 per acre for planting). The resulting growth would be 900,000 board feet per year, which we could immediately add to our annual sales program under sustained yield. At $125 per thousand board feet, that would mean a $112,500 increase in annual income that we could realize immediately from sale of mature timber elsewhere in our holdings. (This of course assumes that we are managing virgin forest, which contains a good deal of old-growth timber.) Looking at our investment opportunity this way implies that we will get our money back in only 1 year, making it very desirable.

This line of reasoning has a second requirement seldom considered in our society. It requires that our business decisions be dependent on and secondary to our moral decisions. It assumes that we place ethics ahead of business. First comes the moral decision to manage our forest resources for sustained-yield timber production while at the same time protecting all the other forest resources previously mentioned. Having adopted that basic policy, the decision to invest in reforestation of that 1,000 acres becomes clearly advantageous—good business, in fact.

I went to Bernie Payne with my idea because I assumed he was much better informed than I was and that it would be a mistake to proceed without concurrence with him or someone of his stature. As it turned out, though, the idea was new to him, and he was very much taken with it. He saw it as a way to approach Congress for increased appropriations to justify increased allowable cuts in the national forests, and he circulated a paper explaining how increased allowable cuts could be justified by appropriations for intensive forestry measures such as planting, thinning young stands, and so on. I was stunned because I believed that the Forest Service had already become overextended in its timber sales, but I could not find fault with his reasoning.*

Bernie Payne's application of my idea regarding intensive forestry was one indication of how the timber industry was beginning to

---

*Later, I discussed this approach to investment analysis with Dennis Schweitzer and Con H. Schallau, forest economists at the Pacific Northwest Forest and Range Experiment Station in Portland. They thought it through and published several papers on the subject, calling it the "allowable cut effect."

influence the Forest Service. But it was not the only example of heightened industry activity. In the 1950s the expanding lumber industry wanted to increase the availability of timber from every conceivable source. I attended many conferences and meetings during this period where I heard foresters and industry spokesmen advocate logging of all of the publicly owned timberland, not just the national forests. The full extent of public forestland includes the following (given in millions of acres as of January 1, 1977):*

- National forests and commercial forestland   89.0
- Bureau of Land Management lands, including the   5.8
  revested railroad grants in Oregon known as the
  O & C lands
- Forestlands held by the Department of Defense, wild-   4.8
  life refuges, the TVA, and miscellaneous other agencies
- Indian reservations   6.1
- Timberland within the national parks and national   NA
  monuments
- State forest lands   23.6
- County and municipal forest lands   7.2

During this same period, industry also embarked on an advertising campaign to encourage public opposition to federal acquisition of land. The objective was to slow down or prevent further establishment of wilderness areas, national parks, and wildlife refuges and to stop the Forest Service from acquiring cutover land.

The Wilderness Controversy

Beginning in 1929, the Forest Service had started establishing "primitive areas" in the national forests. Sixty-three such areas were established by 1933, ranging in size from 5,000 to more than a million acres. These were areas the Forest Service considered important enough to preserve under federal ownership but not significant enough to establish as national parks. (Some thought the Forest Service opposed granting national park status to these areas because jurisdiction over the lands would then pass from the Department of Agriculture to the Department of the Interior.) When timber became scarce, industry urged the Forest Service to "refine" the boundaries of these primitive areas. Regulation U-1, adopted in 1939, established a clear policy for administering primitive areas. It

*Source: *Forest Statistics of the United States* (Department of Agriculture, Forest Service, 1977).

called for public hearings with regard to the boundaries of each one, after which the area would be established as wilderness. In the 1950s, it quickly became apparent that through this procedure, timber industry representatives were persuading the Forest Service to delineate the boundaries of primitive areas to exclude any lands of commercial value. Frequently, sizable areas of land without timber or other exploitable resources were added to primitive areas. In this way, although the acreage of wilderness increased, key forestlands became accessible to industry. Dave Brower, then executive director of the Sierra Club, called this "wilderness on the rocks." Since then, lobbyists for industry have continued to oppose virtually every wilderness and national park proposal that has been advanced.

By 1953, when Dwight Eisenhower assumed office, industry's efforts began to pay off. One of Eisenhower's first moves was to put a ceiling on the number of people who could be employed by the federal government. Shortly after that, a program was initiated to induce federal workers to accept early retirement. Many who responded were old-time foresters in the Forest Service, the very people who had the skills to practice multiple-use forestry. This measure, coupled with natural attrition, resulted in a large-scale turnover of personnel in the Forest Service. At the same time, the timber lobby persuaded Ezra Taft Benson, the new secretary of agriculture, to make sure the Forest Service actually sold their full allowable cut.

The only way the timber management officers could comply with the demands placed on them—to sell timber at a faster rate than ever before, with fewer experienced people to prepare and supervise timber sales—was to go back to places that had already been selectively logged, where roads already existed, and mark the remaining timber for sale. Thus, clearcutting, a technique that until the 1950s had been practiced only in the Douglas-fir region, became widespread in the national forests. The timber industry was understandably gratified, and not only because of the opportunity to buy more timber. They needed to log in the cheapest method possible in order to compete with producers of other building materials, and they believed that clear-cutting was part of the answer.

At about that same time, computer technology began to take hold. It became apparent that the Forest Service could control their inventory of forest resources most easily by computer. All of the commercial forestland in the National Forest System is mapped or photographed from the air and delineated into a mosaic of "cutting blocks" that range in size from 20 to about 150 acres. Statistics relating to each block, such as species composition, age of stand, condition of timber, and so on, are gathered by sampling techniques, and the results are entered into data-processing records. The simplest and most economically efficient system for keeping records of timber resources, therefore, was to "convert" the forests into series of even-aged stands. Thus, in order to keep track of the forests by computer, the Forest Service itself found it convenient if not necessary to simplify the forests. This method of record keeping permitted central planning, which also made it easier for timber industry representatives to deal directly with the White House and with congressional committees in their efforts to secure access to ever-increasing quantities of timber.

Richard E. McArdle was chief of the Forest Service from 1952 to 1962, the period during which pressure was being exerted on the Forest Service to increase timber sales. As such, he was heir and protector of the enlightened management policies that until then had endeared the Forest Service to the American people. McArdle recognized that multiple use and sustained-yield management were policies the Forest Service had developed on it own, under no legal requirement other than the constraints described in the Organic Act of 1897. He was concerned that intense rivalry between the timber industry and other groups that used the forests might force the Forest Service to dedicate the commercial forest-land in the national forests to one dominant use (timber) at the expense of the other uses of the forest. Consequently, he supported the Multiple Use-Sustained Yield Act, which was enacted on June 12, 1960, after 5 years of heated congressional debate. Section 1 of that act reads, "It is the policy of the Congress that the national forests are established and shall be administered for outdoor recreation, range, timber, watershed, and wildlife and fish purposes."* On August 30 of that year, McArdle delivered the keynote address for the Fifth World Forestry Congress in Seattle. The following excerpts from that speech clearly demonstrate his interpretation of that law:

> What is new is the rapidly growing awareness of the need to apply multiple-use management more widely and more intensively. This comes not only from the obvious need to make forest lands more fully useful to the people but also to lessen the pressures to divert forest lands from a combination of uses to some one exclusive use. In most instances forest land is not fully serving the people if used exclusively for a purpose which could also be achieved in combination with several other uses. . . .
>
> . . . The significance of the recent legislative enactment is, first, legislative recognition of multiple-use and sustained-yield principles of management; second, a clear-cut directive to apply

*Multiple Use-Sustained Yield Act of 1960 (74 Stat. 215, as amended; 16 U.S.C. 528-531).

these principles on the national forests; and third, naming the basic renewable resources for which the national forests are established and administered and assuring them equal priority under law. . . .

An essential of multiple use is positive, affirmative management of the several uses involved. Haphazard occurrence of these uses on some particular tract of land does not constitute multiple-use management. Multiple use is not a passive practice. On the contrary, it is the deliberate and carefully planned integration of various uses so as to interfere with each other as little as possible and to supplement each other as much as possible. Multiple use is by no means an assemblage of single uses. It requires conscious, coordinated management of the various renewable resources, each with the other, without impairment of the productivity of the land. . . .

In brief, multiple-use management as we practice it on the national forests requires us to consider all of the five basic renewable resources, although on any specific area we may not have all of them in operation at any one time. It obliges us to coordinate these various uses even though doing this results in less than fullest possible productivity of some uses. The requirement for sustained yield applies to all renewable resources and is aimed both at getting a high level of productivity and at preventing overuse of any resource or impairment of productivity of the land. . . .

And now a closing word to you as eminent leaders in a respected profession. Multiple-use forest management is a challenge to foresters to broaden their vision. We must be forest land managers instead of primarily timber growers. The thinking of foresters is believed to be preoccupied with timber and dominated by silviculture. To some extent this criticism is justified. But multiple use, when properly applied, eliminates this bias. The future success of foresters and the contribution of the forestry profession to the welfare of our countries may depend on our response to the need for a balanced use of forest land resources. May we now and always perform in the best interests of the countries we serve.*

The next day, Edward P. Cliff, McArdle's assistant chief, addressed the same group on the application and opportunities for multiple-use forestry in large publicly owned forests. Ed Cliff was destined to succeed Richard McArdle as chief of the Forest Service in 1962. His speech shows a somewhat different interpretation of the new law. A suggestion of the impending struggle over the meaning of multiple use may be gleaned from a few quotations from his speech:

---

*Proceedings, Fifth World Forestry Congress: Multiple Use of Forest Lands (Seattle, WA: University of Washington Press, 1960), 144-145.

It is important to remember that one of the basic elements of the multiple-use principle followed by the Forest Service is that all resources receive equal consideration. No one resource or use automatically outranks another. However, in application, it is necessary to establish priorities when conflicts occur. It is not until confronted by local conditions in which there is a specific relationship between supply and demand that a decision has to be made that one resource or use might be more important in the public interest than one or more of the others. . . .

I shall give you just a few examples of the coordination measures most commonly applied. In harvesting national forest timber, strips of uncut vegetation are left along fishing streams and around the borders of lakes to protect fishing waters and scenic values. Strips of timber also are left uncut along highways and main forest roads. Timber cutting is permitted in these reserved strips only to salvage dead and dying trees and those which are hazardous to the public. . . .*

We see in these two speeches, given on two subsequent days, both the case for the new multiple-use law and its undoing.

From McArdle, the chief who was to retire: ". . . the need to apply multiple-use management . . . to lessen the pressures to divert forest lands from a combination of uses to some one exclusive use. . . .

". . . Multiple use is . . . the deliberate and carefully planned integration of various uses so as to interfere with each other as little as possible. . . . [It] is by no means an assemblage of single uses.

" . . . We must be forest land managers instead of primarily timber growers."

From Cliff, who was to succeed him: ". . . It is necessary to establish priorities when conflicts occur."

The illustration Cliff gave shows how the Forest Service was to use the new law to justify departures from its original intent, departures that had been piecemeal until that time but that since have become standard practice: ". . . In harvesting national forest timber [a given; there is no discussion of how the timber can be harvested to protect the other uses in that particular part of the forest], strips of uncut vegetation are left along fishing streams and around the borders of lakes. . . . [So much for the watershed, fish, and campers.] Strips of timber also are left uncut along highways and main forest roads. [So much for scenic beauty.] Timber cutting is permitted in these reserved strips only. . . . " [Only if no other excuse can be found to cut them.]

*Ibid., 178-179.

No other single example I know of shows better how the Forest Service has distorted Gifford Pinchot's principles of multiple use or "preservation through use," which were enacted into law in 1960, into its "dominant use" doctrine of today.

And even in the short run, the new law did little to stem the escalating pressure for more logging in the national forests. In 1961, the forest supervisors received instructions from the Washington office to shorten rotations so that forests could be cut at more frequent intervals. The objective was to increase the allowable cuts in their districts by 10 to 25 percent in anticipation of improved utilization standards. It was reasoned that by the time the second rotation came around, industry would be using enough more of the material then considered unmerchantable that the sustained yield would average out. This reasoning so angered many foresters that some even resigned. These new instructions were formally incorporated into timber management plans by changing the rotation from that determined by culmination of mean annual increment in trees 12 inches in diameter at breast height to a 12-inch top, using the Scribner Decimal C log rule, to that of trees 7 inches in diameter at breast height to a 6-inch top, using the International log rule. (See Chapter 6 for an explanation of these terms.) In other words, much smaller trees would be included in the allowable cut. In an average-quality ponderosa pine forest, that meant changing the rotation from 124 years to 90 years. This made it possible to classify more timber as overmature because it was beyond rotation age and therefore available for accelerated liquidation.

THE KENNEDY YEARS

In 1961, shortly after John F. Kennedy announced his appointment of Orville Freeman as secretary of agriculture, exponents of the timber industry joyfully proclaimed, "At last we have someone we can talk to!" On February 21, 1962, they presented Freeman with a formal request titled *Recommendations of the Lumber Industry to the Secretary of Agriculture.*

In the request, the National Lumber Manufacturers Association noted that the lumber industry was becoming increasingly dependent on the federal government for its timber supply. It protested that lumber companies were not getting enough timber from the national forests and that prices were too high. It objected to timber sale procedures (which the Forest Service had developed to protect and manage the national forests) and complained that industry had failed to get satisfaction through fifteen years of negotiation. The association made four recommendations.

Two were proposals for new regulations, which Freeman was urged to write, following the tradition of other secretaries of agriculture who had written twenty-nine regulations over the years under the authority granted them by the Organic Act of 1897.

The first proposal was titled "Sale of the Allowable Cut." It read as follows:

> A prime objective of National Forest management shall be an orderly program of timber sales designed to promote the regular harvest of the full timber-growth potential from *commercial forest areas in such a way* [emphasis added] that there may be community stability, continuity of employment, a continuous supply of improving wood products and an economically healthy forest industry.*

The intent was to urge the Forest Service to sell more national forest timber than the national forests themselves could sustain, based upon growth taking place on intermingled and adjacent private lands. It was to sacrifice the quality of the national forests in order to sustain local industries that were failing because they had not practiced sustained yield on the private lands. It was to encourage the Forest Service to sell timber from the national forests as though the combined acreages of public and private forestlands in a particular area comprised a single working circle. (A "working circle" is a forest area from which a sustained yield of forest products is planned, generally ranging from 250,000 to 1,000,000 acres.)

> To ensure performance in meeting these objectives, the Chief of the Forest Service shall annually report to the Secretary of Agriculture such data, for each national forest, as the allowable cut limit, the volume of timber under contract, the volume that could be sold considering the accumulated undercut or overcut, the volume of timber sold, the estimated average forest growth potential per acre of commercial forest land in the National Forest and the average volume cut per acre over the entire commercial area.†

Not long after this request, the Forest Service began to display charts in regional and forest rangers' offices showing allowable cut and timber sold by year. The curves rose upward and onward.

The timber industry's second proposal, titled "Timber Appraisal," follows:

Recommendations of the Lumber Industry to the Secretary of Agriculture with Respect to National Forest Management (Washington, DC: National Lumber Manufacturers' Association, 1962).
†Ibid., 6.

The Forest Service shall take cognizance of the dominant position of the government as the principal seller of timber in large areas of the United States and the lack of a normal market in those areas where there is no alternative source of supply. The economic well-being and future of numerous communities depend on fairly priced raw materials from the national forests. The Forest Service shall avoid taking advantage of its dominant position in the setting of rates for timber.

Appraisal rates for national forest timber shall be residual values for entire sale offerings as determined by subtracting from product values the sums of operating costs and margins for profit and risk. Product values shall be based on current market experience. Costs shall be those of an operator of average efficiency and related to the conditions of the local terrain and timber. The profit margins shall be based on government reports of profit experience in competing building materials industries with due allowances for differences in risk. . . .*

This procedure actually had been developed by the Forest Service in 1914 and is followed to this day. The appraisals are used as minimum prices for timber offered for competitive bidding, and bids often double or treble the appraised rates. Hence, the intent of this request may have been to induce the Forest Service to sell timber at appraised rates instead of bid rates. Purchasers were seeking ways to avoid having to compete for national forest timber.

The third recommendation requested a new appeals procedure. It proposed a prompt and impartial procedure for resolving differences regarding the contract and its administration and performance. Industry complained that the existing appeals procedure was slow and expensive and that the final decision remained with the seller, the federal agency. (A new appeals procedure was adopted that was much as industry representatives had requested, although the USDA retained the last word.)

The fourth recommendation called for a complete revision of the timber sale contract form in order to establish a normal buyer-and-seller relationship between the Forest Service and the lumber industry. At that time, it was asserted, the contract form established a one-sided relationship in which an excessive amount of power and control rested in the hands of the seller, permitting arbitrary, unilateral seller domination of the buyer-and-seller relationship.

The standard timber sale contract form that had been used before that time contained a number of provisions governing the activities of loggers in the woods and specifying that they should be performed "to

*Ibid., 8.

the satisfaction of the officer in charge." This made it possible for the forester to maintain control of loggers who, if left to their own devices, might drive all over the woods with their bulldozers, knocking the bark off reserved trees, smashing reproduction, and creating erosion problems. Careless loggers often left debris on the ground that created a fire hazard and invited the buildup of pine beetle populations. These activities had led to disputes and sometimes hostility, particularly when inexperienced people were placed in charge of timber sales.

Secretary Freeman responded generously. The Forest Service, part of the Department of Agriculture, made changes in its standard timber sale contract form so that it conformed with civil contracts. Where the previous contract had placed matters such as erosion control and slash disposal following logging under the jurisdiction of the timber sale officer in charge, the new contract had to spell out specific requirements in writing, and the timber sale officers were forbidden to give orders to timber purchasers or their loggers while logging was in progress. To do so would technically make the timber sale officers employers, liable for any damage caused or injuries sustained by the loggers. This made it impractical to supervise the woods operations sufficiently to protect residual stands where multiple-use forestry and uneven-aged management were being attempted. The forest officer in charge could no longer *prevent* damage from occurring and therefore had to rely on collecting for damages after the fact. Unfortunately, the penalties were often worth the price to the operator. This revision of the timber sale contract was one more reason why the Forest Service found it ever more difficult to practice uneven-aged management in the national forests.

Most important, though, was that after receiving these proposals, Edward P. Cliff, the newly appointed chief of the Forest Service, appointed a board of review to consider "policy, procedure, and practical application to specific working circles of any consideration which affects determination of allowable annual cutting rates" in the national forests. On September 3, 1962, the board issued a report titled *Determination of Allowable Annual Timber Cut on Forty-Two Western National Forests*. Two paragraphs from that report are revealing:

> The 42 western national forests, on which primary attention is centered, were designated as representing those on which timber demand-supply relationships are critical, making determination of allowable cuts of particular importance. These forests are in western Montana, northern and southeastern Idaho, Washington, Oregon and California. They are located in Forest Service Regions 1, 4, 5, and 6. . . .

This report was prepared as a result of two weeks of consultation, analysis, and writing in Portland, Oregon. It was initially intended to circulate a draft of the report for general review by Forest Service and other concerned people for 60 days. However, a commitment by the Secretary of Agriculture to report by October 15 on increased allowable cuts on these forests, based on current adjustments and recomputation from latest inventory data and some changes in procedures, made it necessary to complete the report in much shorter time, with very limited opportunity for the Board to obtain review.

Those consulted by the board were as follows:

U.S. Forest Service, representatives of the Washington Office and Regions 1, 4, 5, and 6, and the Pacific Northwest Forest and Range Experiment Station

Bureau of Land Management, Mr. Travis Tyrrell and Mr. Rodney O'Fety, Portland

Bureau of Indian Affairs, Mr. Earle Wilcox, Area Forester, Portland

Western Forest Industries Association, Mr. Joseph W. McCracken and associates

Industrial Forestry Association, Mr. William D. Hagenstein [*] and representatives of four association members

Western Pine Association, Mr. Ernest L. Kolbe

Western Lumber Manufacturers' Association, Inc., Mr. George R. Craig*

The last four were the principal lobbyists for the timber industry. These industry representatives, meeting quietly with officials of the federal agencies that control the country's major remaining old-growth timber resources, rushed their recommendations to the secretary of agriculture under a schedule that gave opponents little chance to object.

This report is the most complete document I know of to show the way in which industry and the Forest Service were beginning to work together. Because it shows so accurately how forest management policies were changing, I will discuss it in detail here. In addition to highlighting key aspects of the report, I will add my own interpretation of the background and implications for day-to-day work in the forests.

The forty-page report begins with a review of the timber supply situation in the forty-two national forests, describes measures that had

*Kenneth P. Davis et al., *Determination of Allowable Annual Timber Cut on Forty-Two Western National Forests: An Analysis of Objectives, Problems, and Methods with Recommendations* (Department of Agriculture, Forest Service, 1962).

already been taken to increase timber sales, and concludes with recommendations as to how even more timber could be sold.

The Review

The report stated that private lands had become largely depleted and industry was becoming increasingly dependent on the national forests. Plant capacity for lumber, pulp, and plywood had been greatly expanded during and following the Second World War. Industry had expanded its production from 17 billion boardfeet of lumber and 2 billion square feet of plywood in the late 1940s to 20 billion boardfeet and 8.8 billion square feet, respectively, in the late 1950s. This converts to about 22 billion boardfeet of logs in 1950 and about 27 billion boardfeet in 1960. Production from private lands had remained about constant, but in the national forests it had increased from 2.9 billion board feet in 1952 to 6.7 billion in 1962. According to the report, this increase in the volume of timber sold annually from the national forests had been brought about by developing more accurate inventories for determining the allowable cut, bringing the allowable cut up to the full sustained-yield potential of the forests, developing a road system sufficient to bring out the allowable cut, and obtaining financing necessary for meeting those objectives. These may appear to be positive accomplishments, but they do not suggest the violations of multiple use and sustained yield that had actually been taking place.

Let us therefore examine the manner in which increased national forest timber sales had been rationalized and achieved between 1950 and 1962.

1. Some working circles had been combined. This resulted in an increased sale of timber in two ways. First, it made it possible to sell the entire allowable cut of a national forest from the few working circles already opened up with logging roads. Up until the 1950s, a national forest generally covered a million or so acres, and was divided into four or five ranger districts, each being a working circle and having its own timber management plan and allowable cut. (Recall that the allowable cut is the amount of timber available for sale under a sustained-yield plan.) At that time, many working circles were inaccessible, so their timber could not be sold. But as the working circles were combined, the allowable cut from the whole forest could be taken just from the areas that were already accessible.

The second way the combining of working circles increased sales was by increasing the allowable cut itself. It just happens that when the

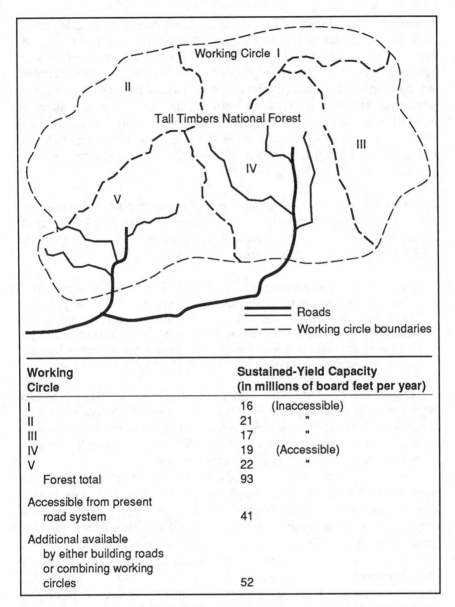

Working Circle	Sustained-Yield Capacity (in millions of board feet per year)	
I	16	(Inaccessible)
II	21	"
III	17	"
IV	19	(Accessible)
V	22	"
Forest total	93	
Accessible from present road system	41	
Additional available by either building roads or combining working circles	52	

FIGURE 1   *Allowable Cut Can Be Increased by Combining Working Circles*

statistics for several working circles are combined, the resulting allowable cut is greater than it would be if it were calculated individually for each working circle (see Figure 1). This is technically known as the "allowable cut effect."

2. Timber access roads had been built. Road construction often made an entire forest accessible to logging. With more logging roads, the Forest Service was able to maintain the annual sale of the increased allowable cut that had been justified by combining working circles. Access roads also enabled the Forest Service to sell high-risk and recently dead trees and to sell thinnings from certain young stands that might otherwise die and be lost. In some cases, the estimated amount of this timber was added to the allowable cut even when the high-risk and recently dead trees themselves were not actually accessible or could not be located.

3. Forest inventories made from aerial photographs inadvertently had led to exaggerated allowable cut calculations. According to the report by the board of review, the forest inventories prepared between 1958 and 1962 had some serious weaknesses:

> Compromises were made on points which weaken the overall value of the information for management planning purposes. These include arbitrary definitions of commercial forest land and adequacy of stocking, use of aerial photographic classifications, types, and averages instead of individual field measurements, [and] occasional lapses into continuing instead of periodic inventories.*

Timber surveys made from aerial photographs are naturally subject to large errors in volume per acre because the trees' diameters and condition are not visible from above. Aerial surveys are far less expensive than ground surveys, and their use is clearly understandable, but they exaggerate the amount of operable timber present.

Conducting a continuing inventory means merely subtracting the volume of timber sold from that established in a previous inventory instead of remeasuring the remaining timber—thus ignoring growth and discrepancies between timber cruised (amount measured in a physical ground survey) and timber actually removed—and continuing to include areas that could not be logged (known as inoperable areas) in the inventory and resulting sustained-yield calculations. Continuing inventories are used because it is far less expensive to merely adjust an old on-the-ground survey than to remeasure the forest. Also, under even-aged management, the entire volume of timber in clearcut blocks can be subtracted from the forest inventory without affecting the accuracy of the

---

*Kenneth P. Davis et al., *Determination of Allowable Annual Timber Cut on Forty-Two Western National Forests: An Analysis of Objectives, Problems, and Methods with Recommendations* (Department of Agriculture, Forest Service, 1962), 12.

figures applying to the logged areas. With this method, the total volume available for harvest is usually overestimated and the locations of inoperable areas are not pinpointed. Inoperable areas are frequently included in the inventory erroneously because samples frequently are taken in small areas where the densities are such that logging appears favorable, but the larger logging area in which the ground sample lies may be inoperable because there are too few trees, because the terrain is too rough or is subject to erosion, or because of the nebulous but real caution imposed by loosely specified multiple-use restrictions such as "scenic values" or "wildlife habitat."

4. Questionable log-scaling practices had been used. Particularly in the Douglas-fir region, questionable log-scaling practices led to a serious underestimate of the amount of timber actually removed from the national forests in timber sales. This was the result of measuring standing timber and preparing timber management plans on the basis of Forest Service short log scale but selling it on the basis of Bureau scale. The Forest Service log scale consisted of measuring no log longer than 16 feet (the maximum length has since been changed to 20 feet), thus taking the taper of the tree into consideration, and measuring log diameters to the nearest inch, fractions being thrown up or down. Thus a log measuring 17.6 inches in diameter would be recorded as an 18-inch log. Likewise, a 30-foot log would be measured as two logs: one 16-foot log and one 14-foot log.

Bureau scale is determined by a scaling bureau that was set up by the timber industry ostensibly as an impartial log-measuring service to ensure accurate statistics for both sellers and buyers. However, Bureau scale requires that logs up to 40 feet long be measured as one log. Therefore, inasmuch as log diameter is determined by measuring inside the bark at the small end of the log, Bureau scale measures the volume of a cylinder the full length of the log but having only the diameter of the small end. Furthermore, Bureau scale discards any fraction of an inch in diameter measurement, so a log measuring 17.6 inches in diameter would be recorded as a 17-inch log. Discrepancy between the two methods of measurement is about 25 percent in typical old-growth timber, and it is sometimes as much as 40 percent. (See Chapter 6 for additional information on log-scaling rules.)

5. Rotations had been shortened. A policy adopted in 1961 based the cutting-age rotation on culmination of growth in terms of International 1/4-inch rule, including trees 7 inches and larger to a 6-inch top instead of trees 12 inches and larger to an 11-inch top. As mentioned earlier in this chapter, this shortened existing average rotations, generally from 10 to 25 years, and sometimes more. This change envisaged economic utilization of smaller trees in the future. The rate of timber sales increased because the shorter the rotation, the faster old-growth stands are cut over and the greater is the consequent current cut.

The increased rate of cutting resulting from these measures had been changing the character of the national forests and threatening future timber supplies even before the board of review's report was written. Hence the report contained a carefully worded warning that the western forest industry could come to be based primarily on fiber rather than on sawlogs. The board was referring to the tendency to develop technology for use of small trees while the forests are being managed for shorter and shorter rotations. Prolonged, excessive cutting could result in such dependency on trees that it would become necessary to cut them before they were large enough to manufacture anything but pulp and chipboard.

Next followed a series of miscellaneous observations. The report showed how excessive cutting had been accomplished, without admitting the excesses, and it recommended measures that would lead to further excessive cutting. Yet this series of comments warned of the results of the very sorts of things the report advocated.

The board stated that about 6 percent of the commercial forestland in forty-two western national forests had been set aside as roadside strips, campgrounds, and so on, and urged that old-growth timber be cut in these areas because "there seemed to be a tendency for forest resource managers on the ground to avoid cutting in such areas because of uncertainty as to policy and procedure." (The Forest Service used these strips along streams, lakes, and highways and around campgrounds to hide its logging operations from the public as well as to give some bit of protection for waterways and recreation. Now industry wanted permission to log even these small areas.)

The board warned that "in some working circles more than 75 percent of the anticipated future cut is expected to come from wood predicted to be grown between [1962] and the time of harvest," due to wide fluctuations in precipitation and even wider fluctuations in tree growth and mortality, and that "many of the future growth and mortality predictions in management plans for the western national forests are based on assumptions of increasingly intensive management practices not yet realized."*

*Kenneth P. Davis et al., *Determination of Allowable Annual Timber Cut on Forty-Two Western National Forests: An Analysis of Objectives, Problems, and Methods with Recommendations* (Department of Agriculture, Forest Service, 1962), 31.

A considerable act of faith is embodied in allowable cut determination on the national forests. In timber management planning, it is assumed that needed additional roads will be built, that stands will be satisfactorily regenerated within the regeneration period allowed for in sustained yield calculations, that adequate protection will be given and productive silviculture applied, that utilization envisaged can be commercially achieved, that timber volumes estimated as available for cutting from complete sampling inventory data can, in fact, be made a reality in terms of operable timber sales, and finally, that sales can be financed and programed to meet the Forest Service objective of making the allowable cut actually available. These things cost money and require continued financial support to achieve.*

So the taxpayer was to foot the bill that would allow the Forest Service to build more logging roads, do more replanting, and hold more timber sales, all to meet industry's demand for a bigger allowable cut.

Conclusions and recommendations. The board made sixteen specific recommendations. Of the sixteen, I have summarized or quoted those that seem most damaging to the national forests and particularly in violation of the principles of multiple use. My comments, in brackets, follow the summaries and quotes.

1. The combining of working circles should be continued.
2. Road financing should be greatly increased through use of appropriated funds. The road program should be geared to the optimum development of the total timber resource rather than being limited to harvesting the allowable cut where the value of the timber sold justifies the cost of road construction. [This proposal clearly was highly favorable to the purchaser of timber. It has led to the present situation, in which the Forest Service's road-building costs often exceed what it makes on a timber sale.]
3. The Forest Service should continue studying the importance of national forest timber to the regional economies. [The hidden agenda has been to justify cutting in the national forests beyond their sustained-yield capacity while the private lands recover from excessive logging in the past. This assumes that the private lands will be protected and will remain available to the timber industry when its forests are again sufficiently mature to exploit. It amounts to a combining of the national forest with intermingled and adjacent

* Ibid., 26.

land in one sustained-yield unit, without a commitment from the owners of the private land to practice sustained yield.

Congress passed the Cooperative Sustained Yield Act in 1944 to stabilize forest production at a sustainable yield, to secure improved cutting and forestry practices on the cooperating private land, and to manage relatively large areas of mixed ownership as one unit. Only one contract pooling private timberland with national forest was adopted under this law. That was with Simpson Logging Company in the Shelton working circle of the Olympic National Forest in the state of Washington. Representatives of the timber industry immediately objected to the law on the grounds that it put a stop to free competition in bidding for public timber. Consequently, no further such contracts were made under this law. However, the Forest Service then attempted to achieve the same results by managing national forest timber as though there were such agreements when they had assurance that adjacent and intermingled private timber was reasonably well managed. The Forest Service has always been interested in stabilizing local forest industry, which, as a matter of fact, is required under the Organic Act of 1897.]

4. Timber management should be geared to utilization standards likely to prevail after removal of all timber older than rotation age. [If and when a market should develop in the future for material not merchantable today, it should be regarded as a bonus and the timber should be added to the sustained yield at that time. It is a distortion of sustained yield to add that quantity to the allowable cut in advance. This proposal also assumed that the western old-growth forests and their high-quality timber would be cut as quickly as possible and would be replaced by even-aged stands to be cut at frequent intervals, yielding small trees of low quality. Management of the new forests was to be entirely determined by the needs of the industry. Again, no mention was made of the needs of the forests, its wildlife, and so on.]

8. A new unit of measure should be adopted that will reflect total utilization. [This would result in the shortest possible rotations consistent with culmination of maximum rate of growth—see Table 5 in Chapter 6.]

12. "A timber harvest should be taken from areas designated for scenic, landscape, or related purposes," to prevent wastage of a utilizable resource. [Again, even the tiny areas that had been off limits to logging, such as campgrounds and reserved strips protecting watersheds, were now to be made available for cutting.]

14. Strong and attractive career ladders should be maintained, particularly in timber management, to minimize user difficulties, as knowledge and experience concerning timber management is requisite to the effectuation of most forest land uses. [Whether intended or not, this resulted in timber management specialists having the final say in management of the national forests and having more authority than specialists in watershed, fish and wildlife, range, and recreation.]

16. "The Board has been fully advised [of steps] being taken to increase allowable cuts to be reported to the Secretary of Agriculture by October 15 [1962]. . . . Making projected annual cuts a reality . . . represents a considerable act of faith in what the future will bring. Allowable cuts now calculated [1962] envisage a substantial increase in future intensity of timber management. To achieve this intensity, strong and continued financial support of the National Forest Program is necessary."* [Again, the taxpayer was to pay for the new logging roads, replanting, fertilizers, and so on that would be needed to bring in the increased allowable cut the industry wanted.]

1964

Next, Congress enacted the National Forest Roads and Trails Systems Act of October 13, 1964, which required the Forest Service to build logging roads to make it as cheap as possible to log out timber—clearly a boon to the timber purchaser. The legislation "authorized the Secretary to provide for the acquisition, construction, and maintenance of forest development roads within and near the national forests and other lands administered by the Forest Service in locations and according to specifications which will permit maximum economy in harvesting timber. . . ."†

To understand the implications of this act, one must realize that the least-cost combination of road construction and log hauling usually occurs when trucks are permitted to carry the heaviest loads they can bear at the greatest speed safety will permit. That is, the cost of road construction plus the cost of hauling logs per thousand board feet of timber in a typical administrative unit is the least when the highest-quality

---

*Kenneth P. Davis et al., *Determination of Allowable Annual Timber Cut on Forty-Two Western National Forests: An Analysis of Objectives, Problems, and Methods, with Recommendations* (Department of Agriculture, Forest Service, 1962), 38.

†National Forest Roads and Trails Systems Act of October 13, 1964 (78 Stat. 1089; 16 U.S.C. 532-538).

timber access roads are built. The Forest Service was therefore required to build timber access roads that were wide, well banked, and gently curved. The destruction resulting from this one act of Congress—in soil erosion, siltation of rivers, damage to fish resources, and obliteration of trails and beautiful camping places—has been enormous.

By 1965, even-aged management, achieved by clearcutting and closely related methods, had become the predominant practice in the entire standard component of the commercial forestlands of the national forests. (The "standard component"—renamed "full-yield component" in 1980—comprises about 50 million acres of the 197-million-acre National Forest System; it is the land on which allowable cuts are calculated and timber sale programs are scheduled.) Alternatives to this management system were no longer seriously considered or openly discussed. The Forest Service's consideration of multiple-use management henceforth applied only to the approximately 150 million acres remaining in the national forests, which are classified as other than "commercial forest land suitable and available for full timber production."

As Gifford Pinchot had feared, the public's prime timberland and remaining old-growth forests had been turned over "for the temporary benefit of individuals or companies."

DOUGLAS-FIR SUPPLY STUDY

In 1969, with the publication of the *Douglas-Fir Supply Study*, the Forest Service publicly acknowledged for the first time that timber sales in the national forests had become seriously overextended. The admission of overcutting was only oblique, however, because the stated purpose of the report was to explore the feasibility of *increasing timber supplies* in the Douglas-fir region of Washington, Oregon, and northwestern California *by applying intensified timber management practices on national forest lands.* Eight alternatives were considered in the report, and all eight indicated a sharp drop in the rate of cutting after the first rotation, which would occur somewhere around the end of the century.

The lowest-intensity alternative reported represented a base level of management, about the level of management practiced in national forests in the region in 1966. It consisted of practicing even-aged management (clearcutting) on a 100-year rotation, allowing 5 years for regeneration after logging, and building 1,100 miles of road per year during the 1970s. The study showed that this alternative would cause a drop in the rate of cutting from the then-current 2.9 billion board feet per year to 1.8 billion board feet per year during the second rotation. That calculation is clear evidence that the Forest Service had already departed from practicing sustained yield.

The highest-intensity alternative described in the report consisted of managing on a 65-year rotation, replanting within a year after clearcutting, and building 1,600 miles of road per year during the 1970s, thus making the region's entire commercial forest area accessible to logging within 20 years, or by 1990. It also assumed that the backlog of nonproducing areas, such as old brush fields, would be reforested within 10 years and that noncommercial thinning (removal of trees too small to have commercial value) would take place in 20-year-old stands. This alternative would increase the annual cut for the remainder of the current rotation to 5.2 billion board feet per year, but the annual cut would drop to 2.5 billion board feet per year during the subsequent rotation. This alternative did not include planting with genetically improved stock or use of fertilizers or irrigation, nor did it consider utilization of trees less than 11 inches in diameter. It thereby left opportunities to rationalize even greater increases in the rate of cut in the future.

The study concluded that high-intensity management was the most appealing of the eight alternatives. The appeal was based strictly on economic considerations, because it justified nearly doubling the allowable cut during the 1970s at the expense of future timber yields and of nearly all multiple-use values. The report did state, however, that adopting the favored alternative would have disastrous effects on watershed, fish resources, and recreation. Only the deer population would reap a benefit, and that merely because of the great increase in browse on the recently cutover land. Unfortunately, these warnings have been ignored as both industry and the Forest Service have continued to seek congressional appropriations to implement the high-intensity alternative.

THE REACTION

During the 1960s many people began complaining about the clearcutting they saw in the national forests. At first there was confusion as to whether the devastation was on national forest land or on privately owned land within the administrative boundaries of the national forests. It soon became apparent, however, that Smokey the Bear had run amok. Hikers found their favorite trails and camping places obliterated. At home they began to find advertising in major magazines that attempted to paint an idealized (and false) picture of intensive forestry. One didn't have to inspect the ads too closely, however, to realize that the pictures of birds and animals contentedly standing around in big rectangles of small trees and stumps were only paintings.

Flying in and out of the Pacific Northwest, especially in winter, when there was snow on the ground, people saw the huge, rectangular patches of bare land left by clearcutting—obviously occupying such a large proportion of the forest that sustained-yield forestry was an impossibility. Soon a variety of conservation organizations became involved. A loose coalition was formed that included the Sierra Club, The Wilderness Society, the National Parks and Recreation Association, the Izaac Walton League, and the National Audubon Society. Many local organizations joined in as well.

It was becoming increasingly clear that the Multiple Use-Sustained Yield Act of 1960 was not working. Because of the rapid destruction of virgin timber and the Forest Service's increasing tendency to permit clearcutting, conservation groups, principally The Wilderness Society and the Sierra Club, lobbied for the Wilderness Bill, which was passed by Congress in 1964. That act required the Forest Service to continue to refine the boundaries of primitive areas, to conduct public hearings on its recommendations, and then to propose that Congress designate the resulting newly defined areas as wilderness. By now, environmental groups had discovered that they could use these public hearings to object to Forest Service and timber industry bias in the proposals and to seek boundaries more to their own liking. The Wilderness Act also established a time schedule for reconsideration of the primitive areas that had not been declared wilderness prior to 1964. The review process, later known as the roadless area review and evaluation (RARE) programs, was applied to additional undeveloped areas of the national forests.

Concern about clearcutting was not confined to the Pacific Northwest. In August 1970, as part of a dispute over the Monongahela National Forest, the West Virginia legislature requested the secretary of agriculture to suspend clearcutting contracts in the national forests of that state. The request went unheeded.

Probably the first and most effective voice opposing the trend toward abandonment of multiple-use forestry on public lands was Guy Brandborg of Hamilton, Montana. Brandy was a retired forest supervisor of the Bitterroot National Forest and a friend of Bernard DeVoto. (DeVoto had been successful in rallying public opinion against destructive policies of the Forest Service in the past through his writings for *Harper's Magazine* and as editor of the *Saturday Review of Literature*.) Brandy succeeded in prodding the Forest Service into appointing a task force to appraise the management practices in the Bitterroot National Forest. The group admitted some mistakes but failed to come to grips with the principal issue: the Forest Service was neither protecting multiple-use values nor practicing sustained yield.

Meanwhile, Brandy had been pleading with Senator Lee Metcalf of his state to get the University of Montana to study timber management practices in the Bitterroot. The university produced the Bolle report, *A University View of the Forest Service*, in November 1970. The report flatly declared that "multiple-use management, in fact, does not exist as a governing principle on the Bitterroot National Forest" and accused the Forest Service of "timber mining" where they authorized logging of timber from noncommercial forestlands.*

In May 1969, the House Committee on Agriculture conducted hearings on a proposed National Timber Supply Act, which would authorize the Forest Service to retain receipts from sales of timber and other income to use to intensify timber management in the national forests. Conservation groups opposed the bill because they thought it would function much as the gasoline tax has: to increase the sale of timber to obtain revenue to finance further increases, and so on, indefinitely. Also, the bill would have specifically authorized the Forest Service to do all the things the timber industry was requesting that were contrary to multiple-use forestry. A companion bill was heard by the Senate Agriculture Committee in October. The House bill was defeated by a vote of 229 to 150 on February 26, 1970, after the coalition of conservation organizations, led by the Sierra Club, got busy and lobbied against it at the last minute.

The Senate Interior Committee conducted hearings on clearcutting practices in national timberlands in April and June of 1971.† Much expert testimony was presented. The record of those hearings is an excellent source of information on the hazards of even-aged management. I deliberately say the hearing *record*, not the actual hearing, because some of the best-qualified experts presented their testimonies by mail, requesting confidentiality because they feared reprisal. The outcome was very disappointing. The committee responded by merely offering guidelines consisting of a few ineffective restrictions on clearcutting. With a bit of fanfare, Forest Service chief Ed Cliff announced that the Forest Service would abide by those guidelines.

In 1970 the Council on Environmental Quality asked for position papers on even-aged management from the Sierra Club, the Society of American Foresters, the American Forestry Association, and the National

---

*Arnold W. Bolle et al., *A University View of the Forest Service* (Washington, DC: U.S. Senate Committee on Interior and Insular Affairs, 1970).
†U.S. Congress, Senate Committee on Management Practices on the Public Lands, *Clearcutting Practices on National Timberlands: Hearings before the Subcommittee on Public Lands of the Committee on Interior and Insular Affairs*, 92d Cong., 1st sess., 1971.

Forest Products Association. In response I prepared "The Sierra Club Position on Clearcutting and Forest Management."* The four solicited papers were sent to the deans of five forestry schools, who were invited to study and comment on them. Each university was asked to evaluate clearcutting from two points of view: timber production and general impact on the environment. In October 1971, Lee Talbot, senior scientist of the Council on Environmental Quality, telephoned to ask me to review the five deans' reports and send comments from the environmentalist's perspective within a week. Two weeks later, all four hundred and fifty pages of the five deans' reports arrived at my office. Obviously, there was no possibility of meeting his deadline. I took a long shot by soliciting the help of experts around the country, but only one of them responded. I never heard from Talbot again.

Meanwhile, in September 1971, President Richard Nixon announced the appointment of a five-member President's Panel on Timber and the Environment. Chairman of the panel was Fred A. Seaton, a newspaper publisher and former secretary of the interior between 1956 and 1961; other members were Stephen Spurr, president of the University of Texas and a professor of forestry; Marion Clawson, director of Resources for the Future; Ralph Hodges, Jr., vice president and general manager of the National Forest Products Association; and Donald Zinn, professor of zoology and past president of the National Wildlife Federation. Two years later, the panel issued its recommendations to increase the cut in the national forests even more: "The annual harvest on lands available for commercial timber production on western national forests can be increased substantially. Analyses based upon nationwide forest inventory data indicate possibilities for increasing the old growth cutting rate in the range of 50 to 100 percent."†

In May 1973, the Izaac Walton League, along with the Sierra Club and others, filed suit to stop clearcutting in the Monongahela National Forest in West Virginia. Plaintiffs charged violation of the Organic Act of 1897 on three counts: that the Forest Service proposed to sell timber other than dead, mature, and large-growth trees, that it proposed to sell timber that was not marked and designated, and that it proposed to permit purchasers to cut trees in the national forests without removing them.

*A shortened version of this paper was later published in the February 1971 issue of the *Sierra Club Bulletin.*
†*Report of the President's Advisory Panel on Timber and the Environment* (Washington, DC: Government Printing Office, 1973), 4.

Judge Maxwell of the Federal District Court handed down his decision in December of that year. He agreed with the plaintiffs and permanently enjoined the Forest Service from allowing the cutting in the Monongahela National Forest of (1) trees that are not dead, mature, or large growth; (2) trees that have not been previously marked; and (3) trees that will not be removed. The judge ruled that nothing in his order was to be construed as affecting the defendant's authority to allow cutting of trees for building roads and trails, protecting the forests from fire and depredation from insects and disease, managing the forests for uses other than lumbering, thinning and improving the forests within sales areas, and conducting experiments in forest management.

The United States Court of Appeals for the Fourth Circuit upheld this historic decision, and the Department of Agriculture did not carry it further because the case was hopeless. But the timber industry and the Forest Service responded by going to Congress for relief.

The House Agriculture Committee scheduled hearings on a proposed National Forest Management Act, which would spell out details for planning in the national forests and repeal those provisions of the Organic Act of 1897 that established multiple use. The committee at that time was strongly supportive of industry and the Forest Service. As each item involved in timber management planning was brought up for consideration, language was offered by both conservationists and industry representatives, and the committee would usually accept the amendments proposed by industry. Toward the end of the hearings, one congressman asked, "Now, will that make it impossible for them to sue us?"

After much debate, Congress finally passed the National Forest Management Act of 1976 (NFMA). That act legalizes all the objections environmentalists have to clearcutting and even-aged management in the national forests, that is, cutting far beyond sustained-yield capacity and managing the forests on short rotations as mere tree farms. It authorizes the Forest Service to depart from sustained yield under certain circumstances so that, in effect, industry is supported where private timber resources have been exhausted and the excessive cutting that had been taking place is legalized. Furthermore, the NFMA establishes elaborate and time-consuming public procedures for management decisions. The act specifically provides that forest plans in effect at the time of passage of the NFMA will remain in effect until new plans under that act have been adopted. So while a new plan is appealed, the destruction continues. That is where it stands as of this writing.

While the NFMA was being debated, the Texas Committee on Natural Resources sued the Forest Service for clearcutting in the state of Texas, using the Monongahela decision as a precedent. On May 24, 1977,

Judge William Wayne Justice in the District Court for the Eastern District
of Texas filed his findings of fact, from which the following paragraphs
are quoted:

23a. Clearcutting results in increased fire hazard, because fire
hazard is a function of fuel moisture content. In a forest, the flammable material on the ground is relatively moist and slow to burn,
because of shade from the tall trees and the moisture of transpiration held under the forest canopy, where air is less free to move
than where there is no forest. When all the trees are removed over
an extensive area, flammable material will be hotter and drier than
under a forest canopy and will therefore burn more readily.

24. Clearcutting probably results in increased hazard from insects and diseases, because it creates stands of trees of the same age
and frequently of the same species, and because most insects and
diseases attack trees of a particular age or species. (It is theorized
by respectable authority that the closer a stand approaches a monoculture, the more susceptible it is to attack by insects and disease,
and the more likely it is that an attack will become epidemic.)

25. Clearcutting impairs the productivity of the land, because it
causes accelerated erosion and loss of the all-important top soil.
Erosion increases exponentially with increase in the size of openings created in the forest by logging, and with the proportion of
timber cut.

26. Clearcutting impairs the productivity of the land, because it
causes leaching of nutrients essential to tree growth.

27. Clearcutting impairs and reduces the amount of habitat essential to various species of wildlife. Some species require relatively mature trees for nesting and for food. Other species require
dead or hollow trees for nesting. Still other species of wildlife require a combination of mature hardwood trees for acorns, nuts, and
other mast, and young hardwoods for browse. As detailed above,
clearcutting results in closed even-age stands a few years after regeneration, and these stands provide inferior food and shelter for
such particular species of wildlife.

28. Clearcutting impairs the productivity of the land by
reducing the number of species and, therefore, eliminating the wide
range of benefits resulting from the subtle interdependencies
characteristic of the natural forest.

29. Except for birdwatching, photography, and some forms of
hunting, even-age management largely destroys the recreational
values of the clearcut area for about thirty years.

31. The Forest Service Manual, Sections 2403.1 and 2471 requires
that "methods of cutting and logging will preserve the residual living and growing timber, promote favorable conditions of

waterflow. . . ." Contrary to the Manual, even-age management, as practiced in the National Forests of Texas, does not promote the younger growth. Further, clearcutting, as practiced in the National Forests of Texas, does not preserve the residual and growing timber, reduce hazards of destructive agents, nor secure favorable conditions of waterflow, but produces contrary effects.*

Then, on June 21, 1977, Judge Justice handed down his decision, which read, in part, as follows:

In accordance with the Findings of Fact and Conclusions of Law signed and entered by this Court on May 24, 1977, Defendants are hereby:
PERMANENTLY ENJOINED from permitting any clearcutting, seed tree cutting, shelterwood cutting, or other cuts designed to regenerate even-aged stands of timber in the National Forests of Texas until such time as: (1) defendant . . . shall have prepared a programmatic environmental impact statement, in accordance with the requirements of Section 102 of the National Environmental Policy Act . . . ; (2) the programmatic environmental impact statement mandated by (1) above has received the approval of this Court; and (3) such programmatic environmental impact statement has, after receiving the approval of this Court, been filed with the Council on Environmental Quality.†

Most unfortunately, this decision was reversed by the United States Court of Appeals for the Fifth Circuit, and the Supreme Court declined to take the case on further appeal. This decision would have had an effect completely opposite to that of the National Forest Management Act if it had prevailed.

MULTIPLE USE REDEFINED

As defined in the Multiple Use-Sustained Yield Act of 1960, multiple-use forestry consists of timber management modified sufficiently to accommodate the various uses of the forest *on the same land, at the same time.* The five uses recognized by the law are outdoor recreation, range, timber, watershed, and wildlife and fish habitat.

In recent decades, however, multiple use has been subverted to mean the exact opposite. It is now interpreted as zoning for a single, dominant use rather than integrating as many uses as possible into each zone. The

Texas Committee on Natural Resources v. *Bergland,* Civil Action No. TY-76-268-CA.
†Ibid.

agency's regulations. As we have seen, it was in direct response to pressure from industry to increase timber production in the national forests to make up for a shortage of private timber.

From the 1950s on, the forest products industry has been successful in persuading Department of Agriculture officials in Washington to repeatedly increase the allowable cut in the national forests and to take whatever measures were necessary to see that the allowable cut was indeed harvested. The Forest Service responded to the directives to sell more timber by allowing clearcutting in areas that had previously been selectively logged, its standard method of logging up to that time. Continued increases in the allowable cut, plus changes in timber sale rules, appraisals, and the like, and instructions and funds to build more logging roads and hold more timber sales, made clearcutting more and more widespread.

These changes in management policies are contrary to the multiple-use law. The Forest Service acts as if the law had been repealed somehow when Congress passed the NFMA in 1976. But the NFMA states six times that its provisions must be carried out in a manner consistent with the Multiple Use-Sustained Yield Act. Furthermore, the NFMA makes specific mention sixteen times of multiple use in management of national forest lands.

A 1970 recommendation of the Public Land Law Review Commission shows that the Forest Service did not have the statutory authority to change multiple use to dominant use:

There should be a statutory requirement that those public lands that are highly productive for timber be classified for commercial timber production as the dominant use, *consistent with the Commission's concept of how multiple-use should be applied in practice.* [emphasis added]*

While I certainly do not agree with the commission's recommendations that the Forest Service get such authority from Congress, it is interesting to note that the commission thought that even if such authority were secured, it should still be applied consistent with multiple-use principles.

Those who are concerned about the future of our national forests are now left with few alternatives. One is to comment on the series of forest plans now being developed by the Forest Service under the National Forest Management Act. But it will be an uphill battle to try to change the

*One Third of the Nation's Land: A Report to the President and the Congress by the Public Land Law Review Commission (Washington, DC: Government Printing Office, 1970), 92.

plans now being developed by the Forest Service under the National Forest Management Act. But it will be an uphill battle to try to change the present course of the Forest Service in this manner. The agency that was once proud to carry out the multiple-use, sustained-yield principles developed by Gifford Pinchot has so shifted its direction that it fails even to mention uneven-aged management as an alternative in these current forest plans.

It is unfortunate, but likely, that comments on forest plans will be considered only to the extent that they indicate what citizens and groups have in mind in the event of litigation. Plans—that is, the printed documents—may be edited to accommodate defects citizens are able to identify, but the proposed activities probably will rarely be modified. At the same time, though, it is vitally important that we make these comments and criticisms of present Forest Service policy, for, as the Forest Service knows, such comments form the necessary basis of any future litigation. Concerned citizens must either appeal or lose their opportunity to litigate, because the courts will throw out their cases if they have not exhausted their opportunities for appeal before suing.

And, indeed, the future of our national forests may ultimately be decided in the courts. Should that come about, it could be to the good, because that is the only arena where conservationists have been successful in dealing with the Forest Service in recent years. So we must continue to challenge inadequate environmental impact statements and timber management plans that are based on the dominant-use policy and that call for excessive logging. We must also keep our congressional representatives aware of our concern and respond knowledgeably and persuasively should legislation affecting the national forests come under consideration.

Currently, the Forest Service has slowed down its acceleration of the allowable cut in some places and increased it in others. The old-growth timber in the forests continues to be liquidated at the behest of the timber industry.

Some glimmers of hope, however, filter out of the experiment stations and forestry schools in the form of research that supports multiple-use forestry and uneven-aged management and identifies the problems with the present policy of even-aged management. We must make it our business to keep track of these research findings and use them and other arguments in any way we can, for if cutting continues at the present level, the subject will be academic by the end of the century.

PART TWO

THE SCIENCE AND PHILOSOPHY OF MULTIPLE USE

Part Two deals with the environmental concerns of forestry. It describes the two basic methods of forest management: tree farming, with its disadvantages, and multiple-use forestry, with its virtues. I refer to multiple-use forestry as "excellent forestry" when it is sensitively applied. Most important, I have tried to clarify the distinction between even-aged and uneven-aged management and to show that even-aged management is incompatible with multiple use.

I have given special attention to soils, which are essential to the continuation of life as we know it on this planet. Forest soils are more fragile than those of agricultural lands and generally are only superficially considered by foresters, if not outright neglected.

CHAPTER THREE
Silvicultural Systems

Forests form and thrive best where there are no people—and hence no forestry, and those are perfectly justified who say: "Formerly we had no forestry science and enough wood; now we have that science, but no wood. . . ."

Germany formerly contained immense, perfect, most fertile forests. But the large forests have become small, the fertile have become sterile. Each generation of man has seen a smaller generation of wood. Here and there we admire still the giant oaks and firs, which grew up without any care, while we are perfectly persuaded that we shall never in the same places be able, with any art or care, to reproduce similar trees. The grandsons of those giant trees show the signs of threatening death before they have attained one-quarter of the volume which the old ones contained, and no art nor science can produce on the forest soil which has become less fertile, such forests as are here and there still being cut down. . . .

Without utilization, the forest soil improves constantly; if used in an orderly manner it remains in a natural equilibrium; if used faultily it becomes poorer. The good forester takes the highest yield from the forest without deteriorating the soil; the poor one neither obtains this yield nor preserves the fertility of the soil.*

The foregoing was extracted from the foreword to *Principles of Silviculture* by the late Frederick S. Baker, professor of forestry and dean of the Forestry School of the University of California. He was quoting from the preface to *Advice on Silviculture*, written in 1816 by a famous German forester named Heinrich Cotta. The piece was also used by Dr. B. E. Fernow in 1902 to introduce the *American Forestry Quarterly*, the predecessor of the *Journal of Forestry*. Thus we have it from three great

*Frederick S. Baker, *Principles of Silviculture* (New York: McGraw-Hill Book Company, 1950), v. Reproduced with permission of McGraw-Hill Book Company.

foresters whose work was spread over a period of 150 years and two continents: the ideal forest exists where there are no people and hence there is no forestry.

But notice that Heinrich Cotta also gives us the notion of good forestry, which can be practiced by "the good forester [who] takes the highest yield from the forest without deteriorating the soil. . . ." If he takes this yield in an "orderly manner," the quality of the forest at least "remains in a natural equilibrium."

Unfortunately, forestry in the United States has too often been that conducted by Mr. Cotta's "poor" forester who, because he utilizes the resources of the forest in a faulty manner, "neither obtains this yield nor preserves the fertility of the soil." And the quality of forestry is getting even lower, despite all the encouraging reports to the contrary from public relations and advertising campaigns.

As we saw in the first two chapters, most companies in the forest industry continue to cut sawtimber faster than it grows and to consume whatever timber they can buy without husbanding their own lands. In recent years, the quality of management of our national forests has been eroding under pressure from industry. Industry, having overcut its own lands, has been increasingly successful in influencing the Forest Service to allow it to do the same in the national forests. Many people are questioning these matters. And well they should, for it isn't as if the Forest Service didn't know how to do a better job and didn't know where its present course was leading.

The Forest Service proudly practiced good forestry for many years, guided by the multiple-use principles formulated by its first chief, Gifford Pinchot, who was a key figure among the social reformers and trustbusters of his time. In 1905, Pinchot set down his policy for the national forests in a letter Secretary of Agriculture James Wilson wrote to Pinchot—which was, in fact, written by Pinchot himself. (It is customary in a bureaucracy for underlings to perform their duties in the name of their superior officers, and the Forest Service is part of the U.S. Department of Agriculture.)

> . . . It must be clearly borne in mind that all land is to be devoted to its most productive use for the permanent good of the whole people and not for the temporary benefit of individuals or companies. . . . The conservative use of these resources in no way conflicts with their permanent value. You will see to it that the water, wood and forage of the reserves are conserved and wisely used for the benefit of the home-builder first of all. . . . Where conflicting interests must be reconciled, the question will always be decided from

the standpoint of the greatest good of the greatest number in the long run.*

In October 1939, Forest Service chief Ferdinand A. Silcox wrote:

National forests are administered on a multiple-use basis. Besides protecting from fire, insects and disease, Forest Service stewardship involves developing and administering these properties—including their land, water, timber, forage, wildlife, and recreational resources and the services they perform—in the public welfare.†

These multiple-use principles were codified into law in 1960 when Congress passed the Multiple Use-Sustained Yield Act, which says in Section 4(a) that the Forest Service must safeguard "the management of all the various renewable surface resources of the national forests so that they are utilized in the combination that will best meet the needs of the American people."

Present management of the timber-growing lands in the national forests—which stresses the dominance of timber production over all other uses of the forest—bears so little resemblance to multiple use that many people have come to believe that the Forest Service no longer has this mandate. This is not the case. Even worse, perhaps, is the fact that since multiple-use forestry is no longer practiced in the national forests, people are beginning to forget what it consists of. I propose, therefore, in the next chapter, to use the term "excellent forestry" in place of multiple-use forestry and to describe its justification, to provide the layman with a basis for judging the quality of timber management wherever it is encountered.

BASIC DEFINITIONS

Since there is much confusion about the terminology used to describe various aspects of forestry, I will begin this section with some basic definitions.

The term *silviculture* refers to the art and science of growing trees. It covers only biological considerations and is parallel to such terms as horticulture and agriculture.

Forest management, in contrast, refers to the economic and financial side of forestry. It determines the size of the annual cut, the age to which

---

*Letter from Secretary of Agriculture James Wilson to Gifford Pinchot, Chief of USDA Forest Service, 1 February 1905.
†Michael Frome, *The Forest Service*, 2d ed. (Boulder, CO: Westview Press, 1984), 76.

trees will be allowed to grow before cutting, the specific areas to be cut, and generally allied matters.

We recognize four basic silvicultural systems and two forest management systems. The silvicultural systems are clearcutting, seed tree, shelterwood, and selection systems. The two forest management systems are even-aged management and uneven-aged management.

Silvicultural Systems

Clearcutting systems involve removal of all the timber from the cutting area at one time. Generally, the area must be larger in diameter than one and one-half times the height of the surrounding timber. This system requires that the species be capable of reestablishment on bare soils in full overhead light. Regeneration may depend on seed existing in the leaf litter at the time of logging, on seed from surrounding trees, or, if the area is very large, on species of trees that have a proven ability to respond to planting.

Seed tree systems also involve clearcutting, but occasional carefully selected, healthy trees or groups of trees are left in the forest, adequately spaced, to provide natural regeneration after logging.

Shelterwood systems involve the gradual removal of the timber over a mere fraction of the time required to grow another yield of trees (a rotation), but over a period of time sufficient to secure and foster the desired reproduction. This is accomplished by logging in several stages. Typically, in virgin forests, three cuts will be made over a period of 10 years. The first cut is designed to remove so-called overmature trees and high-risk trees that may fall or be subject to disease or insect attack. This is referred to as a sanitation-salvage cut. The second cut consists of uniformly opening out the canopy in order to afford sufficient light and warmth to stimulate germination, establishment, and survival of the seedlings springing from seed shed by the overhead trees. The second cut is normally made in a good seed year, and the trees reserved for this purpose are, of course, of seed-bearing size. Finally comes one or more cuttings in which the remaining old trees are removed as fast as necessary for the development of the new stand.

All of the silvicultural systems just described are classed as *even-aged silviculture.*

Selection systems, finally, are aimed at establishing or maintaining an even distribution of trees of various age classes throughout the forest.

Single trees or groups of trees selected to be cut will usually consist of those above a certain diameter limit, but occasionally some of these are left if they are of exceptional thrift or quality or are needed as seed trees in some local area of the forest. Decadent, suppressed, diseased, and insect-infested trees below the diameter limit are also removed. This system may be applied with species that do not regenerate successfully in shade as well as those that can tolerate shade. For shade-tolerant species, openings may be small, but for the proper reproduction of shade-intolerant species, a larger group of trees may have to be taken. It is important to remember that most commercial species of conifers are shade intolerant. Group removal also has certain practical logging advantages, so the group selection system tends to become popularly used in a selectively managed forest. However, in general, the forest is dense and relatively dark at all times.

Forest Management Systems

Forest management may be either even-aged or uneven-aged.

Even-aged management consists of managing timber resources by developing relatively large stands of trees for each age class. Cutting areas generally range from 15 or 20 acres to 300 acres, but they have been as large as 1,000 acres in Alaskan national forests and even more on private lands. The forest inventory is maintained by mapping techniques. Even-aged management is well illustrated by the tree farm advertising that is widespread these days. In an even-aged forest, the first three silvicultural systems described above—clearcutting, seed tree, and shelterwood— may be practiced because all of them can be used to create sizable stands of trees of substantially the same age. However, selection silviculture is never used with even-aged management.

Under this system, formerly well-managed forest has often been converted to large blocks of even-aged stands. The simplest and most common practice for achieving an even-aged forest is large-scale liquidation by clearcutting of old growth and naturally occurring uneven-aged stands. These are replaced by plantations or otherwise regenerated even-aged young stands.

Even-aged management has been adopted in our national forests in response to demands for excessive quantities of timber, with no real regard for wildlife and fish habitat, watershed protection and water quality, recreational values, protection of endangered plant and animal species, or long-range outlook for timber quality. Where forests are converted to even-aged stands and then managed accordingly, major silvicultural decisions are made by managers in the central office rather than by foresters in the forest.

Uneven-aged management consists of employing any or all four of the silvicultural techniques previously described as appropriate for the specific stands or groups of trees the forester is treating. However, the size of the openings created by logging and the size of the areas given silvicultural treatment vary according to the judgment of the forester in charge and are frequently too small to be mapped. Hence, the forest inventory must be maintained in terms of the number of trees by species, age, size, condition, and so on.

Even-aged silviculture—clearcutting, seed tree removal, or shelterwood cutting—may be practiced under a system of uneven-aged management. But no system of uneven-aged silviculture—selection or group selection cutting—is possible under even-aged management. This is mainly because the cutting units in an even-aged forest are so large that the subtle interrelationships between species and age groups, important to a secure forest ecosystem, are entirely lost. Before we go on to a more detailed discussion of multiple-use forestry, it will be helpful to understand the problems that arise when forests are managed under even-aged systems.

PROBLEMS WITH CLEARCUTTING AND EVEN-AGED MANAGEMENT

Clearcutting, particularly the magnitude of clearcutting required to convert forests to even-aged management, has become the subject of great controversy all over the world, particularly in the United States, Canada, and Australia and in the tropical rain forests of Asia, Africa, Indonesia, and South America. Here are some of the problems associated with clearcutting.

Soil Erosion and Nutrient Loss

Clearcutting accelerates erosion and loss of the all-important topsoil, thereby impairing the productivity of the land. Erosion increases exponentially with the size of the openings created by logging and with the proportion of timber cut. This is particularly true after roots of stumps decay on steep slopes, thus releasing their hold on otherwise loose earth.

Clearcutting also results in the leaching of nutrients essential to tree growth. Microscopic organisms, whose bodies contain soluble nutrients, are killed by the drastic changes in their environment, and the roots of living plants are no longer present to absorb those nutrients released through death and transfiguration of biological material. Losses are severe in some soils and minor in others, but leaching occurs and productivity is impaired, at least to some degree, wherever vegetation is removed and the soil is laid bare.

Landslides

Frequently, and most often in the western United States, forested mountain slopes are steeper than the angle of repose of the material composing them. The roots of trees hold the soil in place. After clearcutting, when the roots decay, landslides result. Many studies indicate a major increase in the incidence of landslides following clearcutting. A study in southeastern Alaska reported a ninety-three-fold increase in the incidence of landslides within 10 years following logging, accompanied by a four-and-one-half-fold increase in the acreage of the slides.* The volume of earth movement in those incidents was not reported, but it must have been immense.

Flooding

In the northwestern United States, clearcutting and forest fires have increased floods from both rain-snow melt and snow melt. When new growth occurs in such areas and the forest recovers, the flood peak discharges again decrease.

Liquidation of High-Quality Timber

High-quality timber is most often found in virgin forests and in managed uneven-aged forests. Clearcutting and even-aged management result in the hasty liquidation of high quality timber and will therefore lead to a future scarcity of high-quality wood. Old-growth timber is very valuable, and forest owners and managers are strongly tempted to liquidate it. Hence, on both private land and national forest land there has been the tendency to clearcut old-growth forest and then to grow small trees on short cycles for pulp and low-quality lumber. Once this course is set, it is difficult to hold merchantable trees in reserve until they become mature. On the other hand, if one starts with a mixed forest, or is satisfied with limited income from thinning operations until the principal trees become mature, one can develop or maintain a

*Daniel M. Bishop and Mervin E. Stevens, *Landslides on Logged Areas in Southeast Alaska*, Research Paper NOR-1 (Department of Agriculture, Forest Service, 1964).

frequent periodic income from selling valuable old-growth trees on a selection or group selection basis and can enjoy income from other compatible uses of the land as well.

Reduced Wildlife Habitat

Clearcutting reduces the amount of essential habitat available to wildlife. Some species of birds and mammals that are important links in the food chain require dead or hollow trees for nesting. The commercially desirable species of wildlife, principally deer, require a combination of trees for shelter and small openings for food. Research indicates that deer thrive best in selectively managed forests. A few years after regeneration, clearcutting often results in closed, even-aged stands that provide no food or shelter for most desirable species of wildlife.

Loss of Recreational Value

Clearcutting impairs the recreational value of the forest for many years. Immediately after clearcutting, the land presents a depressing sight. One sees bare earth torn up by heavy machinery; stumps; scattered branches; abandoned logs; and a great tangle of other severely damaged vegetation. A few years later, if we are fortunate, the scene becomes one of a large field of seedlings and saplings, frequently intermingled with brush and hardwood sprouts. It remains essentially in this condition for the next 20 to 50 years, by which time it becomes open enough to walk through. But it is still a monoculture of small trees, with little variety and virtually no wildlife. Fifty years or more are required before the area even starts to become interesting, and of course, it will be 80 to 150 years before an interesting variety of species and sizes of trees develops. If a subsequent clearcut occurs before that time, however, this variety will never be achieved.

Loss of Species Diversity

A wide range of species provides the forest ecosystem with the many benefits that result from subtle, yet strengthening, interdependencies. For example, nitrogen-fixing plants such as ceanothus brush enrich the soil, and insect-eating birds protect the forest trees from destructive pests. Clearcutting impairs the long-term productivity of the land by reducing the number of species and thus eliminating these benefits. Furthermore, even-aged stands, usually composed of a single species, are more susceptible to catastrophic loss from insects and disease because most pests attack trees of one particular species or age.

Increased Fire Hazard

Clearcutting results in increased fire hazard. Of all types of vegetation, the lowest fire hazard occurs in mature, old-growth timber. While the highest fire hazard occurs in dry grass, the second highest occurs in stands of seedlings and saplings or abandoned logging debris on recent clearcuts.

The rate at which a fuel burns depends on its moisture content. Inflammable material on the forest floor is relatively moist and slow to burn because of the shade provided by tall trees and the moisture of transpiration held under the forest canopy, where air is less free to move. When all the trees are removed over an extensive area, inflammable material, including young trees, becomes hotter and drier and therefore will burn more readily and rapidly. This principle has been recognized for many years by the Forest Service in its fire control administration. Old-timers say, "To control a fire, run it up into the woods."

Increased Risk from Insects and Disease

Where clearcutting is practiced, there is always the tendency to establish plantations of a single species without regard to the forest type in which that species naturally occurs. A pure stand—one composed of a single species—creates an ideal situation for a disease or a population of insects to build up to epidemic proportions, as has occurred in the southern pine forests. Infection is direct and rapid from tree to tree, and if that one species is destroyed, there is nothing left. The most hazardous pure stands are even-aged stands because fungus parasites are often virulent during only one stage of the trees' development.

For example, fusiform rust (*Cronartium fusiforme*), which slows the growth of or kills slash pine and loblolly pine, has increased dramatically in the South since the 1930s, when these pines were first planted in even-aged stands. Damage from this disease and from outbreaks of the southern pine beetle (*Dendroctonus valens*) has become so severe that the desirability of investing in pine plantations is being questioned.

Likewise, outbreaks of the hemlock looper have been especially destructive in stands composed of a high percentage of hemlock. Where hemlock is combined with a large proportion of other species, infestations soon thin out and lose their destructive power. Attacks of the spruce budworm also have been most destructive in stands composed of a high percentage of the true firs and Douglas-fir.

Plantations of young pine in California are being invaded by a variety of little-known insects, some indigenous and some imported. The insects reduce the growth of stands by sap sucking and defoliation. Some insects kill the topmost shoots, causing upper branches to turn up in replacement, creating crooked or forked stems. Dead trunks and stubs of dead branches make easy entry for heart rot, and in a number of cases, insects will kill the trees outright. The pine reproduction weevil and the more familiar bark weevils are principal causes of tree death in young stands.

Fomes annosus, the agent that causes decay in the butt logs of a good many fire-damaged old trees, is a minor nuisance in a virgin forest and tends to be elminated almost entirely in an uneven-aged forest. However, where clearcutting is practiced, the disease spreads through the stumps and roots of the felled timber to become an epidemic, killing young trees.

Severe Damage to Soil

Clearcutting also does enormous damage to forest soil. It promotes erosion and compaction of the surface soil, particularly where mineral soil is exposed. In dry climates such as those that characterize much of our western forestland, clearcutting exposes organic matter to heat and air, which allows it to become dessicated, slowing down decay. Clearcutting exposes the forest floor to intense solar radiation, often accompanied by evaporation, and, as a result, the normal soil life of fungi, bacteria, worms, and all types of microscopic plants and animals is destroyed or at least greatly changed. This promotes the growth of open-land fauna and flora, such as brush and seed-eating birds, which are usually undesirable. The brush and other vegetation invited by clearcutting severely competes with forest tree seedlings, and the seed-eating birds replace the insect-eating birds that normally protect the forest.

Conditions in natural stands strongly indicate that tree vigor is the most important factor in warding off disease. Stands on good sites generally are not damaged significantly by native diseases, but those on poor sites often suffer severely. If the soil on a site is allowed to deteriorate by careless logging, particularly by excessive bulldozing, subsequent stands will be less vigorous than their predecessors and more subject to loss through insects and disease.

Tree Farming and Multiple Use

The management systems that I have been describing—clearcutting and even-aged management—are currently practiced in most of our national forests. This means that our national forests have largely been converted to tree farms.

Multiple-use forestry and tree farming are exactly opposite in concept and differ radically. Tree farming, in essence, means mass-producing low-quality wood without regard for other values except as they interfere with that objective. In tree farming, large areas are clearcut, then extensive measures are taken to prepare the site, such as raking up and burning of logging debris and scarifying the soil. The area is then replanted with young seedlings, usually varieties selected for fast growth. Tree farming also involves growing trees on short rotations, stimulated by thinning and fertilizing. Competing vegetation and other wildlife are suppressed with biocides, chemicals used to control broadleaf plants that compete with conifers. These substances work their way from one species to another until they become concentrated in birds and animals that live at the top of the food chain. No one knows what concentrations are lethal to the various species unintentionally subjected to this treatment. Multiple-use forestry, on the other hand, is the husbanding of all the resources of the forest and intermingled wild land. We will learn more about the details of its practice in the next chapter.

CHAPTER FOUR
Excellent Forestry

Multiple-use forestry has five characteristics, each requiring considerable elaboration for clear understanding. First of all, cut must be matched with growth—that is, the amount of timber removed from one's property must not be more than the amount that will grow in the cutting interval. This is generally referred to as *sustained yield*. Where one is working with virgin timber, this means continuous production at an even rate, with the aim of achieving an approximate balance between net growth and harvest at the earliest practicable time, in either annual or somewhat longer periods. If a forest is managed to obtain a sustained yield under multiple-use forestry as I am describing it, the quantity of wood produced may increase and its quality may improve, but neither will ever decline.

Multiple-use forestry also implies growing timber on *long rotations*, generally from 100 to 200 years. The length of a rotation is determined by the age of trees at the time of cutting plus whatever time is required to establish new seedlings after logging. Long rotations permit the dominant trees to achieve physiological maturity before being cut or at least reach a size that produces a sustained yield of high-quality wood, in contrast with mere wood fiber.

A third characteristic of multiple-use forestry is *uneven-aged management,* in which trees within the forest are of various ages. Openings created by logging are no larger than is necessary to meet the biological requirements of the trees in the forest; for example, most commercial species of trees are intolerant of shade once they have passed the seedling stage of development. The size and shape of the openings also depend on the height of surrounding timber, the direction of the prevailing wind, the slope and aspect of the land, the silvics of the species involved, and the condition of the timber. All this implies frequent, light cuts; generally, no more than 10 percent of the volume is removed at one time. Forestry is an art as well as a science, and the preparation of logging operations should be the responsibility of the most experienced and highly skilled foresters.

The fourth characteristic of multiple-use forestry consists of *ecological balance*, which maintains the habitats of all native species of plants and animals in the area. Some trees will be allowed to live out their natural life cycles and die standing, to provide for hole-nesting species. These trees should be well distributed throughout the forest, not merely abandoned trees that are unprofitable to log.

Ecological balance also *preserves the natural biota*, which relies on native species of trees as the source of seed to regenerate the forest and on genetic strains known to be acclimated to the site and capable of withstanding hazards peculiar to the locality. (Type conversion, in which a forest is clearcut and replanted with a single species, is a common violation of this principle.) The roles of many species of plants and animals in the ecology of the forest are unknown; therefore, one must be conservative with regard to altering the environment.

Finally, multiple-use forestry is characterized by *extreme care to avoid damage to the soil*, the all-important resource. Foresters the world over are behaving as though the importance of the top layer of naturally occurring soils has proven to be a myth. Actually, life as we know it on this planet depends directly on that top foot or so of soil. Wherever this has been ignored, civilizations have ceased to exist.

THE ADVANTAGES OF EXCELLENT FORESTRY

The advantages of multiple-use forest management are overwhelming.

Multiple-Use Forestry Reduces Fire Hazard

The lowest fire hazard of all the cover types found in our forests occurs in mature, old-growth timber. Dry grass carries the highest fire hazard, but the two next highest hazards occur in stands of saplings and in logging slash on cutover land. In the mature forest, air is trapped by the full canopy of the trees overhead, creating a microclimate that is kept humid by the transpiration of the trees and is cooled by the shade. Fire hazard is primarily a function of fuel moisture content. In the mature forest, moisture is relatively high and remains so even in the middle of hot summer days. Furthermore, mature trees are mostly free of branches close to the ground, and their bark tends to be fire resistant. Thus, even when fires do occur, they tend to move rapidly along the ground, burning merely leaf litter and debris and occasional patches of young trees.

A dramatic illustration of how a mature forest reduces fire hazard occurred in 1956 in the Haystack fire in northern California's Klamath River country. At one point the fire roared up the south slope of the Siskiyous, going through three adjacent ownerships situated at about the same elevation and having the same cover type. One was a section of national forest that had been logged a few years before in accordance with the Forest Service Region 5 standard marking rules. About 60 percent of the volume of the forest, primarily the oldest and largest trees, had been removed. The second section was virgin timber, and the third was property belonging to a lumber company that had recently cut everything permitted under the California State Forest Practice rules: about 90 percent of the volume of the forest had been cut; only trees under 20 inches or so in diameter were spared.

The fire killed about half of the timber on the national forest parcel; it killed practically every living thing on the lumber company's land; but it only burned a few patches of small reproducing trees in the virgin forest. It did burn the decayed hearts out of the few standing dead trees, which, after falling, left some hollow logs to become habitats for a variety of living things. Clearly, the forester who maintains the full forest canopy as much as possible and practices uneven-aged management is least likely to suffer disaster from fire.

Of course it must be recognized that fire is always a factor in forest ecology and that some regime of controlled burning is essential in many forest types to maintain ecological balance and to prevent disastrous fires. We must also recognize that occasionally there are lightning-caused fire storms that can be neither prevented nor controlled by any known technology.

While foresters usually insist upon felling all dead trees during logging operations because the trees constitute a fire hazard, they frequently overlook the fact that these very trees provide habitats for many birds that perform a great service in controlling the insect enemies of our forests. These birds include woodpeckers, chickadees, titmice, nuthatches, creepers, mountain bluebirds, and violet-green swallows.

Multiple-Use Forestry Reduces Damage from Windthrow

As with fire, occasional uncontrollable disasters are caused by severe windstorms that level patches and sometimes large areas of forest. But trees grown individually or in small groups tend to be wind-firm, in contrast with trees grown in large, even-aged stands. Light selection logging, or clearcutting of groups or small patches of trees, provides maximum assurance against windthrow. During the great Columbus Day storm of 1963 along the West Coast, a tremendous amount of damage occurred in heavily cut stands. Relatively speaking, the damage was much less in virgin timber, even though much of the virgin timber was in naturally occurring even-aged stands.

Multiple-Use Forestry Reduces Damage from Insects and Disease

Damage from insects and disease is far more severe where clearcutting is practiced than it is in forests where selective cutting is the method of management. Where large areas are clearcut, as when forests are converted to stands of trees of the same age, certain insects may breed in the slash in great numbers and later attack the young reproducing trees. Perhaps the best example is the huge epidemic of southern pine beetle that is killing pure, even-aged stands of loblolly pine in the southern states. The outbreak began in eastern Texas in 1982; since then, outbreaks have occurred in Arkansas, Louisiana, Mississippi, and Alabama. In these states, the beetles have killed about 250,000 acres of pine, which would have yielded 1.5 billion board feet of lumber.*

Multiple-Use Forestry Produces High-Quality Wood and Fiber

Forests can and should be managed to produce a continuous, even flow of mature timber. Old growth is far superior to young growth, however you look at it. Stumpage prices are much higher for old-growth than for young-growth timber. Prices of higher-grade commodities have increased substantially in recent years because of the increasing scarcity of old-growth timber. Fine, close-grained redwood used for interior trim has become scarce and extremely expensive; similarly, close-grained, edge-grained Douglas-fir used for flooring and stair steps is becoming rare. The same may be said for boards without knots, commonly used for doors and cabinets. We can expect to see a great increase in the use of pulp, but the great quantities of young growth available will hold pulp log prices down during the forseeable future. In pulp, furthermore, quality of fiber will become an important factor.

Growing timber slowly and on long rotations has another advantage: it greatly increases the quality of the fiber. In the dense canopy of a selectively managed forest, the trees tend to grow slowly. This is not to say

---

*Southwide Suppression Program for the Southern Pine Beetle (Department of Agriculture, Forest Service, 1986), 1.

that the total volume of timber grown is necessarily any less than in even-aged stands. Nakoosa-Edwards Paper Company grows pine for pulp in Wisconsin because the dense, slowly grown wood produces more fiber per acre than can be recovered from the pine plantations in Georgia, which produce four times the volume of much lower-density wood. The fiber from trees grown slowly is longer and stronger than that from fast-grown pine, and longer and stronger fibers are needed in the manufacture of high-quality paper. Quality is also a consideration in veneer. Second-growth Douglas-fir is much less valuable for veneer than is old growth. Second growth not only is undesirable for veneer faces, it also results in rough veneer cuts; the numerous knots in the second growth tend to chip the knife when they are cut. If lumber is produced, the yield of high-grade material is lower from second-growth than from old-growth trees.

The living part of a tree, aside from its leaves and roots, is a single layer of cells between the bark and the woody bole called the cambium layer. These cells divide to alternatively produce wood and bark. As a tree matures and grows in girth, its cambium produces longer and thicker-walled cells. The length of fibers laid down in new growth in conifers increases with the age of the tree. Length generally varies from 1 millimeter at age 1 to about 4 millimeters at age 70, after which time length of fiber tends to remain constant with increase in age. This means that where timber is being grown for fiber, the longest fibers occur only in that part of the tree that has grown after age 70. It would seem to be good business, therefore, to grow trees to an age of 100 to 200 years and to use for pulp chips the residue from squaring or rounding the logs, making high-quality lumber and plywood from the remainder of the core. This is essentially what is done with our virgin timber today, but not with trees grown on a short rotation.

What I have said about the length of fibers is also true of the density or strength of fibers. That part of the tree that has been laid down by the cambium layer after age 70 contains the strongest fibers as well as the longest ones. Also, as trees grow more slowly, which they do as they get older, they tend to have dense fiber in the crown as well as in the lower bole. Consequently, the tops of trees grown on a long rotation are superior for pulp purposes.

That part of the conifer grown before 40 to 50 years of age is inferior for pulp in that it has a high proportion of extractives. The yield of fiber is small, and the amount of dissolved material that must be disposed of is proportionally higher than when pulp is made from slowly grown old wood. This waste material adds to production costs, and it creates severe water pollution problems at pulp mills.

Multiple-Use Forestry Is Economically Sound

We hear a good deal of talk these days from both foresters and industry representatives who say they cannot afford to grow trees on a long rotation or to a great size. They say they must clearcut for economic reasons. But studies on the subject show that this is plain wrong. A study reported by Atkinson in 1967 showed that the cost of felling, limbing, and bucking trees from 45 to 48 inches in diameter cost $7.04 per thousand board feet, in contrast to $18.36 per thousand board feet for trees between 12 and 16 inches in diameter. Similarly, the cost of yarding and loading them onto trucks was twice as much per thousand board feet for trees 12 inches in diameter as it was for trees 30 inches in diameter.* (Bucking means cutting trees up into log lengths, and yarding means collecting the logs for loading.) Although the dollar figures for the costs in this section have changed due to inflation in recent years, the comparisons, which are the point here, remain accurate.

The February 1969 issue of the *Journal of Forestry* reports the findings of a research team studying comparative logging costs under four cutting specifications, ranging from single-tree selection to clearcutting. The team concluded that logging costs from standing tree to truck do not differ appreciably with cutting method, and the forest manager is therefore free to choose a cutting technique on the basis of management and silvicultural considerations other than cost.†

A study by Kenneth N. Boe in the redwood region indicated a logging cost of $11.37 per thousand board feet in a selection system—slightly less than the $11.45 per thousand board feet where clearcutting was practiced. This study was done by the Forest Service in the Six Rivers National Forest.‡ A similar study made in the California pine region showed that where clearcutting was practiced, involving 17,000 board feet per acre, 133 man-minutes per thousand board feet were expended. Heavy selection cutting involving 13,000 board feet per acre required only 118 man-minutes per thousand board feet. But surprisingly, a light sanitation-salvage cut, involving only 3,000 board feet per acre, cost only

---

*William Atkinson, "Economics of Young-growth Management," *Proceedings of a Conference on Young-Growth Forest Management in California* (Berkeley, CA: University of California, Department of Forestry and Resource Management, 1967), 65-74.
†Philip M. McDonald, William A. Atkinson, and Dale O. Hall, "Logging Costs and Cutting Methods in Young-Growth Ponderosa Pine in California," *Journal of Forestry* 67 (February 1980).
‡Kenneth N. Boe, "Tractor-Logging Costs and Production in Old-Growth Redwood," Research Paper PSW-8 (Department of Agriculture, Forest Service, 1963).

119 man-minutes per thousand board feet, considerably less than clearcutting.*

It is fairly easy to explain these figures. Where partial cutting is employed, we are removing a preponderance of larger trees from the forest. This gives us the greatest handling efficiency during each step of the logging process.

The size of clearcut openings is another, though slightly different, consideration. Here, presumably, we would not have the compensating factor of having selected large trees as in partial cutting, although clearcut patches may be selected on approximately the same basis as individual trees to remove patches of large, old trees. An experiment was conducted in 1965 by the Forest Service in the mixed conifer area of the northern Sierra Nevada to determine the relative costs of logging various-sized openings. The openings ranged from 30 feet to 90 feet in diameter. Costs for logging were found to range from $7.04 to $7.99 per thousand board feet, and the author observed that the differences were not statistically significant, concluding thereby that the size of the opening is irrelevant to the cost of logging.†

Multiple-Use Forestry Promotes Better Regeneration

Uneven-aged management—where a forest contains a mix of trees of various ages, which are generally cut only when they reach maturity—provides us with many advantages in obtaining reproduction. This type of management safeguards the rich variety of trees and vegetation within a forest. The small clearings that are made when trees are harvested assure us of a reliable source of seed because the seeds of commercial conifers rarely travel more than a few tree lengths from their source, and partial shade from the edge of the forest prevents excessive heat and drought from killing seedlings. Also, the naturally occurring old growth is composed of genetic strains specifically adapted to the site through having survived all the hazards and peculiarities of the immediate environment.

Collecting seeds in one area for reforestation in another is far more hazardous than is generally realized. Trees grown at a low elevation from seed gathered higher up are apt to be late in starting their spring growth. This can be serious where we experience long summer

*A. A. Hasel, "Logging Cost as Related to Tree Size and Intensity of Cutting in Ponderosa Pine," *Journal of Forestry* 44 (August 1946).
†Philip M. McDonald, "Logging Costs and Production Rates for the Group-Selection Cutting Method," Research Note PSW-59 (Department of Agriculture, Forest Service, Pacific Southwest Forest and Range Experiment Station, Berkeley, CA, 1965).

droughts, as in the Sierra Nevada. Likewise, trees grown at a high elevation from seed collected lower down may burst their buds and start to grow at the first signs of spring, only to be killed back by late frosts.

Other, more subtle, difficulties occur when trees are planted outside their natural range. Silviculturists have warned against this practice since forestry began. It has been found , for example, that a native rust is killing Monterey pine planted on cutover redwood forestland in northern California. It had been assumed that the limited natural range of this pine (the Monterey peninsula) was probably the result of the tree failing to migrate back northward following an ice age. Now we are finding that there must be other reasons for that species adhering to its limited range, reasons subtle and unknown. As another example, loblolly pine planted as few as 50 miles either north or south of the seed source is found to grow at a slower pace than trees grown from local seed.

At best, trees are injured by planting. Stands naturally regenerated in small clearings are less susceptible to disease than those artificially reproduced. Usually, far more seedlings occur naturally than one would plant. The seedlings that survive are those that do not come in contact with decaying roots of the previous generation and thus avoid diseases that so often decimate plantations; the seedlings usually do survive in sufficient numbers to provide adequate stocking. This natural process also provides random spacing, avoiding the jolt many people experience on discovering a forest to be made up of evenly spaced trees in straight rows.

Multiple-Use Forestry Maintains a Natural Mix of Species

Excellent forestry preserves ecological balance because it maintains the natural mixture of species that occurs in the forest. This is best done by relying on natural reproduction and by controlling the size of openings when harvesting timber. There are many reasons to maintain a natural mixture. Only a few are well understood, but these are enough, I believe, to demonstrate a need to maintain the primeval ecosystems. This is of particular importance in forests because of the great length of time between harvests, in contrast with agriculture. Farmers can rotate crops to replenish the soil. They can replace unsatisfactory varieties with newly generated ones developed by geneticists in our fine agricultural colleges. They can correct many kinds of mistakes in a single growing season. But foresters usually do not live long enough to discover their mistakes, and by the time errors become apparent, the evidence needed for understanding failures has been destroyed, or genetic strains peculiarly adapted to a particular site have been extinguished.

Some species make excessively heavy demands on soil nutrients when planted in pure stands. They may grow well in youth, but later may slow and deteriorate. It is often necessary to develop an admixture of species that makes a light demand on the soil and whose leaf litter decomposes readily into a mild, rich humus. Furthermore, pure stands may fail to utilize the site completely. They may be composed of a shade-intolerant species and consequently have thin, open crowns, which presumably fail to utilize the sunlight completely, or they may be shallow rooted and able to utilize only part of the soil. Also, research has revealed examples of certain plants that have very specialized functions. For example, sugar maple has been shown to inhibit growth of its competitors by exuding a toxic substance through its root system; dogwoods intermingled with pine in the South are found to serve as calcium pumps, and calcium is the essential nutrient most frequently lacking in forest soils of that region; and the roots of alder exude a substance that prevents the spread of root-rotting fungi.

Clearly, so much is unknown about interrelationships of plants and other living things that it behooves us to maintain the natural balance as much as we can. After all, the species mix that naturally occurs in the virgin forest is there because the inhabitants are mutually supportive of, or at least benign toward, each other. Otherwise, they would not be there.

I have a particular concern with respect to the Pacific Northwest. The area west of the Cascades and into the northwestern corner of California is known as the Douglas-fir region. Forests there comprise the greatest variety of coniferous species of any forests in the world. Many foresters confuse the Douglas-fir species with the Douglas-fir region. They insist that clearcutting is necessary to obtain satisfactory regeneration of Douglas-fir when actually their objective is to eliminate the associated species, which are commonly regarded as having less value.

The naturally occurring mixtures of tree species and shrubs in this region are fully described in "Natural Vegetation of Oregon and Washington," by Jerry F. Franklin and C. T. Dyrness, General Technical Report PNW-8 (Department of Agriculture, Forest Service, 1973). The naturally occurring mixtures found generally throughout the country may be found in *Silvics of Forest Trees of the United States* (Agriculture Handbook No. 271), published by the Forest Service.

Multiple-Use Forestry Preserves the Natural Biota

Of even greater importance than providing for appropriate mixtures of species is preserving the gene pool found in the natural forest biota. It has long been recognized that identification of species is a purely arbitrary division of a continuous range of variation within plants having generally distinguishable characteristics. During the last 25 years, however, through vast improvements in technology, scientists have discovered ways to identify genetic material. It is now known that there are hundreds of varieties within a species, each having its optimum environment. It is evident that living organisms have migrated up and down the continents with the coming and going of ice ages, and the varieties that have survived under these very stressful circumstances are those best suited to the situation in which they find themselves. Take the loblolly pine, for example. It grows all the way from the Atlantic to eastern Texas. Yet if seed from this species is planted as few as 50 miles either north or south of its origin, the trees do poorly compared with trees grown from the local variety of seed. Likewise, as I pointed out earlier, ponderosa pine planted in the Sierra Nevada at a lower elevation than the seed source is likely to start slowly in the spring and fail to start its annual growth before the summer drought sets in. If it is planted at a higher elevation than the seed source, it is likely to bud out at the first burst of spring, only to be killed back by late frosts.

Here's an interesting story that illustrates how little we know about how plants adapt themselves to specialized environments. It was told to me by Bill Isaacs, a colleague of mine in New Mexico, when I visited the state a few years ago on behalf of the Sierra Club. Bill is a forest mycologist (a mycologist is one who studies fungi). He taught the subject for 2 years at the University of Washington and for 1 year at the University of Michigan. When he was in Michigan, he got a phone call from a friend in New Mexico, who said, "Bill! It's raining and the mushrooms are popping. Come on out!" Bill told him he was crazy. "There are no mushrooms in New Mexico." But his friend insisted, so Bill went.

Now I must digress to give you some background for this story. Do you know what mycorrhiza means? Well, the roots of conifers are relatively large and clumsy. Conifers alone cannot compete successfully with other seed-bearing plants because of their inefficient root systems. But there are mushrooms whose mycelia—that's what the mycologists call roots—penetrate the conifer's roots and draw out synthesized sugars and starches for their own use. (Mushrooms contain no chlorophyll and do not photosynthesize their own food.) In return, these mushrooms extract minerals from the soil and supply them to the trees, minerals that the trees' roots cannot absorb. This relationship is called mycorrhizal, and mushrooms that have this relationship with trees are called mycorrhizae.

Well, when Bill Isaacs made this sudden trip to New Mexico, there were precisely 12 mycorrhizal mushrooms described in the scientific literature. He and his friend headed for the Gila National Forest, near the Mexican border, where they collected 70 pounds of mushrooms under a grove of foxtail pine. After they hauled the mushrooms back to the laboratory, they proceeded to describe over 360 new mycorrhizal species! Three hundred and sixty new species not previously identified, described in a single day from a single site! That shows us something about the magnitude of the unknown.

Multiple-Use Forestry Protects Soils

In Chapter 5 I will enlarge on the importance of protecting the soil during logging, but the subject deserves mention in this discussion of multiple use as well. American foresters notoriously disregard the effects of logging practices on soils. This is particularly true in the post-war era, in which logging has become highly mechanized and much of the remaining timber being logged is on steep ground. The oversized and unwieldy equipment used by logging operators is totally unacceptable in multiple-use forestry. Logging should be conducted with light, small equipment, which can be maneuvered around the trees that are left standing and which functions without disturbing the soil. All logging should be planned and supervised to prevent soil damage, and no logging should be permitted where complete protection of the soil cannot be assured.

Uneven-aged management, in which both road construction and logging are carefully planned, sustains the quality and productivity of the soil. It tends to maintain soil porosity and absorbancy, thus reducing erosion and flood damage.

Multiple-Use Forestry Protects Fish and Wildlife

The care of the soil and maintenance of a full forest canopy that characterize multiple-use forestry also protect the habitat for fish in streams by keeping the water clean and cold and by preserving spawning beds. Silt and slime, the products of erosion, have destroyed untold thousands of spawning beds.

Old trees are required habitat for many species, for a variety of reasons. Very large trees are necessary to support the huge, heavy nests of bald eagles, for example. The red-cockaded woodpecker roosts in cavities in old, live southern pines. In order to peck out their nesting cavities, these birds require pines infected with a heart-rot fungus called red heart, and that fungus does not ordinarily infect trees younger than 80 years of age. The woodpecker needs live trees for its nesting cavities because the resin or pitch that flows from the sapwood of only living trees creates a barrier to tree-climbing snakes that prey on fledglings. The bird also needs extensive pine and pine-hardwood forests to meet its foraging requirements.

Hollow trees and logs are often required nesting places for raccoons and foxes. Standing dead trees constitute nesting sites for a great many birds and small mammals, most of whom protect the forest. Most of the hole-nesting birds live on insects that without population control can become epidemic and destroy large areas of forest trees.

A great deal has been written in recent years about the spotted owl, an endangered species that inhabits forests in the West. This little bird requires for its survival large areas of old-growth forest fairly close to each other and ranging the length of the West Coast. Protection of the spotted owl is important because its habitat requirements coincide with those of a large number of other ecologically important birds and animals.

Multiple-Use Forestry Protects Recreational Value

The uneven-aged management techniques used in multiple-use forestry largely preserve the beauty of the natural forest because only certain trees are selected to be cut at any given time. After 2 or 3 years, the effects of logging are practically invisible. For most people, such well-managed forests will quite adequately serve most wildland recreational needs. If we can maintain the natural beauty of the forests even while logging, we can take a good deal of pressure off our wilderness areas, which have become increasingly popular and crowded. In contrast, present practices, particularly clearcutting, in the national forests and to a greater extent on private forestlands, is creating an ever-increasing demand for more wilderness.

If national parks and wilderness areas become the only places of natural beauty available for outdoor experience, people who object to the inaccessibility of wilderness and the absence of conveniences there will crowd in with those who understand and appreciate it. This not only will increase the use of such places but will add to the clamor for roads and other nonwilderness development. Furthermore, if we should reach the sad state of having no large, old-growth timber except within our national parks, we will surely face a great demand to log that last bit too. Indeed, the overture to this outcry is already being heard. We had a foretaste of it in the ridiculous arguments advanced in opposition to the establishment of the Redwood National Park.

Good foresters have long supported multiple-use or excellent forestry. Joseph S. Illick, who was state forester of Pennsylvania when Gifford Pinchot was governor of that state, wrote as follows in 1935:

> Several hundred years of European forestry and about half a century of experience in the United States offers ample proof that the best forestry rests not upon a single purpose but a number of purposes. On the same area of land it is often possible to grow timber, furnish food and shelter for game animals and other wildlife, provide protection to watersheds, offer healthful recreational opportunities, enhance the beauty of the landscape, and promote the general welfare. The best forestry takes account of all these values and works out a comprehensive and coordinated technique to handle them efficiently. Such a composite plan of management is appropriately called multiple-purpose forestry. Rarely is a single purpose in forestry so overwhelmingly dominant as to warrant the exclusion of other objectives. Multiple-purpose forestry has as its objective the full and balanced development and use of all forest resources and the greatest sustained output of forest products, uses and services. Multiple-purpose forestry programs are not developed by accident, nor are they the result of planless endeavor. Only through conscious, deliberate, and planned efforts are the best results obtained. To exist as a nation, to prosper as a state, and to live as a people, we need forestry, and multiple-purpose forestry offers the best means to get it and keep it.*

As we have seen, excellent forestry costs nothing but restraint and, as Heinrich Cotta wrote two centuries ago, offers the greatest gifts a forest can provide—except in the ideal situation in which there are no people, and hence there is no forestry.

---

*Joseph S. Illick, *An Outline of General Forestry* (Totowa, NJ: Barnes & Noble Books, 1935), 16. Permission granted by Barnes & Noble Books, Totowa, New Jersey.

CHAPTER FIVE
Care for the Soil

At an annual meeting of the California Alumni Foresters in Berkeley some years ago, the speaker at our evening banquet was Walter Lowdermilk. He was a forester who had become famous as a soil scientist; he had worked with Franklin Roosevelt to establish the Soil Conservation Service. He described a trip he made to China, financed by Boxer Indemnity Funds, to study the Gobi Desert, how it had come to be, and what measures might be used to restore the land.

In the Gobi Desert, he found temples on mountaintops surrounded by stone walls that protected good soil and thriving trees. Outside the stone walls, on the slopes of the mountains, he observed nothing but blowing sand dunes for great distances. Now, he knew that under normal conditions, the poorest soil is found on mountaintops because fine silt and humus are carried down the slopes with rain and melting snow, finally making up the alluvial flats near the mouths of rivers.

He explained this anomaly, concluding from this and many other observations that the desert had once been forest. The land had been destroyed by logging, overgrazing, and burning. He told us how this experience in the Gobi desert had led him subsequently to study similar situations around the Mediterranean and how he made a career of warning the world that civilization depends on that top foot of soil, where the nutrients reside. This philosophy was taught as gospel when I attended forestry school in the 1930s and was generally accepted by the scientific community.

Walter was a very gentle and sensitive man. In his address he had revealed an uncanny sense of observation that gave us who listened attentively a feeling of humility. After the lecture we filed out in silence, for we knew we had been in the presence of greatness.

But there in the lobby, leaning over a table, with his neck all red like a turkey, was one of my old forestry professors, hollering, "Bull—! Bull—! That man's a Communist!" The professor couldn't accept any criticism of the practices of his friends in the lumber business.

Foresters today are performing as though our understanding of the dependence of civilization on soil and the importance of soil conservation had somehow been discredited. This is certainly not the case. However, care for the soil during logging has indeed gone out of fashion. One of the worst examples of carelessness to the soil may be seen in the redwood region of California. I worked with the Sierra Club and others in helping to establish the Redwood National Park, and as a result I had many opportunities to observe logging practices in that region. Typically, logging begins with the felling of all the "white woods," as everything other than redwood is locally known. These trees are then cut into 16-foot lengths and pulled up tight by cable to the backs of tractors. Then the bulldozer blade is shoved into the ground and the log and tractor combination is driven downhill, shoving the earth ahead, using the blade as a brake.

Next, strips of uniform slope, called "lays," are bulldozed from each of the big trees to allow the brittle redwoods to fall on flat ground. The trees are then felled, cut into logs, hitched onto cables, pulled up tight against the tractors, and driven down the slope. The bulldozer blade is again used as a brake in this gruesome caravan. By the time logging is completed, the land is crisscrossed with ruts as much as 10 feet deep. I came across some that were 30 feet deep where the tractors had used the same route repeatedly.

When you look at aerial photographs of cutover forest logged this way, you can see that somewhere between 75 and 80 percent of the surface area has been scraped off by the bulldozers. Whoever is responsible for such catastrophe has no conscience and no foresight. He has simply removed the timber in the way that was fastest, cheapest, and most profitable.

After observing such practices on a different occasion, I raised the question of soil value to another professor of forestry, a good scientist and an old friend. We were sitting in a bar after a field trip with members of the California state legislature. The purpose of the field trip had been to consider the adequacy of California's forest practices act, and my old friend the professor was defending industry's practices. I began to question my own understanding of the role that soils played in forestry. I asked him, "It's many years now since I was in school. Am I out of date? Is it no longer believed that we depend on that top layer of soil? Can it be that soil theory has changed? He responded, "No, of course not. What made you ask that question?"

American foresters notoriously disregard the effects of logging practices on soils, ignoring the detrimental impact their careless destruction will have on future forests. Anyone who doubts the importance of protecting the topsoil should read *Topsoil and Civilization* by Vernon Gill Carter and Tom Dale. They point to example after example of civilizations rising and falling according to their use and abuse of the topsoil. In western Iran, northern Iraq, Syria, Lebanon, Greece, and many other now-poor countries that once supported flourishing civilizations, the scenario was the same. People deforested their hillsides to plant crops. When the winter rains came, the fertile topsoil on the slopes was washed away, and the land was ruined in a few generations. "When this happened," the authors write, "the people had to move to new land or eke out an existence on impoverished land. These civilizations declined or perished in a few centuries, as they depleted or exhausted the lands on which they were built."*

A photograph by Walter Lowdermilk in the same book shows one of the four remaining groves of the cedars of Lebanon, which once comprised a magnificent forest of more than a million acres, one of the wonders of the ancient world. It was logged by the Phoenicians, with bronze axes, and erosion set in as soon as the land was cleared. The mountains and hills have eroded to bare rock; the area now produces little except silt.

We in the modern world ignore the importance of the topsoil at our own peril. But, unlike the ancients, we have the lessons of history to warn us of the likely consequence of our carelessness, and we have the tools to do a much better job.

In the remainder of this chapter, I will demonstrate what needs to be done to protect forest soils. But first we need to know something about the makeup of the soil itself and about the natural processes that go on in the forest soil environment.

SOIL STRUCTURE: NUTRIENTS AND MICROORGANISMS

It is generally accepted that fertile soil is composed of 40 to 50 percent minerals, 20 to 25 percent moisture, 20 to 25 percent gases, and 5 to 15 percent humus. Spread among these components are the nutrients and trace minerals crucial to plant growth.

The study of chemistry teaches us that the earth is made up of one hundred or so elements. Plant physiologists tell us that only a few of them are essential for plant life. An interesting way to remember these is to recall the phrase "See Hopkin's Cafe, mighty good!" This is a

*Vernon Gill Carter and Tom Dale, *Topsoil and Civilization* (Norman, OK: University of Oklahoma Press, 1974), 14.

mnemonic device that translates into C HOPKNS CaFe, Mg, the symbols for carbon (C), hydrogen (H), oxygen (O), phosphorus (P), potassium (K), nitrogen (N), sulfur (S), calcium (Ca), iron (Fe), and magnesium (Mg). In addition to these, certain plants also require a few trace elements that sometimes are lacking in the soil. But it is not necessary to get into that amount of detail in this general overview.

For practical purposes, the elements essential to plant life may be considered to be omnipresent throughout the surface of the earth, except for five: potassium, phosphorus, nitrogen, calcium, and magnesium. These elements are available to plants only in soluble form and therefore sometimes are absent. It is important, however, to have a general idea of how those soluble nutrients remain available to plants and how they are stored in the soil.

That top foot or so of earth that we call soil is the most densely populated zone in the biosphere. Ed Munns, former chief of the Division of Forest Influences in the Forest Service, wrote as follows in *Soils and Men: 1938 Yearbook of Agriculture*: "Fungi, bacteria, protozoa and minute animals inhabit forest soil in tremendous numbers. They conserve the vital elements, contribute to soil porosity, and are indispensable in maintaining the supply of colloidal organic matter in the soil. Different species probably have specialized environmental requirements."[*]

In that same publication, Charles Thom, principal mycologist, and Nathan Smith, senior bacteriologist, in the Department of Agriculture's Bureau of Plant Industry wrote that organisms in forest soil "vary in size from the microscopic up to the gigantic and in numbers from a few per acre to billions per ounce. They have in reality changed the surface layer of the soil from an aggregate of mineral particles to a mass teeming with organisms and honeycombed by visible channels made by roots of plants or by burrows of animals and insects."[†] Bacteria carry on the process of decomposition, but they are not alone in that function. Fungi are numerous and active, especially under forest conditions. Some of them, the mycorrhizae, live in close association with the roots of plants, somewhat like the nitrogen-fixing bacteria, in an arrangement that is advantageous to both the plant and the fungus. Then there are protozoa, one-celled animals that feed on bacteria, and slime molds that apparently feed on both bacteria and fungi. Going up the scale of size, there are nematodes, worms, insects, and larger animals living in the soil and each having some effect on it.

---

[*]U.S. Department of Agriculture, *Soils and Men: 1938 Yearbook of Agriculture* (Washington, DC: Government Printing Office, 1938), 226. This great classic is highly recommended to the reader.
[†]Ibid., 940.

In the same publication, Ivan Sims, Ed Munns, and John Auten wrote as follows in a chapter titled *"Management of Forest Soils."*

Reduction of the litter to humus is effected by the fungi, bacteria, and animals that live in and on the litter and soil. The primary attack is by wood-rotting fungi and such vegetarian animal forms as termites, ants, larvae of larger insects, earthworms, millepedes and mites. In the wake of these primary attackers come other organisms that eat them, their offal, what is left of the litter, and each other. The fineness of the resulting material can be visualized by considering that many of the species of animal with chewing mouth parts are only one-tenth of a millimeter (one two-hundred-fiftieth of an inch) broad.

In the soil itself, a similar population converts the dead roots and rootlets and the organic matter brought down from the litter layer. Their burrows and tunnels, although averaging only a millimeter in diameter, contribute in large measure to the lightness and porosity of the soil.

The small size of these useful animals is compensated for, however, by their numbers. Partial catches obtained with special equipment show as many as 5,500 individuals (not including earthworms and nematodes) per square foot of soil to a depth of 13 inches. As many as 70 different species have been collected from less than a square foot of rich forest soil. The total animal population of the soil and litter together probably approaches 10,000 individuals per square foot.*

Obviously, much of the nutrient reservoir in the soil is sloshing around in the bellies of these tiny organisms with chewing mouth parts. These animals, by eating and being eaten, hold soluble nutrients in the soil in this manner, and other living things convert insoluble nutrients in the forest litter and the soil below to forms that can be utilized by plant life.

SOIL NUTRIENT CYCLES

Phosphorus

Low productivity of crops is due more often to a lack of phosphorus than to a lack of any other element. Phosphorus is found in every living cell and is essential in both plant and animal nutrition. The ultimate source of this element is the sea. On land it is found mainly as apatite, a sedimentary rock, and in the bones and shells of living organisms.

*Ibid., 739.

Phosphorus is found in the finest particles of soil and is therefore subject to loss through wind and running water. Because of its relative scarcity in mineral form, life depends on natural recycling of this element.

Nitrogen

Nitrogen comes from various sources, but most commonly from the root nodules of leguminous plants, which are well distributed throughout the world. Many other plants, such as ceanothus and alder, also fix atmospheric nitrogen (convert it into substances that can be utilized by green plants). Alder has the capacity to fix about 350 pounds of nitrogen per acre per year. This is truly phenomenal and is about on par with that produced by an alfalfa field. Interestingly, the acacia species in Australia function in the same way as alder does in our western North American forests. They are understory trees that tend to take over an area after it has been clearcut. The leafy lichens that grow on the branches of trees and are often seen lying on the forest floor are another source of nitrogen. There is estimated to be about 200 pounds of lichens per acre in the rain forests of the Cascades. About 25 percent of those, or about 50 pounds per acre, are nitrogen fixers. This accounts for about 15 pounds of nitrogen per acre per year. Nitrogen is fixed, too, as electric sparks pass through air, so much of it comes from rain, particularly after lightning storms.

Potassium

Potassium is well distributed throughout the surface of the earth, particularly in the form of sand and silt derived from orthoclase, microcline, and muscovite. Under various weathering factors, principally temperature changes and the action of water, these and other potash-containing silicates are converted slowly to an ordinary clay, known as kaolinite, and water-soluble potassium. The potassium cycle is relatively simple, but this element is not available to plants until it is converted to water-soluble compounds by bacteria, mycorrhizae, and possibly other organisms. Normally, soil contains about ten times as much potassium as it does soluble nitrogen. The cycle of soluble potassium is essentially from soil moisture to plant, with the size of soil particles acting as a regulator of solubility; then from the plant to animals of all kinds, including the microscopic; and through animal wastes back to the soil. Potassium is lost from forest soils mainly when it is leached out by erosion and when wood is removed from the land by logging.

Calcium and Magnesium

Calcium and magnesium are widely distributed in the earth, occurring in both igneous and sedimentary rocks. As with phosphorus, these elements are essential to both plant and animal life but are available to plants only in soluble compounds. Hence, plants depend on various microorganisms and a few particular plants that have the capacity to utilize these elements in their mineral form. In nature, they are recycled adequately in most ecosystems. However, in situations in which crops are removed from the land, their cycle is broken. Unless measures are taken to minimize losses, and either to limit harvesting to match the natural rate at which calcium and magnesium can be derived from inert minerals or to artificially replenish them, the soil will become impoverished over a period of time.

HOW NUTRIENTS ARE LOST

The rich nutrient reservoir in forest soils can be lost or depleted in several ways: (1) by removal of the timber itself during logging; (2) by the compaction caused by the use of heavy equipment during logging and road construction, which destroys the microorganisms in the soil and causes the nutrients they contain to be leached out; (3) by erosion, which transports soil nutrients out of the watershed; (4) by exposure caused by removing vegetation that casts shade, retaining a relatively humid atmosphere and preventing the soil from becoming too hot for survival of microorganisms; and (5) by the practice of tree monoculture, particularly when herbicides are used to suppress competing vegetation.

Removal of Trees

In forest trees, approximately half of the essential nutrients taken up from the earth are deposited in the bole, or trunk; about one quarter, in the leaves and small branches; and the remainder, in the stump and roots. This varies greatly with the age and species of trees. With deciduous trees and shrubs, the distribution of nutrients obviously varies with the season. The magnitude of the nutrient reservoir also varies greatly from place to place, depending on climate, slope, and the basic mineral content of the underlying strata. There is no question, however, that nutrients are removed whenever logs are taken off the land, and because of the distribution of nutrients within the trees themselves, it is important to leave the small branches, leaves, stumps, and roots behind to minimize the detrimental impact of logging. Also, the shorter the rotation, the more rapidly will the nutrient reservoir be depleted. It is easy to see that whole-tree logging and short rotations are therefore detrimental to the health of forest soils.

Indeed, some foresters have argued that nutrient cycles should play the determining role in logging. They theorize that the allowable cut and rotation should be calculated by determining the rate at which nutrients are replaced naturally, taking into account the rate at which they are extracted due to logging. This is an interesting theory, and one that I tend to agree with, but I don't believe enough is known to permit such calculations at the present time.

Compaction

Compaction contributes greatly to the reduction of soil quality by destroying large numbers of microorganisms, thus permitting the nutrients they normally store in their bodies to be released into the soil as leachable solutes. In addition, their decreased number reduces the rate at which insoluble minerals are converted into soluble substances that plants can use. Compaction also reduces the ability of the soil to absorb water. When rain falls or snow melts on compacted soil, the water runs off instead of soaking into the earth, so compaction causes erosion as well.

The *Final Environmental Statement and Renewable Resources Program, 1977-2020,* a report presented to Congress on March 2, 1976, by the Forest Service,* enlightens us on the degree of damage done to soils from compaction. Page 351 of that document states:

> Soil compaction during logging, particularly due to road building and use of heavy equipment on skid trails, affects site productivity by reducing soil pore (air) space, which can adversely affect tree growth. The time required for recovery depends upon climate, soil type, and degree of compaction. In areas where soil freezing and thawing occur, recovery normally takes 3 to 10 years; where freezing does not occur, it takes much longer.

So the physical act of compacting the soil reduces the ability of the site to support a new growth of trees. This is over and above the nutrient losses that result when the microorganisms in the soil are destroyed.

*As required under the National Forest Management Act of 1976 (16 U.S.C. 1600 [note]).

Soil Removal and Erosion

Erosion is the most obvious cause of soil loss. However, erosion is not easily noticed because newly eroded soil most often comes to rest in landforms we are so accustomed to seeing that we fail to observe the destruction. The thing to look for, other than obvious gullying, landslides, and washouts, is "castling" and the presence of gravel or small stones on the surface of bare land. Castling consists of stones and little bits of material perched on top of small piles of fine material. The implication is that the smaller particles have been washed away, leaving heavier pieces of stuff on the top of little pedicels. Where sheet erosion has progressed, one sees a flat surface nearly paved with stones, whereas cut banks in the same general area reveal only scattered stones mixed with earth.

Improper logging practices degrade soil quality by removing litter and topsoil during logging itself and by causing the erosion that often follows logging. Research conducted in Japan and reported in 1971 by Hidenori Nakano revealed that erosion sharply increases in proportion to the amount of forest cover removed. The following table shows the relationship of erosion to the intensity of logging of a 30-year-old stand of *Pinus densiflora*:

Intensity of Cutting for Logging	Annual Erosion (tons/hectare)	Rate of Erosion Relative to That on an Uncut Plot
All trees cut, stumps extracted	28.53	78
All trees cut, stumps not extracted	3.66	10
Trees cut on 3/4 of area in upper part of slope	2.06	6
Trees cut on 1/2 of area in upper part of slope	1.14	3
Trees cut on 1/4 of area in upper part of slope	0.75	2
No cutting (control)	0.35	1

SOURCE: Hidenori Nakano, *Soil and Water Conservation Functions of Forest on Mountainous Land* (Tokyo, Japan: Government Forest Experiment Station, 1971), 24.

These findings are verified by studies showing that water runoff increases with the proportion of timber removed and that erosion increases exponentially with increases in runoff. Experimental watersheds throughout the United States show a pronounced increase in annual stream flow after clearcutting. Yet it is doubtful that removal of only 20 percent or less of the forest cover would result in a detectable change in stream flow.

Nedavia Bethlahmy of the Intermountain Forest and Range Experiment Station in Ogden, Utah, developed the following formula for calculating the increase in erosion resulting from a corresponding increase in runoff: $\log_e E = 1.35R - 0.77$, where E = amount of erosion and R = amount of runoff. This equation shows that erosion increases exponentially with a linear increase in runoff, so doubling the runoff results in a fourfold increase in erosion.[*]

The capacity of undisturbed forest soil, with its humus layer intact, to act as a catchment for sediment has led to the unquestioned and widely accepted practice of diverting runoff from skid trails and compacted surfaces into undisturbed soil. By the same reasoning, streamside buffers (unlogged strips of forest beside streams) are used to protect streambeds and water quality. Rice and coworkers, in reviewing literature on the effects of forestland uses on stream environments, commented: "Certainly, bare and compacted soils resulting from logging disturbances are potential sites for erosion and surface runoff. However, because these areas are often not contiguous, eroded soil may come to rest on intervening undisturbed ground rather than move out of the watershed."[†]

We can see from Nakano's and Bethlahmy's work that the amount of erosion increases exponentially with the proportion of timber cut. The total amount of erosion resulting from a series of partial cuts over a rotation will be far less than what would result from one clearcut per rotation on the same area. Above all, the size of clearcuts is the controlling factor with regard to the amount of erosion and nutrient loss caused by logging.

It seems, therefore, that a selection system of management, in which the size of the openings is kept relatively small, tends to preserve the soil-holding properties of the forest. With small openings, only a limited area of bare land is exposed to surface runoff at any given time. And since erosion increases exponentially with a linear increase in runoff, there will be less total erosion from the small or partial cuts in a selectively managed forest, even though there may be more frequent entries into a selectively managed, uneven-aged forest than under even-aged management.

---

[*]Nedavia Bethlahmy, *Effects of Exposure and Logging on Runoff and Erosion*, Research Note INT-61 (Department of Agriculture, Forest Service, 1967), 3.
[†]R. M. Rice, J. S. Rothacher, and W. F. Megahan, "Erosional Consequences of Timber Harvesting: An Appraisal," *Proceedings of a Symposium on "Watersheds in Transition"* (Department of Agriculture, Forest Service, Fort Collins, CO), 1972.

We can also see from the results of Rice et al. that the soil and soil nutrients that do erode can be prevented from moving out of the watershed only if there are nearby areas of undisturbed ground to trap them. However, even-aged management, which is characterized by large clearcuts, will expose much more soil surface to runoff. This will trigger the exponential increase in erosion, and the eroding soil and nutrients will likely travel out of the watershed because there will be no undisturbed land nearby to stop their course.

Donald Gray, Doug Swanston, and others have been investigating the relationship between landslides and clearcutting in the Pacific Northwest and Alaska. (Summaries of their findings are presented in Part Four of this book.) These researchers find that the roots of trees are important in holding soils in place on steep slopes. Clearcutting, especially when the stumps are removed, results in a tremendous increase in the occurrence of landslides. (Pine stumps are sometimes pulled up for making turpentine and resin from the pitch they contain.)

The forested areas in the Ozarks of Missouri and Arkansas tend to be steep and unstable, like those in much of the Pacific Northwest. Local people have pointed out that after the roots of cut trees decay in an area previously clearcut, the mountain slopes tend to slide. This corresponds with the findings of Gray and Swanston mentioned above. So a selection system of management that preserves the soil-holding properties of the forest also reduces landslides and erosion. This particularly applies to coniferous forests. In hardwood forests, stumps of cut trees sprout and are less likely than conifer stumps to lose the binding qualities of their root structures. In the East, small patches of hardwoods in coves and on steep slopes are occasionally selectively logged instead of clearcut because their roots tend to reduce erosion and because the hardwoods provide food and habitat for wildlife.

Exposure

Logging, slash disposal, and site preparation following logging are harmful to soil life forms because these activities lay mineral soil bare and expose it to sunlight, drying it out and elevating soil temperatures. The changes in vegetation that occur through these practices destabilize the soil communities by disrupting the established balance of fauna and flora.

Biochemicals

The use of herbicides and biocides is another contemporary practice that destroys soil nutrients by the deleterious effect these chemicals have on the microorganisms. Many small nitrogen-fixing organisms are sensitive to these poisons. However, that fact is generally overlooked in considering the detrimental impacts of their use. These poisons also tend to accumulate in the forest environment as minute organisms feed on each other and eventually find their way into the bodies of animals that live at the top of the food chain. Furthermore, very little research has been done to determine the nature of chemicals formed through the breakdown of agri-chemicals and their impact on living things.

It has been shown that dioxin is one of the most lethal poisons known. One drop is sufficient to kill 1,200 people. Dioxin is an impurity inevitably present in 2,4-D and 2,4,5-T, both of which are commonly sprayed on cutover forestland to suppress the growth of unwanted vegetation. These chemicals also revert to dioxin when heated by fire or exposed to sunshine in leaf litter; hence, the amount of dioxin introduced into the environment through their use will always be underestimated.

CHEMICAL FERTILIZERS

Many people assume that soil nutrients lost through improper logging can be readily replaced through fertilization and that therefore there is no reason to complain about careless management of forestland on this score. But fertilization is expensive, and in forestry, where returns are not experienced for many years following investment, it is generally impractical.

Furthermore, the effects of fertilization may not always be what one expects. For example, researchers at the Forest Service's Pacific Northwest Experiment Station in Oregon found in 1973 that heavy fertilization in young Douglas-fir forests in western Washington and Oregon resulted in increased winter breakage, primarily in smaller trees. It at least doubled the number and resulting cubic volume of trees lost to mortality over a 7-year period.

Sometimes fertilization may stimulate the growth of competing vegetation rather than crop trees. Additionally, it is not known what effect fertilization programs have on fungi, although nitrates in adequate concentrations are known to be toxic to most life forms. In several experiments referred to in *Tree Growth and Forest Soils*, published by Oregon State University in 1968, fertilizer applications adversely affected tree growth. One study explains that the fungi, which convert insoluble elements to soluble ones that can be taken up by the roots of new trees, are killed by the fertilizer, and hence new growth is reduced.

I can think of no better way to describe proper care for forest soil—care that is sadly lacking under current management practices—than to quote a few paragraphs written by Ivan Sims, silviculturist at the Northeastern Forest Experiment Station in Pennsylvania; Ed Munns, chief of the USDA's Division of Forest Influences; and John Auten, silviculturist at the Central States Forest Experiment Station in Minnesota.

Improvement of forest soils must be achieved by indirection. The direct attack of the agronomist using such methods as plowing under of cover crops, application of fertilizers and lime, and tillage is far too expensive for wide application to forest soils. Experimentally, both in Europe and this country, such treatments have been shown to result in increased growth, but the effects have been short lived. More lasting effects can be obtained by managing the density and composition of the stands.

The agricultural principles of close-growing crops to prevent erosion and assure maximum return of organic matter to the soil underlie, in part, the silviculturist's ideal of full stands. The incorporation of organic matter into the soil can be obtained by the forester by fostering a large and active litter and soil population, and the effects of applying lime, nitrogen, and other fertilizer elements can be achieved by regulating the composition of the stand. The essential results of crop rotation can also be achieved by maintaining mixtures of species in the stands.

The general desirability of mixtures springs from the differences in ability of the species to extract nutrients from the soil and from differences in rooting habits. As an example, the soil under a shallow-rooted pine stand in Sweden was growing steadily more acid and biological activity was decreasing; the lesser vegetation indicated distinctly poor soil. After beech was interplanted among the pines the soil acidity decreased, biological activity increased, and the composition of the herbaceous growth indicated a much higher quality site. The roots of the beech were tapping a calcareous soil layer below the zone occupied by the pine roots and returning the calcium to the litter layer. Analysis of tree leaves in the Hudson Highlands of New York indicates that even when the roots of several species occupy the same soil layers there is marked difference in their ability to extract nitrogen, phosphorus, calcium, and potassium. This differential ability, in the light of the minimum requirements of the species, goes far toward explaining the often observed successional trends in forests.

The implication is clear that species characteristic of good sites and fertile soils contribute most to the maintenance of soil quality. The species with high requirements, such as ash, maple, beech, and basswood, return large quantities of nutrients to the soil in litter. The conifers generally have lower nutrient requirements than hardwoods, and coniferous litter has lower nutrient content.

This difference in nutrient content of litter explains in part the richer and more abundant soil life generally associated with hardwood stands. This in turn accounts for the better incorporation of organic matter in hardwood soils.

The general principles by which silviculture should be guided, then, are: (1) to maintain full stands; and (2) to encourage mixtures and direct their development along the lines of natural ecological succession.*

CONCLUSION

It seems only common sense that preserving the quality and presence of soil nutrients and respecting the naturally occurring soil communities are of prime importance if we are to maintain a healthy and productive forest. The top foot or so of soil is as important to the continued productivity of our forests as it is to our agriculture. We can best preserve forest soils by forest management practices that (1) keep openings in the forest no larger than is necessary to satisfy the biological requirements of the tree species being harvested, so as to encourage natural regeneration; (2) provide for long rotations, which will supply high-quality timber, because the timber will be allowed to achieve optimum growth, and minimize disturbance to the soil; (3) rely on natural controls to protect the forest from insects and disease, so as not to harm the microorganisms in the soil that carry much of its nutrient load; and (4) use methods of logging and road building that prevent the soil from being compacted and keep erosion to a minimum. Small, lightweight equipment should be used for logging, and roads should be laid on the land rather than cut into it.

*U.S. Department of Agriculture, *Soils and Men: 1938 Yearbook of Agriculture* (Washington, DC: Government Printing Office, 1938), 747-748.

PART THREE

FOREST PLANNING

As I said before, it takes timber to grow timber. Obviously, wood grows on land stocked with trees regardless of their age or size. But the rate of growth on any particular piece of land increases in both quantity and quality as the trees become larger. Unfortunately, timber may be merchantable at a very young age; hence, there is a temptation to cash in one's forest resources long before the timber reaches its optimum rate of growth and well before high-quality forest products are produced and multiple-use values have developed. We observe by studying ancient civilizations that once forests have been cut down to below the optimum age for maximum production, there is no turning back. People in need of wood for fuel are forced to cut young trees before they reach their optimum size and age, and from there on forest destruction progresses exponentially with the increase in population. The world's forests today are largely past the point of no return, and the forests of the United States are perilously close to that point.

The purpose of Part Three is to explain the mathematics of forestry in as simple terms as possible, to enable you to find that point of no return by examining the documents relating to our national forests and to help you identify the most important points in commenting on national forest plans.

CHAPTER SIX

Mensuration

This chapter may seem unnecessarily technical to the general reader. You might be asking yourself, Do I really need to know forest mathematics to influence forest policy? However, I urge you to forge ahead, for in my experience, application of this subject has been the single most important way in which the commercial forest industry has influenced the Forest Service to increase its allowable cut and shift its policies away from multiple use and sustained yield. The numbers and calculations used to determine how much wood can be cut in a forest, just like any other statistics, are subject to interpretation and bias. It's time people concerned with the future of the national forests knew how to use the rules of forest mathematics. It's too important a subject to be left to industry representatives.

One major misconception prevalent among foresters, probably more than any other, has led to excessive logging in the national forests. This is the belief that, other things being equal, an even-aged stand at maturity will produce about twice the volume per acre as will virgin forest. In fact, the two will produce about the same amount of wood.

A forest usually starts from bare land and at first supports many more trees than can occupy the same space when the trees are mature, simply because large trees occupy more space than small ones. Hence, we can assume that most forests start out as even-aged stands following the death of an old tree or group of trees. For the first few years, there is no measurable volume in terms of board feet because the trees are too small to produce lumber. After the trees reach a size at which lumber can be fabricated from them, we can measure the volume of lumber per acre that can be manufactured from all the trees of such a forest. That figure gradually rises with the increasing age and size of the trees until it approaches the maximum the species and quality of land can produce. As it approaches that maximum volume, the rate of increase slows until finally the figure levels off and starts to decline. Over the centuries, and over a large area, the average figure declines as some trees die and are replaced with patches of seedlings, repeating the process. Generally, though, the trees do not all die at once, so eventually the forest breaks down through natural processes into a mosaic of even-aged stands of all ages.

At that time, the average volume per acre, in terms of lumber that may be recovered from merchantable-sized trees, is about one-half the volume the even-aged stand had when it reached its peak. This is understood by every forester, presumably. But most foresters jump to the conclusion that even-aged management in a properly regulated forest under sustained yield will produce twice the volume encountered in virgin forest, and therefore excessive cutting during the first logging of virgin forest will be of no consequence in the long run. This conclusion is exactly wrong. The difference between the virgin forest and the regulated forest under even-aged management is in the size of the even-aged stands. In the virgin forest, the individual even-aged stands are random in size and distribution, whereas under even-aged management, they are large and clearly visible. However, the volume per acre *for the forest as a whole* will be about the same for both.

Two anecdotes illustrate this point. When I was a student at U.C. Berkeley, during a course in silviculture, Professor Frederick Baker had our class debating the pros and cons of even-aged versus uneven-aged forest management. The discussion continued through three or four class sessions. Finally, I asked Baker to tell us which alternative would produce the most timber. He looked off into space and said, "Well, I'll tell you. The Germans have been practicing even-aged management for a long time—planting trees in straight rows, thinning them periodically, and doing all the things required to maximize production. The French, on the other hand, size up each tree and decide whether to remove it or leave it, rake away leaf litter to make way for natural regeneration where trees have been cut down, and practice what we call uneven-aged management. I've examined the records of both as far back as they go, about four hundred years, and as near as I can tell, in the long run they get about the same results, except the French have a lot more fun doing it."

In 1973 I went to Norway with a group of people who were working on a new forest practices act for the state of California. My objective was to find out how the Norwegians managed to require private forest owners to practice sustained-yield management. We met first with the secretary of agriculture, who greeted us but didn't say much of substance. Then we met the chief forester. (Apparently their forest service is set up much the same as ours, in a Department of Agriculture. They all spoke fluent English, incidentally.) Whenever the chief forester said something that touched on my concern, I interrupted with a question about the techniques or laws they used to require sustained yield. After several such attempts on my part, he finally departed from his prepared speech. He told us that 80 percent of the forestland in Norway is in small ownerships. Eight hundred years ago the country passed a law forbidding sale or purchase of land without a permit, and permits are virtually impossible to obtain. Norway has no land taxes; its government is financed in some other way, which he didn't explain. When the country industrialized and people moved into the cities, they retained ownership of those small, timbered holdings. Consequently, Norway is the most outdoor-oriented country in the world. It is not unusual to find two hundred thousand people out on skis on a winter weekend. Owners will sell a few trees under carefully controlled conditions from time to time, but the people love their forests and refuse to allow their lands to be clearcut; basically, there is no incentive to sell timber in large quantities. The chief forester lamented, "If we could only get these people to practice even-aged management, we could expand our pulp and paper industry by as much as fifty percent, or even double it."

The next day we visited an experimental forest consisting of about 2,200 hectares. The director told us that the Department of Agriculture had purchased the forest around 1915. When they acquired it, they began practicing uneven-aged management and had a sustained yield of something like 2,800 cubic meters per year. (Numbers in this anecdote are not exact, for I have to rely on my memory.) Every 10 years they made a new inventory of their timber resources, measured the rate of growth, noted the condition of the forest, and recalculated their sustained yield. With each new survey, the sustained yield increased. Around 1936 it reached 3,200 cubic meters. Then they switched to even-aged management, and the sustained yield continued to increase with each subsequent survey until it reached 4,200 cubic meters in 1966. At this point, they discovered a mistake. Each survey had been made with the assumption that the bare openings in the forest would be planted, and the anticipated plantings had been taken into account in the calculations. It had finally become apparent that for some reason, those openings were incapable of growing trees. So they had to recalculate their sustained-yield measure using *actual* stocking as the realistic measure of stocking capacity. When they did this, they went back to the sustained-yield figure they'd had when they practiced uneven-aged management. (The actual figure was somewhat larger than what they had started out with in 1915 because of changes in utilization: they were able to include very small material that was formerly ignored, because trees too small for lumber are now used for pulp.)

This story also illustrates the importance of the many small decisions that must be made in taking an inventory of forest resources and in calculating sustained yield. It shows too that few, if any, of these decisions are subject to precise determination. For example, one needs to determine the minimum size of tree that is considered merchantable, the top diameter of a merchantable tree, and the age at which a stand of trees will reach its maximum volume in order to determine rotation. Numbers selected for these and many other calculations will play an important part in determining the allowable cut.

Lobbyists for industry have a habit of encouraging the Forest Service's timber management officers to pick numbers that, in combination with others, tend to maximize the allowable cut. The foresters frequently go along with these little distortions, partly because each one seems small and inconsequential, but mainly, I think, because they believe that production under even-aged management will be much greater than could be achieved by working with the natural forest under uneven-aged management, as they used to do. They think that in the long run, the even-aged forests are going to produce far more than they could get from the virgin forest.

People who want to challenge forest plans need to be able to understand the consequences of all these little distortions, which when combined tend to exaggerate the allowable cut, for it is not possible to tell whether sustained yield is being practiced by merely looking at a forest. One may be practicing even-aged management and doing a very bad job of cleaning up, thus leaving the land in a deplorable condition, but at the same time limiting removal of timber to quantities consistent with growth. On the other hand, one might be removing timber under a sophisticated system of selection management and taking exquisite care to prevent damage to residual trees and other values, yet be cutting at a far greater rate than can be sustained.

Therefore, in order to judge the validity of a timber management plan, one needs to understand the mathematics peculiar to forestry. That mathematics is called *mensuration*.

UNITS OF MEASURE

Forest products are measured in a variety of ways: lumber is sold in board feet; firewood and pulp bolts are sold in cords; plywood statistics are kept in square feet of 3/8-inch three-ply; wood chips are reckoned in "units." The basic unit of measure used to determine the volume of wood in a forest, regardless of the products that might be manufactured from the cut trees, is called the *log rule* (rule as in ruler, not rules of the road).

LOG RULES

A log rule is a table that shows how much wood is contained in logs of various sizes and indicates the quantity of products that can be fabricated from them. The Scribner rule, for example, indicates the number of 1-inch boards that can be cut from round logs of various lengths and diameters. More than forty different rules were used in the United States as the lumber industry evolved during the latter part of the nineteenth century, but no single rule has ever been adopted as standard by the lumber industry or by professional foresters. Log rules were initially designed to provide information needed in buying and selling wood, but they are also used for measuring trees and forests and even for predicting growth.

Log rules are used to build *volume tables,* which measure the amount of lumber and other products, such as wood chips, that can be manufactured from whole trees.

Volume tables, in turn, are the basis for developing *yield tables,* which indicate projected volumes per acre in growing forests.

Finally, yield tables are used for determining *rotation*—the number of years a series of even-aged patches of trees should be allowed to grow in order to maximize growth of a forest in the long run.

The Forest Service uses three log rules in gathering and publishing forest statistics and in their business of forest management. The three rules are the Scribner Decimal C rule, the International 1/4 Inch rule, and the Huber rule. The first two indicate the amount of *lumber* that theoretically can be cut from logs of various lengths and diameters, measured in board feet, and the third indicates the *total content* of logs, measured in cubic feet.

A board foot is a piece of wood 1 foot long, 1 foot wide, and 1 inch thick, hence one-twelfth of a cubic foot. A board-foot log rule represents the contents of the rectangular section that can be cut from a tapered cylindrical log, a shape known as a truncated paraboloid (see Figure 2). The figures exclude mill waste consisting of saw kerf, end trimmings, and slabs. Hence, a considerable volume of wood material in a log does not show up in board-foot tables. One cubic foot of solid wood in a round log will produce from 4.6 to 7.0 board feet of lumber, depending on the size of the log.

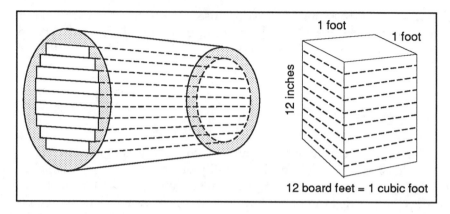

FIGURE 2 *Lumber Accounts for Only Two-Thirds of the Cubic Content of the Log*

The Scribner Decimal C Rule

The Scribner rule was developed from diagrams. These are merely circles drawn to scale to represent the small ends of logs of different lengths and diameters, on which the various boards that might be sawed are marked off. The Scribner rule allows for the thickness of the saw blade, but it does not include boards that might be shorter than the log, nor does it consider logs smaller than 6 inches in diameter at the small end. "Decimal C" refers to the fact that the numbers are rounded to the nearest ten and the last digit is dropped; thus, 2 is really 20 board feet, 63 is 630 board feet, and so on. This rule was developed in the Lake states and has long been used by the forest industries in most of Canada as well as many parts of the North and the West. It underestimates volumes in small logs and altogether ignores logs less than 6 inches in diameter. Despite the Scribner rule's inaccuracies, the Forest Service uses it in measuring timber sold from the national forests because people both in the timber industry and in the Forest Service are accustomed to it and understand it.

When the Scribner rule is used to measure the volume of wood in a forest, only logs 6 inches or larger in diameter inside the bark at the small end are normally included. This size of log corresponds to trees that are about 12 inches in diameter outside the bark 4 1/2 feet above the ground. That is, a tree measuring 12 inches in diameter outside the bark 4 1/2 feet above the ground will measure about 6 inches in diameter inside the bark 16 feet above the ground.

Four and one-half feet above the ground is the accepted height for measuring the diameter of a tree. This measurement, which includes the bark, is called *d.b.h.*, short for "diameter at breast height." It is generally assumed that d.b.h. is the same as the diameter inside the bark at stump height, 1 1/2 feet above the ground. This generalization is quite accurate for most species, and where it wouldn't apply, as with a species such as redwood, which characteristically flares broadly at the base, the error resulting from making this assumption is small and negligible.

The International 1/4 Inch Rule

The International rule was designed by the Forest Service in an attempt to establish an accurate international standard for measuring logs, to avoid conflict over the many rules being used in various parts of this country and Canada.   It was derived with a mathematical formula worked out to give the yield of logs in terms of their diameters and lengths: $(0.22D^2 - 0.71D)$ for a 4-foot log,* in which D is diameter in inches. This rule measures logs as small as 4 inches in diameter inside the bark at the small end, in contrast with the Scribner rule, which includes only logs 6 inches or more in diameter. When the International rule is used, the corresponding minimum-breast-height size for measuring trees is 8 inches d.b.h. The International rule is considered to be more precise than the Scribner Decimal C log rule.

The Huber Rule and Other Cubic Measure Formulas

One might assume that complications would cease if only the industry would be content to reckon wood volumes in terms of total cubic content of logs of whatever size, condition, or degree of manufacture one is concerned with: lumber, plywood, pulp, or any combination thereof. But such is not the case.

There are at least three formulas in use for determining the cubic content of round logs. One method, the Huber rule, multiplies the length of the log by the area of a circle representing the middle of the log. Another averages the areas of the two log ends and multiplies that number by the log's length. A third applies an average taper to the log according to the log's length and the area of a circle representing the small end of the log.

Cubic-foot tables may include logs as small as 1 inch in diameter inside the bark at the small end and 4 feet in length.   Under the McSweeney–McNary Forest Research Act of 1928, the Forest Service periodically surveys and publishes reports on the country's timber supply. Statistics for cubic feet of wood in those reports, and in forest plans, include the merchantable portions of trees over 5 inches d.b.h.

*Donald Bruce and Francis X. Schumacher, *Forest Mensuration* (New York: McGraw-Hill, 1935), 156.

Cubic measure is coming into general use because of the development of integrated forest products industries. Companies that turn out lumber, plywood, chipboard, and pulp and paper products can make use of the total content of logs brought to the mill. Board-foot rules give only the amount of lumber that can be cut from logs of various dimensions, but cubic measure gives the total volume of wood regardless of its proposed use. However, cubic-foot rules can lead to disastrous results when they are employed to determine rotations, particularly when multiple-use considerations are involved.

Table 1 illustrates how the three major log rules compare with one another. The table indicates the contents of only 16-foot logs from 4 inches through 25 inches in diameter. Actual rules cover many log lengths and include larger diameters than those shown here.

TABLE 1 *Content of Logs by Various Log Rules (example)*

Diameter (inches)	Contents in Board Feet (16-foot logs)		Solid Contents (cubic feet)
	Scribner Decimal C Rule (in tens)	International 1/4 Inch Rule	
4	—	—	5
5	—	10	6
6	2	20	7
7	3	30	9
8	3	40	10
9	4	50	11
10	6	65	12
11	7	80	13
12	8	95	15
13	10	115	16
14	11	135	17
15	14	160	18
16	16	180	20
17	18	205	21
18	21	230	22
19	24	260	23
20	28	290	25
21	30	320	26
22	33	355	27
23	38	390	28
24	40	425	29
25	46	460	31

SOURCE: *National Forest Log Scaling Handbook* (Department of Agriculture, Forest Service, 1969).

Note that a 16-inch log contains 160 board feet by the Scribner rule and 180 board feet by the International rule. This shows how the Scribner rule underestimates the lumber content of small logs. Note also that the same log contains 20 cubic feet of wood, which would amount to 240 board feet if it were possible to make it all into 1-inch boards.

VOLUME TABLES

Log rules are used to compile volume tables. A volume table is similar in appearance to a log rule but represents the amount of timber contained in whole trees instead of simply in logs (see Table 2). Volume tables are compiled using various log rules, and they also vary with the degree of utilization anticipated from the trees. Some tables include only that portion of trees up to a 10-inch or more diameter inside the bark. Others include volume up to other minimum diameters or even for the total height of trees. Volume tables are prepared for each species or group of species. They are also prepared to reflect the productivity of

TABLE 2 *Content of Trees 100 Feet in Height by Various Log Rules (example)*

| Diameter at Breast Height (inches) | Contents in Board Feet | | Solid Contents (cubic feet) |
	Scribner Decimal C Rule (in tens)	International 1/4 Inch Rule (in tens)	
10	4	10	20
12	11	17	29
14	18	25	40
16	24	34	52
18	34	44	66
20	44	56	83
22	54	68	100
24	66	82	119
26	79	98	139
28	94	114	160
30	109	131	182
32	124	148	204
34	140	164	226
36	156	180	250
38	172	197	274
40	188	214	298

SOURCE: Tables 32, 33, and 34 in Walter H. Meyer, *Yield of Even-Aged Stands of Ponderosa Pine*, Technical Bulletin 630 (Department of Agriculture, Forest Service, 1938 [rev. 1961]).

the land, a factor foresters refer to by the term "site." (We shall explore that further on.) In practice, volume tables are prepared for each site quality, and each table provides figures for a variety of tree heights and diameters.

YIELD TABLES

The log rules are next used to compile yield tables. Yield tables also resemble log rules in appearance, but they show the volume *per acre* that may be expected for trees of each age class. As with volume tables, these too are based on tree measurements using a specified log rule and particular utilization standards.

TABLE 3   *Volume per Acre by Various Log Rules (example)*

Age (years)	Scribner Rule (board feet)	Volume per Acre (site index 100) International Rule (board feet)	Solid Contents (cubic feet)
20	—	600	1,700
30	1,000	5,400	3,000
40	4,300	11,900	4,100
50	9,200	19,300	5,050
60	14,800	27,000	5,850
70	20,500	34,000	6,500
80	26,000	40,200	7,100
90	31,200	45,600	7,650
100	36,100	50,300	8,100
110	40,600	54,500	8,500
120	44,600	58,200	8,850
130	48,300	61,600	9,150
140	51,700	64,800	9,450
150	54,800	67,800	9,750
160	57,600	70,600	10,000
170	60,100	73,300	10,250
180	62,400	75,900	10,500
190	64,600	78,400	10,750
200	66,700	80,800	10,950

SOURCE: Tables 16, 11, and 6 in Walter H. Meyer, *Yield of Even-Aged Stands of Ponderosa Pine*, Technical Bulletin 630 (Department of Agriculture, Forest Service, 1938 [rev. 1961]).

The choice of log rule is of particular importance in forest planning and has immense significance with regard to multiple-use values, as we shall see.

ROTATION

The fourth and final use for log rules in forestry is determining the length of rotation. Rotation is defined as the planned number of years between the regeneration of a stand and its final cutting. Technically, the term refers to even-aged forest management, but where uneven-aged management is practiced, the rotation age may be used as criteria for identifying mature trees.

Rotation can be determined by any of various techniques. It may be merely an arbitrary figure, or it may be determined with the objective of providing a sustained yield of trees of a certain size or quality. Most commonly, it is calculated from yield tables to determine the age that will produce the maximum volume per acre per year from a *sustained-yield management unit*. In American national forests, this is generally an area of several hundred thousand acres.

To determine a rotation that will maximize long-range production, we must prepare yet another table from the log rule. If we turn to a typical yield table (such as Table 3) and divide the volume per acre by the corresponding age, we develop a table called *mean annual increment* or *average annual growth* (see Table 4).

TABLE 4   *Mean Annual Increment, Ponderosa Pine (site index 100)*

Age (years)	Scribner Rule	Board Feet per Acre International Rule	Cubic Measure
20	—	30	85
30	33	180	100
40	108	298	102
50	184	386	101
60	247	450	98
70	293	486	93
80	325	502	89
90	347	507	85
100	361	503	81
110	369	495	77
120	372	485	74
130	372	474	70
140	369	453	68
150	365	452	65
160	360	441	62
170	354	431	60
180	347	422	58
190	340	413	57
200	334	404	55

SOURCE: Tables 25, 23, and 21 in Walter H. Meyer, *Yield of Even-Aged Stands of Ponderosa Pine*, Technical Bulletin 630 (Department of Agriculture, Forest Service, 1938 [rev. 1961]).

A close look at these figures shows that the average rate of growth rises to a peak, then levels off and declines. The peak of that curve occurs when the trees have attained their highest average annual growth, after which time growth will slack off. In forestry this peak is called the "point of diminishing returns" or the *culmination of mean annual increment*. Here, using the Scribner rule, the peak occurs between 120 and 130 years; with the International rule, the peak occurs at 90 years. (Remember, these two log rules measure *lumber*.) Using cubic measure (which reckons the total content of the logs for lumber or for pulp), the maximum growth per acre per year occurs at 40 years. The mean annual increment from Table 4 using the Scribner rule is shown graphically in Figure 3.

Now, if a forest is divided into as many areas as there are years in the rotation, with one area representing each age, the forest will be producing the maximum volume the land is capable of sustaining in terms of the product or utilization standard planned for. For example, if we were managing a 1,200-acre tract of forestland on a 120-year rotation, we would have 10 acres stocked with 1-year-old trees, 10 acres stocked with 2-year-olds, and so on, up to 120-year-olds (see Figure 4).

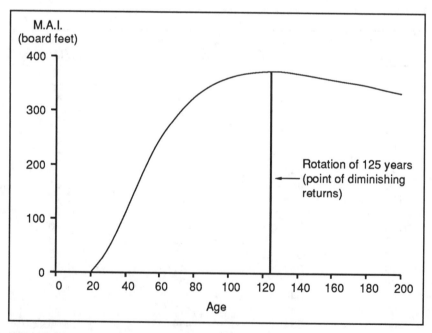

FIGURE 3   *Mean Annual Increment in Board Feet, Using the Scribner Rule: Ponderosa Pine, Site 100 (from Table 4)*

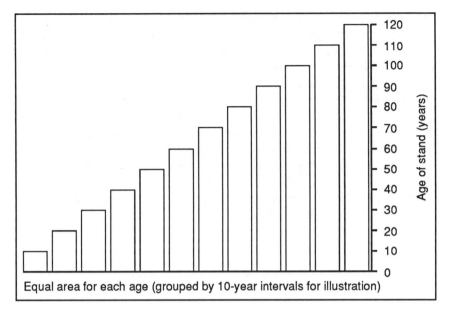

FIGURE 4   *Area by Age of a Fully Regulated Forest*

ROTATION VARIES WITH SEVERAL FACTORS

The length of rotation as determined by culmination of mean annual increment, the age at which a forest (not individual trees) will achieve its highest average annual growth, is affected by a variety of factors: the log rule used; the quality of the site; whether net or gross yield tables are being used; utilization standards (such as the minimum size of tree included in the yield table and the minimum top diameter of merchantable logs); and finally, the quality of wood that is wanted. We shall explore these factors separately.

Log Rule

Choice of log rule is extremely important in determining length of rotation. Scribner Decimal C rule renders the longest rotation of the three rules used by the Forest Service. International rule is intermediate, and cubic-foot rules render the shortest rotations. Figure 5 demonstrates how the choice of log rule can affect rotation age. As we saw in the ponderosa pine illustration in Table 4, on an average site with an index of 100, the rotation age is between 120 and 130 years if we use the Scribner rule, 90 years if we use the International rule, but only 40 years if we use cubic measure. (It should be noted that in this case, cubic-foot content of trees 1 inch d.b.h. and over is used; if, for example, cubic-foot content of trees 6.6 inches d.b.h. and over were used, the rotation would be 60 years. This illustrates the importance of utilization standards.)

Rotation is determined on the basis of the product or variety of products a forest is being managed for. A pulp company would use a cubic-foot log rule because sustained-yield management under the rotation determined with that rule would maximize cord wood production. For that reason, timber companies managing loblolly pine plantations on the better lands in the South today generally operate on a 25-year rotation.

Similarly, a board-foot rule is used if a forest is being managed for lumber production. Where multiple-use forestry is being practiced, the

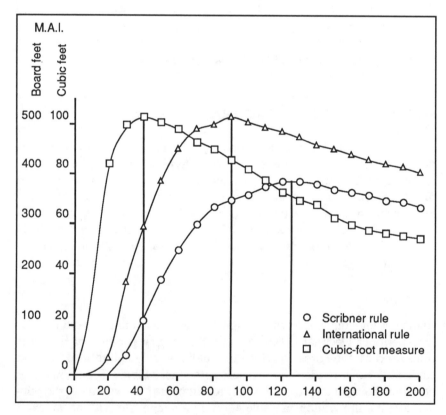

FIGURE 5   *Rotation by Various Log Rules: Ponderosa Pine, Site 100 (from Table 5)*

rotation should be based on the Scribner rule, because it renders the longest rotations of the various rules in use. Multiple-use values are proportional to the length of rotation; the longer the rotation, the greater are the multiple-use values of the forest.

People in the timber industry generally want the Forest Service to use the cubic-foot rule because it renders the shortest rotations. When used in determining the sustained-yield capacity of a forest, a short rotation tends to justify hasty liquidation of valuable old-growth forest. It is frequently argued that the national forests should be managed in a businesslike manner, which means maximizing income and minimizing cost in the short term.

Site Quality

Site quality, usually just referred to as "site," is a measure of the productive capacity of forestland. In the United States, site quality is determined by estimating the total height that dominant and codominant trees will attain at a particular age on a particular piece of land. Site quality is one of the most important factors affecting length of rotation: the higher the site quality, the shorter the rotation; the poorer the site, the longer the rotation.

Standards for determining site quality are established by measuring the height and corresponding age of a large number of trees and plotting a curve from the data to represent the average tree height at each age. A family of curves of the same shape is then drawn to cover the full range of site qualities. Site quality is identified by tree height at a particular age, usually 50 years but occasionally 100 years. Hence, "site 80" refers to land capable of growing trees 80 feet in height at 50 years of age. The examples of volume and yield tables shown in this chapter apply to a single site. In practice, however, volume and yield tables are prepared in sets covering the full range of site qualities applying to each commercial species; an example is shown in Figure 6.

The term "site index" refers to the actual average height in feet that dominant and codominant trees in a particular stand will attain at a certain age (usually 50 years). "Site class" refers to a general indication of site quality, usually expressed by roman numerals. Site I means excellent, Site V means poor, and so on. Volume tables and yield tables are generally classified by site index rather than site class to provide for precision in forest mensuration.

Rotation age varies greatly with site rating. For instance, using the Scribner rule, the mean annual increment culminates at 87 years in a stand having a site index of 160. This means that on forestland with a

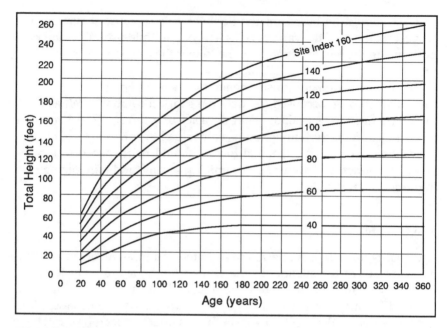

FIGURE 6   *Height of Dominant and Codominant Trees (site index represents height at 100 years)*

SOURCE: From Walter H. Meyer, *Yield of Even-Aged Stands of Ponderosa Pine*, Technical Bulletin 630 (Department of Agriculture, Forest Service, 1938 [rev. 1961]), 9.

site index of 160 (where the quality of the land is such that trees will grow to an average height of 160 feet in 50 years), it will take 87 years for trees to reach their highest point of average annual growth (culmination of mean annual increment); 87 years will also be the rotation age for this stand. If the site index is 60 (trees will grow to an average height of 60 feet in 50 years), culmination of mean annual increment and rotation age will not occur until the trees are 196 years old. Using the Scribner rule, rotation age will come at 124 years on land with a site index of 100 (see Table 5).

Net or Gross Yield Tables

The first reliable yield tables prepared by the Forest Service for American commercial species were based on studies of naturally occurring even-aged stands of the various species throughout their ranges. In October 1930, the Forest Service published Technical Bulletin 120, *The Yield of Douglas Fir in the Pacific Northwest*, by Richard E. McArdle et al., and in October 1938, Technical Bulletin 630, *Yield of Even-Aged Stands of*

TABLE 5   *Rotation Ages for Even-Aged Stands of Ponderosa Pine by Cubic-Foot and Board-Foot Measure*

Site Index (Height at 50 years, in feet)	Cubic-Foot Measure	Board-Foot Measure	
		International Rule	Scribner Rule
40	70	—	—
60	54	161	196
80	42	107	148
100	40	90	124
120	39	76	107
140	41	70	97
160	45	64	87

Ponderosa Pine, by Walter H. Meyer.   The yield tables in these publications did not account for the volume of trees that die as stands grow older. They reported only the net volumes that may be expected in fully stocked stands at various ages.

Gross yield tables, which include net yield *plus* estimated mortality, are designed to indicate the volume that may be realized if stands are systematically thinned throughout their rotation and the thinnings are added to the yield. When trees that die naturally are harvested and become part of the forest's yield, the culmination of mean annual increment is delayed.

When the age of culmination, either in volume or in value, is a controlling factor, rotations for managed stands, in which periodic thinnings are removed and utilized, will be longer than those for stands that are not periodically thinned. The increase in yield available through harvesting thinnings will amount to no more than 25 percent over a rotation, and it will usually be considerably less than that because of the improbability of accurately determining which trees will die between cutting cycles and the difficulty of picking up all dead trees before they deteriorate.

Utilization Standards

Rotations become shorter as we anticipate improved utilization standards. The smaller the minimum diameter of tree included in the yield table and the smaller the utilized top we reckon with, the shorter will be the rotation when determined by culmination of mean annual increment. This means the more of a tree we can make use of, the shorter the rotation, if we are managing the forest mainly for pulp and low-quality lumber. This is why figuring in cubic feet leads to short rotations.

Quality Considerations

Finally, we must consider the impact on rotation of planning for high-quality forest products. Dense, clear lumber comes from the butt logs of old trees. The highest-priced lumber and plywood are manufactured from physiologically mature timber. The longest and strongest fiber comes from wood that has grown after the tree is about 70 years old. Therefore, if we are determining a rotation that will give us the highest *value* of yield at harvest, we will make some estimate of culmination of mean annual increment of value of our anticipated yield, or of volume of high-quality wood, such as yield of number 1 and 2 sawlogs. (In the trade, logs are generally graded on the basis of diameter and number of knots. The older the tree, the greater it will be in diameter and the more free of knots the lower logs will be.)

Planning for Multiple Use

Multiple-use values are clearly proportional to the length of rotation. If we are concerned with minimizing the loss of soil, maximizing the quality of water runoff from the forest, maximizing opportunities for wholesome recreation, taking care to protect habitat for those species that live at the top of the food chain, and making sure we have a continuous supply of high-quality wood products, we will select the longest rotations for our national forests that we can possibly persuade the public to accept.

CHAPTER SEVEN

Reviewing Forest Plans

GENERAL CONSIDERATIONS

You will most likely have some particular concern in mind when you undertake to review a forest plan. You may be disturbed by the unsightliness of cutover land or concerned about how logging will affect your favorite fishing streams. Perhaps you are troubled about the effects of herbicides on wildlife and the health of people in your community. Whatever your specific concerns may be, there are two general considerations that are basic to your review. These are the following:

1. The volume of timber being offered for sale, now called the "allowable sale quantity" or "programmed annual harvest."
2. The impact of logging and road construction on the land, that is, the degree to which these activities will impair the productivity of the land for all of the uses described in the multiple-use law.

First, let us consider the volume of timber being offered for sale. In order to determine whether this volume is excessive, you must examine the sustained-yield or allowable cut projections in the forest plan. As I mentioned earlier, there is a strong tendency among foresters to be recklessly optimistic about future growth following clearcutting. Inasmuch as multiple-use values are greatly affected by logging, it is important to be sure that logging is kept within reasonable limits. Any of the following conditions can lead to excessive logging:

1. The length of rotation is too short.
2. Sustained yield is overestimated.
3. Adequate regeneration is not realized.

You should always be alert to the possibility that various alternatives have been considered in making each specific decision and that the alternatives chosen are those that tend to maximize the programmed allowable harvest or sustained yield.

CHECKING THE ROTATION

Determination of the length of rotation is thoroughly discussed in Chapter 6; suffice it to say here that in order to be sure multiple-use values are given sufficient consideration, the rotation should be based on culmination of mean annual increment of high-quality material. Many factors affect the length of rotation. Choice of log rule is one of the most important; board-foot rules generate longer rotations than do cubic-foot rules. Gross yield tables render longer rotations than do net yield tables, and large minimums in tree and utilized top diameters render longer rotations than do small tree and top diameters. (The yield tables used should include only relatively large trees and should not include treetops smaller than the diameter generally used for manufacture of lumber.) Certainly, the minimum size of tree in the yield table used for calculating rotation and sustained yield should not be smaller than the minimum size of tree presently considered merchantable. In the West, the Forest Service generally considers the minimum size of merchantable tree to be 12 inches d.b.h. At present, the timber industry in the eastern United States generally accepts 16 inches d.b.h. as a minimum size for hardwood trees, although the Forest Service may require purchasers to log considerably smaller trees in national forest timber sales.

Site is another factor affecting rotation. High-quality sites produce shorter rotations than do low-quality sites. Hence, any overestimate of site quality leads to an excessive allowable cut.

CHECKING THE SUSTAINED YIELD OR PROGRAMMED ANNUAL HARVEST

All the information needed to check Forest Service calculations is available to anyone who wants to examine it. Section 2416.3 of the *Forest Service Manual*, dated December 1980, states the following:

The early stages of the planning process involve myriad decisions and assumptions by a variety of resource specialists. Many may be seemingly minor decisions in the mathematical program. In the analysis of alternatives, the effect of these early decisions may not be recognized. Therefore it is essential that the decision rationale be documented in the planning records and be available for public review.

Sustained yield is calculated in a variety of ways, and calculations are complicated due to the many variable factors. In recent years, foresters have applied computer technology to the problem in hope of improving the accuracy of their predictions. I have observed that with each new development in forest technology, estimates of sustained yield increase, lending support to my concern about the underlying bias that seems to pervade the profession. Whether I'm right or wrong about this bias, an overoptimistic calculation of sustained yield can lead to serious difficulties in the future. We will never be able to make a reliable long-range prediction of timber growth because we cannot predict some of the most important factors that determine it: temperature, precipitation, and difficulties with insects and disease. Because of these uncertainties, the Forest Service develops new plans for each national forest every 10 years. Nevertheless, these frequent redeterminations are insufficient assurance that long-range sustained-yield predictions will be realized, because corrections of overestimates are often postponed until the subsequent planning period. Where this is the case, the forest inevitably experiences a consistent decline in quality and sustained-yield capacity.

Regardless of the method of calculation used, the most important items to consider in reviewing a plan are its basic assumptions. We have already discussed rotation. We also need assurance that the volume of timber to be sold is consistent with the volume of timber used in forest planning. If, for example, purchasers are buying only logs of a certain size or species yet smaller trees or trees of additional species are included in sustained-yield calculations, the forest may inadvertently be selling timber beyond sustainable quantities.

After checking the validity of the basic assumptions, the next step is to check the calculations. Formulas used to calculate sustained yield vary, depending on the condition of the forest and on the management objectives. To review national forest plans, you don't need to know all the technical complexities. In most cases it will be sufficient to understand two basic methods, one used for old-growth forests and the other more suited to eastern national forests.

The most appropriate and easily understood method for calculating sustained yield in a forest containing substantial quantities of old growth is the *Hanzlik formula:*

$$AC = \frac{V_m}{R} + I$$

in which AC = allowable cut for a decade
       V_m = volume of old-growth timber
       R = rotation
       I = growth for the decade

In the eastern national forests, which are generally made up of abandoned farmland and are composed largely of young stands, the *Austrian formula* is more appropriate for estimating sustained yield. The allowable cut in these forests may be checked by using this formula:

$$AC = I + \frac{V_p - V_d}{A}$$

in which AC = allowable annual cut, in volume
       A = adjustment period, in years
       I = average annual increment during the adjustment period
       V_p = present volume
       V_d = desired volume at the end of the adjustment period

If the Forest Service cannot provide estimates of the increment of growth, a reasonable estimate may be made by noting the difference in volume per acre from each age class to the next. This difference may reasonably be considered to represent the rate of growth. The volume difference must be divided by the number of years in an age class to obtain growth per acre per year.

IS THE ALLOWABLE SALE QUANTITY CONSISTENT WITH EVEN-FLOW SUSTAINED YIELD?

To answer this question, simply divide the total quantity of timber in that part of the forest dedicated to full timber production by the programmed allowable harvest, then add the current growth. To make this test, you need to ask the Forest Service for a table or tables showing the following information for the *standard component of commercial forestland* in the *working circle* with which you are concerned (since 1983, the standard component of a forest has been defined as the commercial forestland suitable and available for full timber yield, excluding lands designated as "reserved," "marginal," or "special") (see Appendix A):

1. Net volume of timber, in board feet.
2. Area by age class, in acres.

3. Net volume of timber, by age class.
4. Programmed allowable harvest or allowable cut.
5. Rotation.

You must be certain that all of the factors shown here in italics apply to the figures you obtain. If, for instance, timberland designated as reserved, marginal, or special is included in the totals, the allowable cut (which really applies only to the area designated for full timber production) will appear conservative when in fact it may be too high for sustained yield. Additionally, a working circle may be divided into several groups for planning purposes; the forest may be segregated by site class, by species group, or by both. If this is the case, you will have to obtain statistics for each group.

Some national forests are managed for two rotations: a short rotation for the first cutting cycle, in which all the old-growth forest is removed, and a long rotation for all subsequent rotations. If you should find this to be the case in a plan you are reviewing, you can object that this is "anticipating the tomorrow that never arrives," merely appearing to justify present excessive cutting but actually having no influence on future activities.

A plan adopted by the Six Rivers National Forest in California in 1969 offers a good example of why it is necessary to question the validity of long rotations. The forest was reported to contain 12,984 billion board feet of timber on 455,249 acres of standard component of commercial forestland. The Forest Service claimed to be operating on a 140-year rotation, with an allowable cut of 206 million board feet. But by dividing the total volume of timber by the allowable cut, it was obvious that the 12.984 billion board feet would last only 63 years. And growth in the small proportion of young even-aged stands that would be 140 years old in 63 years would furnish the allowable cut for only about 3 more years, at the most.

This is a practical application of the Hanzlik formula. Obviously, more sophisticated methods of calculation are available, but here this simple test was certainly sufficient to reveal that sustained yield was by no means being practiced and that the staff probably had deluded themselves with overoptimism in their calculations.

MAKING A FIELD INSPECTION

When commenting on a forest plan, you should take a careful look at the forest and the actual field practices being used. You may need to make some simple measurements to determine whether reforestation is being accomplished according to plan, whether the forest plan is reasonably conservative in predicting tree growth, and whether sustained yield is actually being practiced. You may want to inquire as to whether any restrictions are being applied to logging equipment in order to protect young trees and minimize damage to the soil. Remember, too, that logging debris should be lopped and scattered so it will decay rapidly and return nutrients to the soil. This practice is also essential to minimize hazard from fire and from insects whose populations often breed up in logging slash. Several of the more important considerations in making a field inspection are discussed below.

Conducting a Stocking Survey

Clearcuts often fail to regenerate according to plan, even after several attempts are made to plant them and sometimes even after competing vegetation is suppressed with toxic sprays. A *stocked quadrant* survey is fast, accurate, and statistically sound. It is an ideal method for determining the percentage of stocking of an area that has been clearcut. The survey consists of sampling plots of appropriate size to determine whether each is stocked or not stocked. The percentage of stocking is then the same as the percentage of stocked plots. This method avoids distortion by considering only the well-distributed seedlings.

To determine the appropriate plot size, we work backward from standard planting specifications used by the Forest Service, generally 680 trees per acre (1/680 of an acre is about 64 square feet). The radius of a circle containing 64 square feet is almost exactly 4.5 feet. (This figure, by coincidence, is the height above ground level used in standard forestry practice for determining tree diameters. It is therefore easy to remember as well as convenient to use.) If we are concerned only with seedlings, as in the case of clearcuts, the percentage of plots of this size that are stocked is exactly the same as the percentage of stocking of the area. For example, if in our plot of 4 1/2-foot radius (64 square feet) we find a tree of commercial species, healthy and free to grow, that plot is stocked. It makes no difference in our tabulation if the plot contains several such trees, but if there is no tree within the 4 1/2-foot radius of the center of the plot, the plot is not stocked and is tallied accordingly. To make a stocking survey, one merely follows a straight line across the topography and notes, every so many feet or paces, whether a plot at that point is stocked or not stocked. The number of stocked plots divided by the total number of plots, multiplied by 100, gives us the percentage of stocking. Technically, sixteen plots should be a statistically significant sample;

however, it would be wise to run one or two transects across the area being examined, counting a larger number of plots in order to avoid dispute over the accuracy of your figures.

In some national forests, 240 trees per acre is considered adequate stocking. In that case, the plot radius for a stocking survey is 7.6 feet. (The area of 1/240 of an acre is 181.56 square feet, and the radius of a circle of that area is 7.60 feet.)

If, however, the area to be examined is stocked with various sizes of trees, as is the case in uneven-aged silviculture, this procedure must be modified by applying a correction factor. In this case, stocking is based on the presence of the tallest tree on each plot that is of a commercial species and free to grow. The correction factor used depends on the size of the largest tree occupying the plot. Young trees are classified as follows:

Name	Symbol	Size	Correction Factor
Seedlings	Se	Trees up to 6 feet tall	1
Saplings	Sa	Trees from 6 feet tall to 4 inches d.b.h.	1
Small poles	SP	Trees 4–8 inches d.b.h.	1.3
Large poles	LP	Trees 8–12 inches d.b.h.	3.4
Piling	P	Trees 12–16 inches d.b.h	6.9

A form for conducting a stocking survey is given in Figure 7.

Checking for Soil Disturbance

One of the main difficulties with clearcutting is the damage it causes to the soil. Forest soils are fragile; generally, the higher the elevation, the greater the fragility. Soil erosion is often not noticeable because the natural configurations of waterborne deposits are commonplace and generally to be expected. I have observed that the landforms visible from an airplane window over the southwestern deserts are essentially the same as those found in silt deposits along our gutters after a rain. (They also look like the landforms discovered on Mars, which are thought to be evidence of there once having been an atmosphere on that planet.) In a forest that has been logged, you should look for evidence of recent earth movement to determine whether the soil is eroding. This may consist of castling, evidenced by the occurrence of pebbles resting on top of little vertical piles of silt, or similar vertical streaks or half-castles on cut banks. Places where soil has been washed away often are paved with flat stones that occupy a far greater proportion of the surface area than

STOCKING SURVEY					
Plot No.	SE < 6' tall	SA 6' tall to 4" d.b.h.	SP 4"–8" d.b.h.	LP 8"–12" d.b.h.	P 12"–16" d.b.h.
A Totals (stocked plots)					
B Correction factor	1	1	1.3	3.4	6.9
C Product (A x B)						**D** (total of all C)
E	Total number of plots (stocked and not stocked) ———→				
F	Percentage of stocking (D ÷ E x 100) ———→				

At each point, note whether stocked (+) or not stocked (–). Consider only dominant or codominant trees of commercial species that are vigorous and free to grow.

FIGURE 7   *Stocking Survey Tally Sheet*

do similar stones embedded in cut banks. Another sign of erosion is fresh deposits of silt and fine sand in streambeds draining cutover areas, in contrast with the greater-sized pebbles and rocks found in the beds of streams draining uncut areas. Compaction is indicated where marks of logging equipment fail to grow grass and herbs to the same degree as adjacent soils.

Estimating Timber Volumes

As I mentioned earlier, the Forest Service uses various log rules in timber management planning. However, the layman can make a fairly accurate estimate of the volume per acre in board feet of a stand of timber. This can be accomplished quickly and easily by using a 20-factor prism* (I'll explain this in detail) and reckoning that every 16-foot log within the average plot will count for 1,000 board feet per acre. You simply count the number of such logs in at least sixteen randomly selected plots, average the number of logs per plot, and multiply the result by 1,000. The result will nearly always be accurate within 10 percent. This method, called *systematic sampling,* renders results identical to those obtained by random sampling, providing that the timber stand being measured is uniform in spacing and density. In systematic sampling, plot measurements are taken at regular intervals along a straight line, such as by following a compass. The technique is derived from the following formula:

$$V = C \times PF \times A$$

in which V = volume in board feet
C = constant:

Lodgepole pine	45
Old-growth ponderosa pine	53
Second-growth ponderosa pine	39
Average/unknown	50

A = average number of 16-foot logs per plot
PF = prism factor

Here is how it works: Decide on a method for locating a series of plots, either by following a compass line or by using some other technique that will avoid conscious choice of plot location. The line should cross the topography whenever possible. If the field to be measured appears to be uniform in size and spacing of trees, sixteen plots should be sufficient. Otherwise, adopt a plan that covers the area.

*Prisms may be obtained from any forestry supplier, such as Ben Meadows Company, P.O. Box 2781, Eugene, OR 97402, or Forestry Suppliers, Inc., P.O. Box 8397, Jackson, MS 39204.

Place the prism at the center of the plot. Walk around the prism; do not move the prism around the point on which you are standing. This may be accomplished by holding the prism on the top of a staff kept at plot center as you survey the plot.

Looking through the prism, examine all the trees in the plot, but count only those whose trunks do not appear to be split by the prism when you look at them at 4 1/2 feet above their high ground level (breast height) (see Figure 8).

Count the number of 16-foot logs contained in all of the trees in the plot, but count only those that are at least 10 inches in diameter outside the bark at the small end, thus discarding the treetops. Learn to estimate top diameter by placing a 10-inch piece of paper on a tree trunk. Judge the place on the upper trunk of the tree that has the same diameter.

Compensate for the slope of the land by tilting the prism to the same angle as the slope. To make a simple instrument for measuring slope, obtain a small semicircular metal protractor. Fasten a piece of wire through the apex so that the wire hangs down over the curved, calibrated edge of the protractor as you align the straight edge with the slope of the land. You can then read the angle of slope where the wire intersects with the calibrated edge of the protractor. To adjust your prism to compensate for slope, simply hold the wire in position, indicating the slope, and hold the prism on the straight edge of the protractor while sighting a tree, at the same time keeping the wire vertical.

Average the number of logs per plot by dividing the total number of logs by the number of plots. Multiply that result by 1,000 to obtain the average number of board feet per acre. Then, of course, multiply that by the number of acres in the area being examined to obtain the total volume of timber under consideration. The logs may be segregated by species, if desired.

Determining Site Index

Although it is not likely to happen, you may have occasion to check the site quality of forestland on which an allowable cut is in question, since there is a different yield table for each site index. You may recall that the site index is the height in feet that trees will attain at a given age (normally 50 years) as indicated on a particular table. To determine the timber-growing capacity of a piece of land supporting a young, uniform stand, the height and age of a number of trees are measured and compared with a set of curves to see on which curve most points fall. In old-growth virgin forests, the convention is to measure the height and age of the tallest 10 percent of the trees and match those figures with the curve.

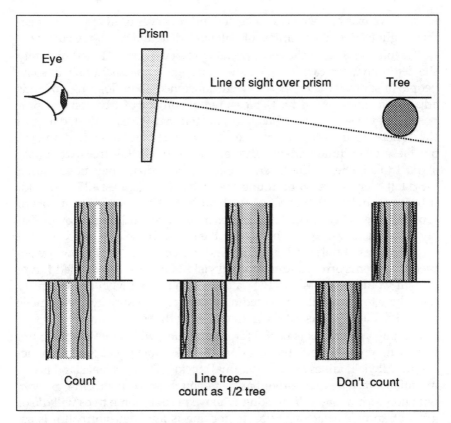

FIGURE 8 *How the Prism Works*

There are other ways of determining the site index; for example, the basal area per acre can be compared with age. Basal area is the surface per acre in square feet occupied by tree trunks at stump height (1 1/2 feet above the ground). In determining basal area, it is assumed that the diameter outside the bark at breast height (4 1/2 feet above the high ground level) is the same as the diameter inside the bark at stump height. Studies show this to be accurate for most species. This method may sometimes indicate a different site index from that indicated by the height-age relationship.

Several sets of site index curves have been prepared for our most important commercial species. Hence, you may want to determine not only whether the correct site has been identified but also whether the most appropriate curves were chosen for determining site in the first place. Normally there will be no need to go into the technicalities suggested here. The important point is merely to determine whether there is any evidence of bias either in choosing site index curves or in applying them that might lead to overestimate of potential yield and excessive cutting.

The following story shows how yield prediction errors based on faulty site determinations can occur. A few years ago, I was asked to help some people in southern Oregon who were concerned about logging on lands adjacent to their property. I measured a number of trees on the proposed logging site, and the height of the dominant trees indicated a good site. There were a few mature trees that were tall and large in diameter, but these were quite widely scattered. Most of the tall trees were only about 1 to 2 inches in diameter. I counted the growth rings in several of these tall, slender trees and found that many were at least 125 years old. It became obvious that most of the land in that site was not capable of growing trees larger than 2 or 3 inches in diameter, although they probably would achieve normal height for their age. If the site index for that area were based only on height of the dominant trees, and growth were predicted from corresponding normal yield tables, the anticipated future growth would be grossly exaggerated. I don't know what caused many trees there to grow tall but exceedingly slender; probably it was a genetic anomaly. But this illustrates the kind of error that can occur.

Although site index is useful for determining which yield table to use in making growth predictions, it does not take stocking capacity into account. All yield tables assume "normal stocking." A normal stand is one in which every desirable tree has just enough space for thrifty growth, with no space wasted. If stocking is above normal, some trees will die or grow at an unsatisfactory rate. If stocking is less than normal, it is assumed that stocking will automatically improve because trees occupy ever-increasing space as they grow, thus reducing the proportion of unstocked area. Often the Forest Service will repeatedly replant open areas, and in some situations success may never be achieved.

Unfortunately, there is hardly any place in the world where normal stocking occurs over a sizable area. Failure of a spot of land to grow trees may have many causes. There may be bedrock hidden close to the surface; an area may be too poorly drained to permit tree growth; a tree-killing root disease may be latent in the soil, ready to attack as soon as it comes in contact with the roots of new seedlings. Therefore, it is essential to determine the actual stocking capacity of a given piece of land as well as its site index in order to properly apply a yield table. In California, the practice has been to assume that commercial species all grow at the same rate. However, even though the height-age relationship for species that grow together is often the same, sometimes it is not. For example, in the spruce-hemlock forests of Alaska, the hemlock doesn't grow quite as tall as the spruce. If the heights of the spruce, and not of the hemlock, were considered, the calculations would indicate a higher site index than if the heights of both species were used. So it is important to look closely at the characteristics of each site to get an accurate picture of its ability to grow timber.

Checking for Multiple Use

Is the forest obviously being managed for timber, with multiple use being considered only to the extent that protection of outdoor recreation, livestock grazing, watershed, wildlife, and fish do not interfere with timber production? Or is timber management modified to accommodate the other uses we expect of our national forests on the same land at the same time? Are standing dead trees available as nesting sites? Is there an ample supply of species that the native wild creatures require for food? Is the area still attractive after logging? Does the method of management require dependence on extraordinary measures, such as use of herbicides or major disturbance of the soil to remove vegetation that competes with planted seedlings?

It is obvious that we cannot apply multiple-use forestry as I have described it to areas that have already been converted to large, even-aged stands of trees. These areas will remain even-aged and thus monotonously uniform for the next one or two hundred years. But the principles of multiple use can be applied to what remains of old-growth timber in those parts of our national forests now designated for full timber production. I also maintain that if any logging is to be permitted in the remainder of the commercial forestland identified as special, modified, or reserved, these principles must be applied.

As I mentioned earlier, multiple use costs us nothing but restraint. And it is restraint that will yield enduring benefits.

If we manage our commercial timberland for sustained yield, using long rotations, we will reap the benefits of high-quality wood products in perpetuity. If we practice uneven-aged management in our forests, keeping the logged areas no larger than is necessary for biological considerations, we will protect the forest soil, enhancing the forest's ability to regenerate itself. At the same time, we will protect the quality of our wildlife, our fishing streams, our municipal water supplies, and the ability of the forest watershed to reduce floods. Selective or group selection cutting also protects the beauty of the forest so that it can still be used for recreation. It eliminates the need for expensive replanting programs, because the small openings in a conservatively cut forest will likely regenerate on their own with native species already adapted to that particular site.

As we have seen, the Forest Service was once proud to implement the principles of multiple use and did so for many years. It is still bound by law to do so under the Multiple Use–Sustained Yield Act of 1960.

However, in recent years the Forest Service has turned its back on its tradition and substituted "dominant use"—timber production—in its management of the nation's commercial timberland. Clearcutting has become the norm rather than the exception. If the agency is allowed to continue on its present course, the nation's old-growth forests will vanish forever, perhaps as soon as the end of this century. People who now use these lands for outdoor recreation—for camping, hunting, fishing, and the like—will have to pursue these activities in wilderness areas or in parks, many of which are even now overcrowded. And when the old growth is gone, surely there will be a concerted effort by the timber industry to log the wilderness areas and parks as well.

Is this the direction in which we want to go? Or can we citizens, the owners of these old-growth forests, using the information in this book and others and the findings from the Forest Service's own research stations, succeed in convincing the agency to take a more prudent path?

PART FOUR

SUPPORTING RESEARCH AND INFORMED OPINIONS

The numbered statements that follow are included to give you the opportunity to document your reports and comments on forest plans without having to visit a forestry library or send away for obscure publications. Some entries are direct quotations, some are summaries, and others are paraphrases of material originally appearing in cumbersome language. A code follows each entry to indicate which applies:

Q   quotation
O   observation
P   paraphrase
S   summary
C   comment

It must be clearly understood that these entries are often my interpretation of research, sometimes in contrast with the reported conclusions. For example, in 004, *Landslides on Logged Areas in Southeast Alaska*, the authors state, "The number and acreage of slides since 1953 increased four and one-half or more times. It shouldn't be overlooked, either, that these increases occurred in a period of less than 10 years." But Table 1 of that publication clearly shows that while only twelve landslides had occurred in the area during the 100 years preceding logging, one hundred sixteen landslides occurred within 10 years after logging, and the largest number of occurrences in any single year was 68. So they could just as honestly have stated that "the number . . . of slides since 1953 increased 68 or more times . . . in a period of less than 10 years." In summarizing that same research, *NCASI* Technical Bulletin No. 456* states, "Frequency of failures increased by 93 times." My division yields 97.

I have not always followed the usual method of citing sources in footnotes in Parts One through Three of this book because in view of the amount of material referenced, it would be too cumbersome to do so. Instead, in places I have simply named the principal researchers whose publications I have relied on. You can easily find the source of research material referred to by looking up the researchers' names in the author index. You can often find additional supporting research in the subject index.

*National Council of the Paper Industry for Air and Stream Improvement, Inc., 260 Madison Avenue, New York, NY 10016, April 1985.

001   Offord, Harold R. *Diseases of Monterey Pine in Native Stands of California and in Plantations of Western North America*, p. 10. Research Paper PSW-14. Department of Agriculture, Forest Service, 1964. **Q**

"In summary, successful planting of Monterey pine in West Coast areas of North America is definitely limited by frost, midsummer heat, disease, and other pests. The most generally suitable sites for planting . . . are the coastal counties of central California. To date the Western Gall Rust and the Sweetfern Blister Rust have placed some limitations on the desirability of planting Monterey pine outside its optimum range in California."

002   Roth, L. E., H. H. Bynum, and E. E. Nelson. *Phytophthora Root Rot of Port-Orford-Cedar*, pp. 4–5. Forest Pest Leaflet 131. Department of Agriculture, Forest Service, 1972. **P, Q**

Phytophthora root rot is causing widespread damage to Port Orford cedar in the lowlands of the Pacific Northwest, and its spread into the mountains is accelerating. No method of control is known. Although it is not stated in this quote, wilderness classification or other restrictive classification may be the best way to stop disease.

"Wherever possible, a policy of nonentry of people, animals, and equipment should be followed in stands containing cedar of any age. Where old-growth timber is involved this will be possible only in a limited way. Probably entry should be allowed where there are concentrations of infected, salvable young timber; however, entry to salvage widely scattered, diseased young-growth should not be allowed."

003   Hughes, Ralph H., George W. Bengtson, and Thaddeus A. Harrington. *Forage Response to Nitrogen and Phosphorus Fertilization in a 25-Year-Old Plantation of Slash Pine*. Research Paper SE-82. Department of Agriculture, Forest Service, April 1971. **S**

Sometimes fertilization of forest trees may stimulate growth of competing vegetation instead. In Florida, a well-stocked 25-year-old slash pine stand was treated with 0, 100, and 200 pounds of nitrogen per acre and 0 and 44 pounds of phosphorus per acre. The chemicals used were ammonium nitrate and superphosphate. None of the treatments produced an increase in growth of merchantable wood sufficient to justify the application, but yields of indigenous herbage increased by 500 to 1,000 pounds per acre for every 100-pound-per-acre increase in the nitrogen level.

004   Bishop, Daniel M., and Mervin E. Stevens. *Landslides on Logged Areas in Southeast Alaska*. Research Paper NOR-1. Department of Agriculture, Forest Service, 1964. **S**

In an area of southeastern Alaska, a drastic change in the landslide pattern occurred after logging. In a period of 100 years before logging, 27.3 acres were affected, but in a period of only 10 years after logging, 119 acres were affected, a 43-fold increase in area. There were only 12 landslides within 100 years prior to logging, but 116 landslides occurred within 10 years after logging, a 97-fold increase. The authors believe that tree roots had held the steep soil in place and that after clearcutting, when the roots of stumps decayed, the land slipped.

005 Myers, Diane. 1973. Unpublished. **Q**

"When a large area is clearcut, the bird population changes from insect-eating to seed-eating birds. Then there are no predators to check subsequent insect outbreaks."

006 Reynolds, Hudson G. *Effect of Logging on Understory Vegetation and Deer Use in a Ponderosa Pine Forest of Arizona.* Research Note RM-80. Department of Agriculture, Forest Service, 1962. **Q, S**

"Deer use . . . tended to reflect the amount of understory vegetation present in overstory classes. . . . Mature residual stands were slightly preferred over openings, and deer tended to avoid dense, pole-sized stands of timber. This suggests that factors other than understory vegetation may influence use of an area by deer."

Therefore, management practices leading to formation of extensive pole-sized stands, such as short rotations and even-aged management, should not be practiced.

007 Zon, Raphael. *Timber Growing and Logging Practice in the Lake States.* Bulletin 1496. Department of Agriculture, Forest Service, 1928. **S**

A study of silviculturally sound selective logging versus clearcutting in hardwood forests around the Great Lakes showed that actual cost per thousand board feet was about the same either way. In one instance, in which 30 percent of the volume was removed, the cost of selective logging was actually less than the cost of clearcutting.

008 Patric, James H. *Some Environmental Effects of Cable Logging in the Appalachian Forests.* General Technical Report NE-55. Department of Agriculture, Forest Service, 1980. **S**

Forestry literature was reviewed for reports concerning effects of logging on soil, water, residual stands, wildlife, and visual appeal. In all cases, cable logging caused fewer unwanted effects than did other logging systems. Even though the cable logging technique is well established, machinery fully suited to harvesting eastern hardwood forests by this method has not been developed.

009 Person, Hubert L., and William E. Hallin. "Natural Restocking of Redwood Cutover Lands." *Journal of Forestry* 40 (1942): 683–688. **S**

Timbered edges of clearcut units have effective seeding distances of only 200 feet uphill and 400 feet downhill under average redwood stand conditions.

010 Brink, David L., and Michael M. Merriman. "Influence of Young-growth on Characteristics and Utilization of Fiber." *Proceedings of a Conference on Young-Growth Forest Management in California,* pp. 7–22. Berkeley, CA: University of California, Department of Forest and Resource Management, 1967. **S**

Fiber density, fiber length, and fiber strength are the principal properties controlling strength of paper. Two measurements are used in evaluating paper strength: burst factor and tear factor. Burst factor is independent of length and strength of fiber; it depends on the bond strength per unit area and the conformability of fiber. This is enhanced by the presence of hemicellulose, which hydrates during beating. If fiber is too short, however, bonding is impossible.

A high tear factor comes from long, strong fibers, which occur in slowly grown wood, older parts of trees, and suppressed trees. Thus, young-growth wood produces paper having a high burst factor and a decreased tear factor, but short fibers tend to decrease both.

011 Resch, Helmuth. "Considering the Physical Properties of Wood in Managing Forest Trees." *Proceedings of a Conference on Young-Growth Forest Management in California*, p. 23. Berkeley, CA: University of California, Department of Forest and Resource Management, 1967. Q

"In the past, judging the quality of trees was often confined to the major criteria of rapid growth, pest resistance and the formation of clear, straight, cylindrical stems. More recently fiber qualities, specific gravity and proportions of latewood also have been considered."

012 Brink, David L., and Michael M. Merriman. "Influence of Young-growth on Characteristics and Utilization of Fiber." *Proceedings of a Conference on Young-Growth Forest Management in California*, p. 12. Berkeley, CA: University of California, Department of Forest and Resource Management, 1967. Q

"Extractives are higher in corewood, decreasing rapidly to the sapwood of conifers. Upper portions of the stem contain somewhat smaller amounts of extractives than lower portions."

013 Resch, Helmuth. "Considering the Physical Properties of Wood in Managing Forest Trees." *Proceedings of a Conference on Young-Growth Forest Management in California*, p. 25. Berkeley, CA: University of California, Department of Forest and Resource Management, 1967. Q

"As a tree matures and grows in girth, the cambium produces longer and thicker walled cells. Thus a pattern of increasing latewood percent and specific gravity evolves from pith to bark and from crown to tree base."

014 Resch, Helmuth. "Considering the Physical Properties of Wood in Managing Forest Trees." *Proceedings of a Conference on Young-Growth Forest Management in California*, p. 24. Berkeley, CA: University of California, Department of Forest and Resource Management, 1967. Q

"Natural decay resistance is of importance among the California species— especially in cedars and redwood. However, only the heartwood is rich in fungicidal extractives, therefore the percentage of heartwood within trees becomes an important feature."

015 Resch, Helmuth. "Considering the Physical Properties of Wood in Managing Forest Trees." *Proceedings of a Conference on Young-Growth Forest Management in California*, p. 25. Berkeley, CA: University of California, Department of Forest and Resource Management, 1967. Q, P

"Tree age is of major importance, because juvenile wood is generally formed during the immature period in a tree's life. It is characterized by short tracheids, by a small amount of latewood, often by wide growth rings, and a large angle between the direction of microfibrils in the secondary layer of the cell walls and the longitudinal axis of a tree."

Juvenile wood is low-density, inferior wood. A greater amount of sapwood is generally found in young-growth trees than in old-growth trees, and a relationship exists between the percentage of heartwood and the diameter of the tree.

016 Schniewind, Arno P. "Influence of Forest Management on Utilization Values—Mechanical Properties." *Proceedings of a Conference on Young-Growth Forest Management in California*, p. 33. Berkeley, CA: University of California, Department of Forest and Resource Management, 1967. **Q**

"Second-growth redwood is definitely inferior to old-growth:"

	Specific Gravity	Modulus of Rupture (psi)	Maximum Crushing Strength (psi)
Virgin or old growth	.40	10,000	6,150
Young growth			
Closely grown	.34	8,300	5,240
Openly grown	.30	6,400	3,810
Random sampling	.35	7,900	5,220

017 Poletika, Nicholas B. "Summary Comments on Young-growth Management as Related to Utilization." Proceedings of a Conference on Young-Growth Forest Management in California, p. 43. Berkeley, CA: University of California, Department of Forest and Resource Management, 1967. **Q**

"An appearance wood, such as Redwood, presents . . . complex marketing problems. A converter of young-growth Redwood is lucky to obtain 25 percent clear lumber as compared to 50 percent or more in old growth."

018 Harris, A. S., and W. A. Farr. *The Forest Ecosystem of Southeast Alaska.*, p. 79. General Technical Report PNW-25. Department of Agriculture, Forest Service, 1974. **Q**

"Evidence from long-term European studies indicates that maximum yields are obtained from lightly thinned, well-stocked stands where anticipated mortality is salvaged. Redistribution of growth through heavy thinning allows for larger sized trees and greater return on investments but generally does not increase gross yield unless moisture, nutrients, soil temperature, or other limiting factors are influenced by the thinning."

019 Erickson, H. D., and G.M.B. Lambert. "Effect of Fertilization and Thinning on Chemical Composition, Growth and Specific Gravity of Young Douglas-fir." *Forest Science* 4 (1958):307–315. **S**

Intensity of thinning in stands of young timber has a pronounced effect on a number of wood properties. In particular, heavy thinning often produces wood of lower density (specific gravity) and decreases the percentage of latewood.

020 Grantham, John B. et al. *Energy and Raw Material Potentials of Wood Residue in the Pacific Coast States—A Summary of a Preliminary Feasibility Investigation.* General Technical Report PNW-18. Department of Agriculture, Forest Service, 1974. **S**

Wood has a heating value of about 9,000 Btu per pound, dry weight.

021 Grantham, John B. et al. *Energy and Raw Material Potentials of Wood Residue in the Pacific Coast States—A Summary of a Preliminary Feasibility Investigation,* p. 21. General Technical Report PNW-18. Department of Agriculture, Forest Service, 1974. **Q**

"For thermodynamic reasons and under typical boiler conditions, one kwh of thermal energy yields about one-third kwh of electrical energy."

022 Gardener, R. B., and David Hann. *Utilization of Lodgepole Pine Logging Residues in Wyoming Increases Fiber Yield.* Research Note INT-160. Department of Agriculture, Forest Service, 1972. **S**

A 35 percent increase in weight of fiber harvested was obtained by addition of a chipper to conventional utilization methods in lodgepole pine. Under conventional practices, this material would have been burned. No cost figures are given.

023 Goldstein, Irving. "Potential for Converting Wood into Plastics." *Science* 198 (1975):851. Copyright 1975 by the AAAS. **Q**

"The conversion of wood into chemicals for production of most of our synthetic plastics, fibers and rubbers is technically feasible. With refinements in technology a large integrated plant utilizing all components of wood for production of ethanol (to be further processed to ethylene and butadiene), phenols and furfural would also be approaching economic feasibility at current petrochemical prices. If crude oil prices continue to climb at a faster rate than wood costs, the economic feasibility of chemicals for polymers from wood would become certain.

"Although technical feasibility has not been established, synthetic oils from liquefaction of wood might serve as feedstocks for cracking to chemicals in the same way that crude oil is presently used.

"The fulfillment of all our polymer needs from wood as a raw material should not place an impossible burden on our wood supply, but might actually improve the availability of wood for lumber, plywood and pulp by providing a use for less valuable wood which would allow reforestation and improved forest management."

024 Merkel, Edward P. *Slash Pine Seedworm.* Forest Pest Leaflet 126. Department of Agriculture, Forest Service, 1971. **P**

Cones of pitch pine, also known as slash pine (*Pinus elliottii*) are often damaged by the slash pine seedworm (*Dioryetria* sp.). Economically important losses are confined to production stands and seed orchards. Damage is to seeds in second-year cones. Natural control is partially accomplished by parasitic wasps of the families Trichogrammatidae and Braconidae which destroy 50 percent of the seedworm larvae and eggs. Phanerotoma fasciata, a braconid wasp, emerges in great numbers simultaneously with the seedworm moth and controls its population.

025 Stevens, Robert. *Pine Needle-sheath Miner.* Forest Pest Leaflet 65 (revised). Department of Agriculture, Forest Service, 1971. **P, Q**

The pine needle-sheath miner attacks and defoliates jack pine, ponderosa pine, Jeffrey pine, and lodgepole pine.

"Parasitism appears to play an important part in regulating needle-sheath miner populations. At Placerville in 1957, six species of parasites were reared from either larvae or pupae of the pine needle-sheath miner. Several species that are possibly parasitic also were reared. The most numerous parasites were of the wasp families (Ichneumonidae), (Braconidae), and (Chalcididae)."

026 Keen, F. P. *Insect Enemies of Western Forests*, p. 215. Miscellaneous Publication 273 (revised). Department of Agriculture, Forest Service, 1952. **Q**

"Many species of birds are insectivores. Nuthatches, chickadees, creepers, warblers, kinglets, and many other species search for insects on tree trunks and foliage, while woodpeckers dig through the bark and feed on larvae of bark and wood borers. Counts have shown that fully seventy-five percent of the western pine beetle population in patches of pine bark worked over by woodpeckers have been destroyed by these industrious workers."

027 McCambridge, William F., and Fred B. Knight. "Factors Affecting Spruce Beetles During a Small Outbreak." *Ecology* 53 (1972): 830. **Q**

"In 1957, spruce beetles, *Dendroctonus rufipennis*, developed into outbreak numbers in logging slash at a north-central Colorado site, entered living spruce trees, but remained epidemic for only two years. Reduced beetle fecundity was the first indication of outbreak decline; this was caused by nematodes and unknown agents. Significant summer mortality agents were pitch, intra- and interspecific competition for food, predation by woodpeckers and flies, and parasitism by wasps. Desiccation of both food and beetle larvae, enhanced by woodpecker feeding activity, contributed significantly to outbreak decline. Winter mortality was attributed mainly to woodpeckers, although temperature of -29 C caused additional losses."

028 Denton, Robert. *Establishment of Agathis pumila for Control of Larch Casebearer, and Notes on Native Parasitism and Predation in Idaho.*" Research Note INT-164. Department of Agriculture, Forest Service, 1972. **S**

Since 1957, the larch casebearer (*Coleophora laricella*) has infested more than half of the western larch in its natural range. Serious deterioration and mortality of stands is evident in northern Idaho. The parasite *Agathis pumila* effectively reduces larch casebearer populations and can maintain a high level of parasitism at low host densities. Native parasites numbered sixteen in 1968, and they accounted for 17 percent of the parasitism. Their role in limiting populations is questionable. Mites and hemipterous bugs are also known predators. Birds, notably the black-capped chickadee, are important predators in the winter period.

029 Schmid, J. M. "A Problem in the Front Range: Pine Beetles." *Colorado Outdoors* 21 (1972): 138. Q, C

"During [its] annual [life] cycle numerous organisms parasitize or prey on the beetle populations. Adult flies and clerid beetles prey on adult mountain pine beetles. Immature stages of flies, wasps and clerid beetles feed on the eggs, larvae or pupae of the beetle. Nematodes reduce the egg production of the female beetles. Woodpeckers pry off the bark to feed on beetle larvae and pupae. In so doing, they indirectly kill more beetles by reducing the thickness of the bark, thus exposing the immature beetles to either increased dehydration or inundation during rainstorms. During the flight period, nuthatches capture adults on the bark, while fly-catchers capture beetles in flight."

Despite this impressive list, during major outbreaks natural enemies rarely reduce populations of the beetle sufficiently to minimize tree losses. However, they certainly minimize the number and frequency of outbreaks.

030 Otvos, I. S. "Avian Predation of the Western Pine Beetle." *Studies on the Population Dynamics of the Western Pine Beetle (Dendroctonus brevicomis),* p. 124. University of California, Division of Agricultural Sciences, 1970. Q, P

"A total of 11 species of birds from 4 families were observed to prey on some stage of the western pine beetle, and 3 other species from 2 additional families were suspected predators."

The most common of these species are the mountain chickadee, the white-headed woodpecker, the western flycatcher, the red-breasted nuthatch, the brown creeper, and the hairy woodpecker. All but the western flycatcher are hole-nesters, according to Peterson.*

031 Otvos, I. S. "Avian Predation of the Western Pine Beetle." *Studies on the Population Dynamics of the Western Pine Beetle (Dendroctonus brevicomis),* p. 124. University of California, Division of Agricultural Sciences, 1970. P, Q

Woodpeckers feed on bark beetles by scraping the bark off trees harboring overwintering beetle larvae and preying on the exposed larvae. "Woodpecker predation constituted the major part of the avian-caused mortality of the immature stages of the western pine beetle."

The woodpeckers decrease beetle populations in three ways: by direct feeding, by changing the beetle's environment (due to thinner bark), and by increasing parasitism of beetles (easier entrance due to thinner bark).

032 Solomon, J. D., and R. C. Morris. "Woodpeckers in the Ecology of Southern Hardwood Borers." *Proceedings of the Tall Timbers Conference on Ecological Animal Control by Habitat Management,* p. 315. Department of Agriculture, Forest Service (Southern Forest Experiment Station), 1971. S, Q

Red-bellied, hairy, downy, red-headed, and pileated woodpeckers were observed in hardwood stands heavily infested by borers. The birds were less efficient in stands with average or low borer populations.

*R. T. Peterson, *A Field Guide to Western Birds,* 2d ed. (Boston: Houghton Mifflin, 1961).

"Borer species that infest small trees, especially those under 6 inches in diameter, are more apt to be captured by woodpeckers than those that attack larger trees. . . . Although the holes made by woodpeckers may cause additional wind-breakage and disease incidence in infested trees, the benefits from reduced borer populations are far more valuable than the lost timber."

033 Brown, L., et al. "Lindane Registration Should Not Be Retained." *Lindane in Forestry . . . A Continuing Controversy.* General Technical Report PSW-14. Department of Agriculture, Forest Service, 1976. **P**

Direct control of insects with lindane (or other biocides) has several shortcomings: its high economic cost, the difficulty of finding all (or even a high percentage) of the infested trees, and its temporary effect (i.e., it doesn't remove the conditions that caused the outbreak).

034 Norris, Logan A., and Dwane Moore. "The Entry and Fate of Forest Chemicals in Streams." *Proceedings of a Symposium, Forest Land Uses and Stream Environment,* pp. 138-158. J. T. Krygier and J. D. Hall, editors. Corvallis, OR: Oregon State University, School of Forestry and Department of Fisheries and Wildlife, 1971. **P**

Significant quantities of aerially applied herbicides miss their targets. At a Christmas tree plantation in Oregon, only 75 percent of wettable powder formulations of atrazine and simazine applied by fixed-wing aircraft reached the ground. During a helicopter application of amitrole, only 60 percent was accounted for. When 2,4,5-T (low-volatile esters) in diesel oil was applied by fixed-wing aircraft, only 25 to 40 percent reached the first intercepting surfaces. Similar results were noted for the pesticides malathion and DDT.

035 Wikstrom, J. H., and S. Blair Hutchison. *Stratification of Forest Land for Timber Management Planning of the Western National Forests.* Research Paper INT-108. Department of Agriculture, Forest Service, 1971. **Q**

"The area of forest land suitable and available for timber production on National Forests of the West has been overestimated, probably as much as 22 percent. Forest land misclassified for timber use includes 1) highly unstable land, 2) land low in timber productivity, 3) forest land devoted to non-timber use, and 4) patches and stringers of forest land too small and/or too isolated to be used in timber production."

036 Hudlund, Arnold. "Arkansas Delta Forest: A Vanishing Resource." *Forest Farmer* 30 (1971): 13. **Q, P**

"Forests are rapidly vanishing from the Arkansas Delta. Between 1959 and 1969, forest land declined by almost 1.3 million acres, or 39 percent, in this portion of the state."
A large variety of hardwood species provides ideal habitat for wildlife.
"Statewide land reassessment made the annual returns from soybeans more attractive than long-term gains from timber."
Massive land clearing and conversion to soybean production occurred. During this period, 800,000 cubic feet of merchantable hardwoods were removed,

and only 23 percent of that land was utilized. Other decreases in forested land occurred as a result of increased flood-control projects and drainage projects.

037 Bolsinger, Charles L. *Changes in Commercial Forest Area in Oregon and Washington, 1945–1970.* Resource Bulletin PNW-46. Department of Agriculture, Forest Service, 1973. **S**

The following physical changes occurred in Oregon and Washington between 1945 and 1970:

Land Use	Resulting Loss of Forestland (acres lost and percentage of total loss)	
Road construction	347,000	35%
Urban and industrial construction	285,000	29%
Farm and pasture clearing	159,000	16%
Power lines	149,000	15%
Reservoirs	55,000	5%
Total	995,000	100%

As of 1945, this total comprised 2.2 percent of the total commercial forestland in these states. Commercial forestland reserved for parks, wilderness, natural areas, and botanical areas increased by only 362,000 acres between 1945 and 1970.

038 Boyce, J. S. *Forest Pathology*, p. 515. New York: McGraw-Hill, 1961. Reproduced with permission. **Q**

"Where forest conditions have been largely destroyed over extensive areas by fire or by unregulated cutting, the new stand, particularly in its juvenile stages, is likely to suffer more severely from disease than would normally be the case. . . . It is evident that in cutting timber the selection method or one of its modifications should be practiced, where possible, instead of clearcutting."

039 Godman, Richard M., and Carl H. Tubbs. *Establishing Even-age Northern Hardwood Regeneration by the Shelterwood Method—A Preliminary Guide*, pp. 4–5. Research Paper NC-99. Department of Agriculture, Forest Service, 1973. **Q**

"Logging while the ground is snow covered has advantages over summer logging. . . . It results in lower seedling mortality, less ground compaction, and less damage to seedling stems. . . . Summer logging will require a much longer time to establish regeneration because of competition from herbaceous vegetation. The stocking may also remain sparse because of seedling loss from skidding."

040 Godman, Richard M., and Carl H. Tubbs. *Establishing Even-age Northern Hardwood Regeneration by the Shelterwood Method—A Preliminary Guide*, pp. 4–5. Research Paper NC-99. Department of Agriculture, Forest Service, 1973. **S**

Shelterwood silviculture proved more reliable in terms of stocking density than either heavy diameter-limit cutting or clearcutting. The latter two often resulted in grassy patches, sparsely stocked with early pioneer species. Data were taken in northern Wisconsin and Minnesota.

041   Baker, F. S. *Principles of Silviculture*, pp. 17–18. New York: McGraw-Hill, 1950. **S**

Clearcutting (even-aged management) promotes erosion and compaction of the surface soil, particularly where mineral soil is exposed. In dry climates, as in California, clearcutting allows organic matter to become very desiccated, slowing down decay. Clearcutting also exposes the forest floor to intense insolation and evaporation, and as a result, the normal soil life of fungi, bacteria, worms, and microscopic plants and animals of all kinds is destroyed or at least greatly changed, with fauna and flora of open lands coming in. This is usually undesirable. Finally, clearcutting invites invasion of vegetation that severely competes with forest tree seedlings.

042   Gill, Don. "Forestry Operations in the Canadian Subarctic: An Ecological Argument Against Clearcutting." *Environmental Conservation* 1 (1974): 91. **Q**

"Environmental and floristic evidence shows that, after removal of White Spruce and Willow-Alder canopies from exposed sites within the boreal woodland of the MacKenzie River Delta, Northwest Territory, Canada, environmental degradation such that secondary succession of low-arctic tundra heath, mosses, and lichens, has taken place. The extreme exposure of cleared sites enables a hardy group of tundra plants to compete with the local flora and invade the previously forested location."

043   Patric, J. H. *Frost Depth on Forest Soils Near Juneau, Alaska*, p. 6. Research Note PNW-60. Department of Agriculture, Forest Service, 1967. **Q**

"It now seems unlikely that clearcut soils can be expected to freeze much deeper than forested soils. In this study, frost penetrated only 4 inches deeper on clearcut than on forested plots."

044   Lynch, Donald W. "Mechanical Thinning of Young Conifer Stands." *Transactions of the American Society of Agriculture Engineers.* 16 (1973): 34. **S, Q**

After a fire or clearcut, extremely dense regrowth of several western conifers may occur (especially lodgepole pine, western larch, and ponderosa pine). Such stands may stagnate on medium- and poor-quality sites when none of the poles express dominance. Hand thinning, even with power saws, is "all but an impossible physical job. Furthermore, economic justification of such a costly pre-commercial treatment is questionable. Consequently, foresters generally have left these stands untreated. The production loss—not only of timber and pulp products, but also of wildlife forage—has been significant."

Mechanical thinning of such stands has been tried on an experimental basis; although this approach shows some promise (according to the author), it has not yet been successful. Mechanical thinning generally requires tractors and some sort of roller-crusher device.

045 Phillips, Robert W. "Effects of Sediment on the Gravel Environment and Fish Production." *Proceedings of a Symposium, Forest Land Uses and Stream Environment*, p. 65. J. T. Krygier and J. D. Hall, editors. Corvallis, OR: Oregon State University, School of Forestry and Department of Fisheries and Wildlife, 1971. **Q**

"Since salmon and trout are primarily sight feeders, water made turbid by suspended sediment is not as productive to the angler. Fishing success declines once the turbidity exceeds 25 ppm. Turbid water makes it possible for fishes that are more tolerant of this condition and less dependent on sight for feeding, such as squawfishes and suckers, to better compete thus reducing the production of trout and salmon."

046 Heede, Burchard. *Flow and Channel Characteristics of Two High Mountain Streams*, p. 11. Research Paper RM-96. Department of Agriculture, Forest Service, 1972. **Q, C**

"It appears that sanitation cutting [removal of dead and dying trees] should not be practiced along small mountain streams at dynamic equilibrium; the movement of bed material in such streams should be minimized. Such equilibrium is necessary, for instance, for maintenance of spawning beds for fish."

Note: "Dynamic equilibrium" is the state of a stream that is moving the maximum size of particles that its flow will allow, varying with its stages. Such a stream is "in balance" with its topography and bed load. For a further discussion of this concept, see Gilbert's *Dynamic Equilibrium Model of Landscale Evolution*.

047 Lantz, Richard. "Influence of Water Temperature on Fish Survival, Growth and Behavior." *Proceedings of a Symposium, Forest Land Uses and Stream Environment*, p. 185. J. T. Krygier and J. D. Hall, editors. Corvallis, OR: Oregon State University, School of Forestry and Department of Fisheries and Wildlife, 1971. **Q**

"In general, the toxicity of chemicals usually increases with increased temperature, and organisms subjected to toxic materials are less tolerant of temperature extremes. Since chemical reaction rates increase with increased temperature and metabolic rates generally increase at higher temperatures, these results should be expected."

048 Lantz, Richard. "Fish Population Impacts." *Proceedings of a Symposium, Forest Land Uses and Stream Environment*, pp. 246–248. J. T. Krygier and J. D. Hall, editors. Corvallis, OR: Oregon State University, School of Forestry and Department of Fisheries and Wildlife, 1971. **P**

A decrease in dissolved oxygen is detrimental to salmonid fish. In the Needle Branch of the Alsea Watershed Study in Oregon, an entire watershed (175 acres) was clearcut. Dissolved oxygen levels remained lower than prelogging levels for 4 years after logging and as of 1970, did not yet appear to be returning to previous levels.

049 Campbell, Homer. "Economic and Social Significance of Upstream Aquatic Resources on the West Coast." *Proceedings of a Symposium, Forest Land Uses and Stream Environment*, p. 14. J. T. Krygier and J. D. Hall, editors. Corvallis, OR: Oregon State University, School of Forestry and Department of Fisheries and Wildlife, 1971. Q

"The South Fork of the Salmon River in Idaho once held about 20 percent of Idaho's total salmon run and provided 30 percent of Idaho's salmon harvest. It was an important segment of the downriver commercial and the upriver sport fishery. Prior to 1952 the drainage was in good condition and the average escapement was 10,000 chinook and 5,000 steelhead. Land use, road construction, and logging created conditions that accelerated the sediment load through landslides and slumps generally associated with intense climactic storms. The magnitude of activity is reported at 326 million board feet removed from the study area. Platts reports that in the South Fork of the Salmon River some spawning areas were blanketed with four feet of bedload sediment.* Platts estimates that Idaho is losing an annual value of $350,000 because of silting in that particular river."

050 Campbell, Homer. "Economic and Social Significance of Upstream Aquatic Resources on the West Coast." *Proceedings of a Symposium, Forest Land Uses and Stream Environment*, p. 15. J. T. Krygier and J. D. Hall, editors. Corvallis, OR: Oregon State University, School of Forestry and Department of Fisheries and Wildlife, 1971. Q

"California fishery biologists estimate that the spawning habitat for 14,000 king salmon in a 16-mile stretch of the Trinity River has been destroyed. Accelerated erosion caused by logging and road construction is considered to be the major contributor to the problem while dam construction has reduced the sediment transport capacity of the river to a level far below the needs to disperse the load produced by tributaries. Although post-logging sediment yields have been reduced considerably by natural revegetative processes in the past 13 years, continued deterioration of the fish habitat is recorded."

051 Campbell, Homer. "Economic and Social Significance of Upstream Aquatic Resources on the West Coast." *Proceedings of a Symposium, Forest Land Uses and Stream Environment*, pp. 11, 13. J. T. Krygier and J. D. Hall, editors. Corvallis, OR: Oregon State University, School of Forestry and Department of Fisheries and Wildlife, 1971. Q, P

"Anadromous fishery resources are almost entirely dependent on upstream watersheds in the Pacific Northwest for their perpetuation. Where data are available known values of spawning areas range from $1,000 to $300,000 per acre annually."

Fisheries are valuable to local economies as well as to anglers. A 6-mile stretch of Rock Creek in California had a value of almost $94,000 per mile in 1948.

052 McKean, John. "Oregon's Fishery Programs and Policies in Relation to Forest Land Uses." *Proceedings of a Symposium, Forest Land Uses and Stream Environment*, p. 210. J. T. Krygier and J. D. Hall, editors. Corvallis, OR:

---

*William Platts. *South Fork Salmon River Fishery Impact and Rehabilitation Evaluation*, unpublished report (Department of Agriculture, Forest Service, Intermountain Region, 1969).

Oregon State University, School of Forestry and Department of Fisheries and Wildlife, 1971. Q

"Oregon's fishery resources currently provide about 6.6 million man-days of angling and a commercial pack of about 9,000 tons of anadromous fish. All of this production whether it is a salmon in the ocean, a trout in the Deschutes River, or a bullhead in the Willamette, is dependent upon the wise management of Oregon's forested watersheds."

053 Narver, David. "Effects of Logging Debris on Fish Production." *Proceedings of a Symposium, Forest Land Uses and Stream Environment*, p. 104. J. T. Krygier and J. D. Hall, editors. Corvallis, OR: Oregon State University, School of Forestry and Department of Fisheries and Wildlife, 1971. Q, P

As "organic debris breaks down it has a high biochemical oxygen demand . . . caused by the respiration of bacteria, fungi and protozoa. Soluble organic substances such as wood sugars, leached from logs exert a considerable chemical oxygen demand . . . as well as biological demand, and the rate of leaching does not decrease for up to 80 days. . . . Secondarily, growth of algae stimulated by nutrient release from decomposing debris and by warming streams when velocity is reduced by debris and the stream is exposed to increased radiation after removal of streamside cover, may result in significant oxygen demands both from respiration (nocturnal) and from the decay of dead algae. . . ."

All stages of salmonid fish are adversely affected by low concentrations of dissolved oxygen.

054 Phillips, Robert W. "Effects of Sediment on the Gravel Environment and Fish Production." *Proceedings of a Symposium, Forest Land Uses and Stream Environment*, p. 64. J. T. Krygier and J. D. Hall, editors. Corvallis, OR: Oregon State University, School of Forestry and Department of Fisheries and Wildlife, 1971. Q

"Research in the field is summarized. Sediment influences fish in several ways. In suspension, (1) it blocks the transmission of light, reducing algae production, and (2) it damages the gill membranes, causing death where concentrations are high and exposure is prolonged.

"When sediment settles on the gravel beds, it is harmful in the following ways: (1) It fills the interstices reducing interchange between surface waters and waters within the gravel bed. This reduces the supply of dissolved oxygen to the egg, and interferes with the removal of metabolites (carbon dioxide and ammonia). (2) Sediment also forms a barrier to fry emergence by blocking the route of egress. (3) Low dissolved oxygen and the physical barrier effect of sediment appear to be additive in reducing survival. (4) Survival after fry emergence is impaired because of a loss of escape cover and a reduction of aquatic organisms that are food for fish. Examples are cited showing that pink and chum salmon survival is inversely related to the amount of sediment in gravel beds."

055 Narver, David. "Effects of Logging Debris on Fish Production." *Proceedings of a Symposium, Forest Land Uses and Stream Environment*, p. 107. J. T. Krygier and J. D. Hall, editors. Corvallis, OR: Oregon State University, School of Forestry and Department of Fisheries and Wildlife, 1971. Q, P

"Much of the dissolved oxygen in the intragravel water of spawning grounds comes from interchange with surface water, and an accumulation of small logging debris on or in the gravel can substantially reduce this interchange and the permeability of the gravel."

These accumulations of debris also fill interstices of the gravel, decreasing living space for stream invertebrates and refuge for young salmonids.

056   Edwards, Clive. "Soil Pollutants and Soil Animals." *Scientific American* 220 (1969): 88–99. **S**

Many animals live by disintegrating and digesting plant residues, breaking the debris down into its organic and inorganic constituents and working the end products into the soil structure. Most important are earthworms, wood lice, millipedes, mites, springtails, termites, and larvae of beetles and flies. Their population may weigh more than 1,000 pounds per acre in temperate zones.

Many commonly used pesticides are lethal to these invertebrates and persist in the soil for long periods of time. When the population of these animals is greatly reduced, soil structure deteriorates and the process of soil formation slows or stops altogether, with drastic ultimate effects on fertility.

057   Rice, R. M., J. S. Rothacher, and W. F. Megahan. "Erosional Consequences of Timber Harvesting: An Appraisal." *Proceedings of a Symposium on "Watersheds in Transition,"* pp. 321–329. Department of Agriculture, Forest Service, Fort Collins, CO, 1972. **S, C**

It is feasible to prevent surface erosion from roads and logged areas but quite difficult (nearly impossible) to prevent mass erosion on steep terrain. The costs of erosion control tend to increase geometrically with the erosion potential.

Note: If the amount of anticipated erosion is doubled, the cost of control is quadrupled.

058   Rice, R. M., J. S. Rothacher, and W. F. Megahan. "Erosional Consequences of Timber Harvesting: An Appraisal." *Proceedings of a Symposium on "Watersheds in Transition,"* pp. 321–329. Department of Agriculture, Forest Service, Fort Collins, CO, 1972. **S**

In many cases, landslides have increased greatly 5 to 20 years after clearcutting. This is because part of the strength of a soil mass comes from the anchoring effect of the tree roots. As the roots decay, susceptibility to landslides gradually increases.

059   Rice, R. M., J. S. Rothacher, and W. F. Megahan. "Erosional Consequences of Timber Harvesting: An Appraisal." *Proceedings of a Symposium on "Watersheds in Transition,"* p. 326. Department of Agriculture, Forest Service, Fort Collins, CO, 1972. **Q**

"Roads undercut upslope soils and may alter the natural drainage from a hillside. By exposing formerly buried material to weathering they may also change the strength of the slope. Road fills place additional weight on the underlying soil mass. The fills themselves are frequently over-steepened slopes of reduced strength and are prone to failure. Consequently, it is not surprising that roads are frequently associated with landslides."

060 Swanston, Douglas. "Principal Mass Movement Processes Influenced by Logging, Road Building, and Fire." *Proceedings of a Symposium, Forest Land Uses and Stream Environment*, p. 36. J. T. Krygier and J. D. Hall, editors. Corvallis, OR: Oregon State University, School of Forestry and Department of Fisheries and Wildlife, 1971. Q

"Root systems of trees and other vegetation can serve as cohesive binders or, if they penetrate entirely through the soil zone, can anchor the soil mantle to the substrate, and thus provide an effective stabilizing influence. In some extremely steep areas this may be a dominant factor in shear strength of the slope soil. Under natural conditions the destruction of such effective mechanical support by logging, windthrow, or fire can produce substantial decreases in mechanical soil strength. Shear strength tests on roots taken from clearcut units of a variety of ages in southeast Alaska . . . have indicated a marked decrease in strength three to five years after cutting, a time period that roughly corresponds to the lag between time of logging and massive debris avalanching in Maybeso Creek Valley, Prince of Wales Island, Alaska."

061 Anderson, Henry. "Relative Contributions of Sediment from Source Areas, and Transport Processes." *Proceedings of a Symposium, Forest Land Uses and Stream Environment*, p. 61. J. T. Krygier and J. D. Hall, editors. Corvallis, OR: Oregon State University, School of Forestry and Department of Fisheries and Wildlife, 1971. P

In the 1964–1965 floods, occurrence of landslides in the H. J. Andrews Experimental Forest was as follows:

Land Use	Landslides per 1,000 Acres (number of slides)
Undisturbed forest	0.4
Logging	3.9
Road construction	125.9

SOURCE: C. T. Dyrness, *Mass Soil Movements in the H. J. Andrews Experimental Forest*, Research Paper PNW-42 (Department of Agriculture, Forest Service, 1967).

A general survey in western Oregon forests of 725 soil and debris slides after the same floods showed similar results:

Land Use	Slides (percent)
In undisturbed areas	22
Associated with logged areas	24
Associated with roads	54

SOURCE: Department of Agriculture, Forest Service, *A Report of the Region 6 Storm Drainage Evaluation Committee. Part I*, unnumbered publication (1965).

062 Fritz, Emanuel. "Some Popular Fallacies Concerning California Redwoods." *Madrono* 1 (1929): 221–223. **Q**

"Virgin redwood forests sometimes are incorrectly called even-aged and overmature, when, in fact, thee is no other forest in the world that can match many redwood stands in range of ages and mixture of vigorously growing and decadent trees. On a typical 30 acre tract, not counting more than 1,000 trees under 12 inches in diameter, the trees were [as follows]:"

Age (years)	Number
0–200	696
201–400	197
401–600	183
601–800	105
801–1000	65
Over 1000	17

063 Lantz, Richard. "Fish Population Impacts—Alsea Watershed Case Study." *Proceedings of a Symposium, Forest Land Uses and Stream Environment*, pp. 182–193. J. T. Krygier and J. D. Hall, editors. Corvallis, OR: Oregon State University, School of Forestry and Department of Fisheries and Wildlife, 1971. **Q**

"The virulence of many diseases can be strongly influenced by increasing water temperatures. For example, kidney disease, furunculosis, vibriosis, and columnaris disease become more pathogenic in young salmon as the water temperature rises. . . ."

064 Lantz, Richard. "Fish Population Impacts—Alsea Watershed Case Study." *Proceedings of a Symposium, Forest Land Uses and Stream Environment*, pp. 182–193. J. T. Krygier and J. D. Hall, editors. Corvallis, OR: Oregon State University, School of Forestry and Department of Fisheries and Wildlife, 1971. **Q**

"Logging activities that increase water temperatures can be expected to have their greatest influence on juvenile salmonids rearing in small streams and on embryonic stages developing in streambed gravels. It is probable that effects during the time that juveniles are rearing in freshwater, in terms of lethal temperature changes, are the most significant. Temperature increases can also affect fish survival by increasing the virulence of many diseases and modifying the effects of toxic materials."

065 Brown, George. "Water Temperature in Small Streams as Influenced by Environmental Factors and Logging." *Proceedings of a Symposium, Forest Land Uses and Stream Environment*, pp. 175–181. J. T. Krygier and J. D. Hall, editors. Corvallis, OR: Oregon State University, School of Forestry and Department of Fisheries and Wildlife, 1971. **Q, P**

"Clearcut logging can produce large changes in the temperature of small streams. The principal source of heat affected by clearcutting is direct solar radiation. Shade removal may increase radiation loads by six to seven times."

In various studies of streams in the Pacific Northwest, mean monthly maximum stream temperatures in midsummer increased by 7 to 12 degrees Fahrenheit. In one case, in which an entire drainage basin of a small stream in the Alsea Watershed was clearcut, the temperature increased by 28 degrees Fahrenheit. There is an inverse relationship between the volume of water flow and the increase in temperature caused by clearcutting. Buffer strips of sufficient width to provide adequate shading are the only effective way of minimizing increases in stream temperature.

066 Swift, Lloyd W., Jr., and Samuel E. Baker. *Lower Water Temperatures within a Streamside Buffer Strip.* Research Note SE-193. Department of Agriculture, Forest Service, 1973. S

This article shows the effect of leaving a streamside buffer strip in a clearcut area. A stream that flowed through an unprotected area was quickly cooled when it entered a protected area by dilution from cool groundwater. The strip protected the downstream trout habitat from thermal pollution. (Note: Important point—the stream was cooled not by the shade but by the inflow of groundwater.)

067 Lantz, Richard L. "Influence of Water Temperature on Fish Survival, Growth and Behavior." *Proceedings of a Symposium, Forest Land Uses and Stream Environment,* p. 190. J. T. Krygier and J. D. Hall, editors. Corvallis, OR: Oregon State University, School of Forestry and Department of Fisheries and Wildlife, 1971. Q, P

"From an economic standpoint, fishery values can often equal or exceed the value of commercial Douglas fir left in even a 100 foot wide buffer strip."

The argument that timber in buffer strips is subject to increased windthrow does not hold true in all cases. In the Alsea Watershed Study, no more windthrow occurred in the timber left in a buffer strip than in that in an unlogged watershed.

Buffer strips serve many purposes—they can minimize temperature increases, sediment deposition in stream channels, and placement of logging slash in stream channels.

068 Farmer, Eugene E. "Relative Detachability of Soil Particles by Simulated Rainfall." *Soil Science Society of America Proceedings* 37 (1973): 629–633. S

By simulating rainfall in the laboratory, researchers sought to determine which factors are most important in detachment of soil particles by raindrops. Surprisingly, slope and rainfall intensity are far less important than the presence or absence of water on the soil surface. Soil particle detachability is greatly increased when a thin layer of water covers the soil surface, such as when overland flow occurs. Thus, it is critical to ensure that bare soil areas remain highly permeable so that no water surface layer can form. Compaction is seen as a serious problem.

069 Larse, Robert. "Prevention and Control of Erosion and Stream Sedimentation from Forest Roads." Proceedings of a Symposium, Forest Land Uses and Stream Environment, p. 77. J. T. Krygier and J. D. Hall, editors. Corvallis, OR: Oregon State University, School of Forestry and Department of Fisheries and Wildlife, 1971. **Q**

". . . Selection of any road route should be the product of several coordinated skills. For example, the soil scientist, geologist, biologist and others will often recognize specific problems and be able to offer acceptable solutions or alternatives. But, all too frequently the location of a specific road is a one-man effort, with little consideration or recognition of alternative opportunities, watershed values, landform or soil characteristics and stability, or other environmental conditions."

070 Larse, Robert. "Prevention and Control of Erosion and Stream Sedimentation from Forest Roads." *Proceedings of a Symposium, Forest Land Uses and Stream Environment*, p. 79–80. J. T. Krygier and J. D. Hall, editors. Corvallis, OR: Oregon State University, School of Forestry and Department of Fisheries and Wildlife, 1971. **P, Q**

The following are recommended ways to reduce erosion potential:

1. "Fit roading to terrain with minimum of road width. Traffic speed geometry, for predominately single-use log-hauling roads, should be subordinated to this objective."
2. "Minimize excavation with a balanced earthwork design . . . compacting embankments under controlled moisture conditions. Bench or terrace and drain natural slopes to provide sound foundations for embankments. Endhaul excavated material from full-bench sections to stable waste areas and compact."
3. "Design rolling grades to reduce surface water velocities and requirements. . . ."
4. "Design cut and fill slopes as steep as possible. . . ."
5. "Use retaining walls. . . ."
6. "Vary ditch and surface water relief culvert requirements. . . ."
7. ". . . Design . . . . the drainage structures to accommodate the flow of live streams on at least a 25 year flood frequency. . . ."
8. ". . . Forest roads should be surfaced. . . ."
9. "Provide for vegetative or artificial stabilization of cut and fill slopes. . . ."

071 Larse, Robert. "Prevention and Control of Erosion and Stream Sedimentation from Forest Roads." *Proceedings of a Symposium, Forest Land Uses and Stream Environment*, p. 78. J. T. Krygier and J. D. Hall, editors. Corvallis, OR: Oregon State University, School of Forestry and Department of Fisheries and Wildlife, 1971. **P, Q**

The following are recommendations for prevention and control of erosion and stream sedimentation from forest roads:

1. "Plan roads to take advantage of natural log landing areas, thereby reducing soil disturbance. . . ."

2. "Take advantage of benches, ridge tops, and the flatter transitional slopes. . . . Avoid steep midslope locations on unstable slopes. The road gradient can be steepened up to 14–15 percent to avoid unstable slopes, reduce road length, and minimize soil disturbance due to present day vehicle capabilities."

3. "Provide natural vegetation buffer between roads and streams. Position roads on transition between toe slope and terrace to protect from flood erosion, being careful to avoid undercutting toe slope or an old slide. Valley bottoms should not be roaded where the only choice is encroachment on streams."

4. "Ridge top roads should avoid headwalls, as these are often extremely unstable slopes, and slope failure will flow directly into live streams."

5. "Vary road grades . . . to reduce culvert and road drainage ditch flows, road surface erosion, and concentrated culvert discharges."

6. "Select stream crossings with particular care . . . to minimize channel disturbance, approach cuts and fills. . . ."

072 Brink, David L., and Michael M. Merriman. "Influence of Young-growth on Characteristics and Utilization of Fiber." *Proceedings of a Conference on Young-Growth Forest Management in California*, p. 12. Berkeley, CA: University of California, Department of Forest and Resource Management, 1967. Q

"In general, lignin content is highest in the corewood and decreases to the outer sapwood. There is some indication that increasing heights above one to four feet show decreasing lignin contents. Therefore, corewood from butt logs can be expected to show the highest lignin content. Within an annual ring, earlywood has slightly higher lignin content than latewood."

073 Brink, David L., and Michael M. Merriman. "Influence of Young-growth on Characteristics and Utilization of Fiber." *Proceedings of a Conference on Young-Growth Forest Management in California*, p. 12. Berkeley, CA: University of California, Department of Forest and Resource Management, 1967. Q

"Alpha-cellulose content is lowest near the pith and increases radially following the increase in cell-wall thickness. . . . This is true of both conifers and hardwoods. Alpha-cellulose remains nearly constant or decreases with increasing height."

074 Resch, Helmuth. "Considering the Physical Properties of Wood in Managing Forest Trees." *Proceedings of a Conference on Young-Growth Forest Management in California*, p. 24. Berkeley, CA: University of California, Department of Forest and Resource Management, 1967. Q, C

"The paint holding ability is greater on vertical grained than on flat grained surfaces, partly because vertical grained surfaces shrink and swell to a lesser extent. Grain raising on flat sawn lumber and veneer is all too common. Type of grain, latewood per cent, shrinkage, and the presence of defects not only affects the paint holding ability but also the weathering of wood products."

Note: To avoid trouble with paint, lumber must be cut from trees large enough for vertical grain sawing.

075 Oswald, Dan. "Young-growth Inventory Data." *Proceedings of a Conference on Young-Growth Forest Management in California,* p. 1. Berkeley, CA: University of California, Department of Forest and Resource Management, 1967. **P, Q**

Young growth in California is defined as "trees less than rotation age, provided the rotation age is set at 120 years or more."

076 Schniewind, Arno P. "Influence of Forest Management on Utilization Values—Mechanical Properties." *Proceedings of a Conference on Young-Growth Forest Management in California,* p. 35. Berkeley, CA: University of California, Department of Forest and Resource Management, 1967. **Q**

"There is a choice in the length of rotation. A longer rotation will mean a reduction in the proportion of low density and low strength material, i.e., the core or juvenile wood."

077 Harris, A. S. *Natural Reforestation on a Mile-Square Clearcut in Southeast Alaska,* p. 9. Research Paper PNW-52. Department of Agriculture, Forest Service, 1967. **Q**

"One must allow five years for reforestation to take place following logging. Therefore a one hundred year rotation actually requires one hundred five years for purposes of field calculation."

078 Boyce, J. S. *Forest Pathology,* p. 515. New York: McGraw-Hill, 1961. Reproduced with permission. **Q**

"In general, naturally regenerated stands are less susceptible to disease than those artificially reproduced. Seedlings are preferable to sprouts because sprout growth is usually more susceptible to disease. . . . At best trees are more or less injured by planting. Roots are particularly subject to injury, thus increasing the incidence of root rots."

079 Minore, Don. *Germination and Early Growth of Coastal Tree Species on Organic Seed Beds,* p. 2. Research Paper PNW-135. Department of Agriculture, Forest Service, 1972. **P**

In heavy shade (less than 10 percent full sunlight), most coastal tree species regenerate best on rotten logs covered with duff (decaying organic matter). The same principle is true for moderate shade, but in light shade both rotten logs and forest floor duff are excellent seedbeds. Both are unsatisfactory seedbeds in full sunlight as occurs after clearcutting.

080 Franklin, Jerry. *Natural Regeneration of Douglas-fir and Associated Species Using Modified Clearcutting System in the Oregon Cascades,* p. 13. Research Paper PNW-3. Department of Agriculture, Forest Service, 1967. **P, Q**

Satisfactory natural regeneration doesn't always occur on clearcuts, due to high soil surface temperatures and distance from the seed source. Shading markedly enhances seedling establishment.

"It is recommended that consideration be given to the use of modified cutting methods such as east-west strip clearcuts, small patch clearcuts, and seed-tree cuttings to improve natural restocking of Douglas fir on sites difficult to regenerate. Such cuttings should be laid out primarily to provide shade and secondarily to favor seed dispersal."

081   Boyce, J. S. *Forest Pathology*, p. 516. New York: McGraw-Hill, 1961. Reproduced with permission. **Q**

"There is always a tendency to establish plantations of one species, rather than mixtures, without regard to how the planted species occurs naturally, because both silviculture and utilization are simplified in pure stands and because of the economic pressure to favor a more valuable species over its less valuable associates. Pure stands are more susceptible to disease, particularly those caused by introduced parasites, than mixed stands. Mixtures of conifers and hardwoods are especially desirable because these two classes of trees in general have their own groups of fungus parasites. A pure stand forms an ideal situation for a pathogen to build up to epidemic proportions. Infection is direct and rapid from tree to tree, and if the one species is destroyed there is nothing left. The most hazardous pure stands are even-aged because fungus parasites are often virulent during only one stage in the development of a tree. Pure stands of trees outside their natural range are particularly liable to difficulty."

082   Baker, F. S. *Principles of Silviculture*, p. 9. New York: McGraw-Hill, 1950. Reproduced with permission. **Q**

"Pure stands may fail to utilize the site completely, either because they are composed of an intolerant species and in consequence have thin, open crowns which presumably fail to utilize the sunlight completely, or because they are shallow rooted and utilize only part of the soil."

083   Baker, F. S. *Principles of Silviculture*, p. 10. New York: McGraw-Hill, 1950. **S**

Some species make excessively heavy demands on soil when planted in pure stands. They may do well in youth, but later may slow and deteriorate. It is often necessary to form an admixture of species that makes few demands on the soil and whose leaf fall decomposes readily into a mild, rich humus.

084   Baker, F. S. *Principles of Silviculture*, p. 10. New York: McGraw-Hill, 1950. **S**

Some pure forests, notably those composed of conifers, may cause a slow deterioration of the upper soil layers. The needles of pines and spruces in particular decompose very slowly and form deep layers of raw humus in which seedlings cannot grow. If trees with leaves that decompose readily are mixed with the conifers, they improve the humus layer and cause decomposition of the coniferous needles as well.

085   Baker, F. S. *Principles of Silviculture*, p. 10. New York: McGraw-Hill, 1950. Reproduced with permission. **Q**

"Since most insects and diseases of forest trees are limited rather sharply to one or a few host plants, mixed stands offer far less opportunity for epidemics than do pure stands. In the case of insects, every tree in a pure stand offers food and a breeding ground. In the case of fungi, the liberated spores find favorable substrates everywhere. In both cases, destructive concentrations can readily be built up in pure stands."

086 Keen, F. P. *Insect Enemies of Western Forests*, p. 219. Miscellaneous Publication 273 (revised). Department of Agriculture, Forest Service, 1952. **Q**

"Pure stands—those composed of a single tree species—are particularly susceptible to disastrous outbreaks [of insects]. For instance, outbreaks of the hemlock looper have been especially destructive only in stands composed of a high percentage of hemlock. Where a heavy mixture of other species occurs the infestation soon thins out and loses its destructive power. Attacks of the spruce budworm also have been most destructive in stands composed of a high percentage of true firs and Douglas fir. It is particularly important that cuttings, in stands that normally grow as mixed types, should not favor the leaving of a single species."

087 Baker, F. S. *Principles of Silviculture*, pp. 8–9. New York: McGraw-Hill, 1950. **S**

In Europe, foresters have debated the issue of pure versus mixed stands for two hundred years. The theorists and schoolmen point out the natural biological advantages of mixed forests, while the timberland owners defend pure stands, which have undeniable financial advantages. Early in the nineteenth century, an influential German forester, G. S. Hartig, became a strong proponent of pure stands; his support led to wide establishment of pure forests of Norway spruce throughout Germany. As these stands matured, weaknesses developed, and toward the end of the century a strong reaction against pure stands developed.

088 Baker, F. S. *Principles of Silviculture*, p. 19. New York: McGraw-Hill, 1950. Reproduced with permission. **Q**

"Even-aged stands are attractive to European foresters, for they are easily managed, readily completely sold, and are easily logged. Planting is well understood and is economically feasible. The biological disadvantages are real and, like the similar disadvantages of pure stands, they have long been stressed by silvicultural writers. But the financial advantages being what they are, the even-aged stand policy goes on. There is much more appreciation of the dangers in recent years, however, and there has been a strong movement toward the abandonment of the pure, even-aged forest management through plantations in favor of a more natural uneven-aged forest form."

089 Oswald, Dan. "Young-growth Inventory Data." *Proceedings of a Conference on Young-Growth Forest Management in California*, p. 1. Berkeley, CA: University of California, Department of Forest and Resource Management, 1967. **Q**

"I contend . . . that if substantial amounts of large old-growth timber are available, harvesting of young stands at rotation determined by either [financial maturity or culmination of mean annual increment] might not take place."

090 Benson, Paul H. *Juvenile Wood in Conifers.* Forest Products Laboratory Report 2094. Department of Agriculture, Forest Service, 1957. S

Density of fiber, and therefore its strength, increases with the age of the tree. The most dense fiber is found near the surface and within the first 10 feet of height of most trees. Suppressed trees, however, tend to have dense fiber in the crown as well. Correlations with age are lacking.

091 Pessin, L. J. "Forest Associations in the Uplands of the Lower Gulf Coastal Plain (Longleaf Pine Belt)." *Ecology* 14 (1933): 1–14. P

Myrica cerifera (wax myrtle), a nonleguminous nitrogen fixer, is common on some sites on the Gulf Coastal Plain. *Drosera* (sundews) are also present and may add nitrogen. Legumes present are *Pitcheria galactoides*, *Cracca spicata* (devil's shoestring), and *Cassia chamaecrista*.

092 Kuhlman, E. G. *Susceptibility of Loblolly and Slash Pine Progeny to Fomes annosus.* Research Note SE-176. Department of Agriculture, Forest Service, 1972. S

Susceptibility of southern pine to *Fomes annosus* is not genetically determined. In a test of 10,000 seedlings from 300 families, no difference in susceptibility was noted after repeated tests. Differences initially noted turned out to be functions of temperature. Quantitative differences in resin production also showed no correlation.

093 Lewis, Clifford E. *Cultivation, Grazing, Insects and Disease Affect Yield of Slash Pine Planted in Sod.* Research Paper SE-174. Department of Agriculture, Forest Service, 1972. S

Slash pine was planted in dense carpetgrass sod; in one experiment, some pines were cultivated to improve growth for overcoming attractiveness to cattle. In another experiment, some were fertilized.

Results: After 11 years, survival was 76 percent without cultivation and only 36 percent with cultivation, although cultivated trees grew faster. Losses were due to fusiform rust and pitch moth, as well as cattle. Cultivated trees were far more susceptible than uncultivated trees.

094 Grano, Charles. *Conditioning Loessial Soils for Natural Loblolly and Shortleaf Pine Seeding*, pp. 1, 3. Research Note SD-116. Department of Agriculture, Forest Service, 1971. Q

"Despite increasing popularity of direct seeding and planting, most Loblolly (*P. taeda*) and Shortleaf (*P. echinata*) pine stands continue to be reproduced through natural seedfall. . . .

"In general, burning can be expected to improve seedbeds and improve stocking, particularly if the timber cut is light."

095 Trappe, James M. "Biological Control—Forest Diseases." *Proceedings of an Annual Meeting of [the] Western Forest Pest Committee*, pp. 16–19. Portland, OR: Western Forestry and Conservation Association, 1971. **S**

The best control of *Poria weirii* (root rot) is alder. *Poria* is the principal enemy of Douglas-fir and many other conifers that grow with it in the Pacific Northwest.

Poria is controlled by inhibiting compounds produced by alder as well as by numerous bacteria and fungi that grow beneath the ground and suppress *Poria* in buried wood. The latter are stimulated by organic nitrogen fixed by alder's root nodules.

096 Gaby, L. I. *Warping in Southern Pine Studs*, p. 8. Research Paper SE-96. Department of Agriculture, Forest Service, 1972. **Q, P**

"Studs which contain pith, in part or completely, are prone to warp considerably in excess of current National Grading Rule limitations."

Studs containing pith may warp in the wall as they did in drying from the green condition; their moisture content may drop from 19 percent to 10 percent. The maximum allowance of 19 percent in the National Grading Rule is too high for these studs. Environmental changes may lower their moisture content to 10 percent or less, with resultant warping. Small, young timber contains a large percentage of pith; hence, it is inferior for lumber.

097 Reukema, Donald L., and Leon V. Pienaar. *Yields with and without Repeated Commercial Thinnings in a High-site-quality Douglas-fir Stand*. Research Paper PNW-155. Department of Agriculture, Forest Service, 1973. **S**

Douglas-fir stands older than 50 years of age on high-quality sites thinned at 5-year intervals show a negligible net increase in total yield by 80 years of rotation age. This study shows a net increase of only 5 percent in total usable production, but even that is exaggerated because of a change in form factor.

098 Burwell, Dave. "Prevention of Debris Accumulation in Streams by Uphill Felling." *Proceedings of a Symposium, Forest Land Uses and Stream Environment*, p. 118. J. T. Krygier and J. D. Hall, editors. Corvallis, OR: Oregon State University, School of Forestry and Department of Fisheries and Wildlife, 1971. **Q**

"Felling trees uphill using a truck-mounted donkey and climber to attach the line, prevents breakage and distributes limbs and tops on slopes instead of in stream bottoms. Costs are two to three times those of comparable conventional cutting. Savings include the intangibles of increased safety, lessened breakage, reduction of slash to eliminate burning and enable quicker regeneration, and reduction of expensive creek cleaning. These may more than offset additional costs."

099 Marlega, R. R. "Streamside Strips and Management Problems—North Umpqua Case Study." *Proceedings of a Symposium, Forest Land Uses and Stream Environment*, p. 229. J. T. Krygier and J. D. Hall, editors. Corvallis, OR: Oregon State University, School of Forestry and Department of Fisheries and Wildlife, 1971. **P, Q**

This study offers practical management implications for minimizing or eliminating increases in water temperature:

1. "Small streams heat up faster than large streams."
2. "South-southwesterly exposure streams heat up more than other oriented streams."
3. "Smaller streams can be effectively shaded by low-growing brush."
4. "Even narrow streamside buffer strips can reduce temperature increases."
5. "Influence of tributaries on main stream temperature depends on volume of flow."
6. "Increases in temperature by shade removal can be predicted."
7. "Larger streams need taller vegetation in buffer strip."

100 Gilliard, E. Thomas. *Living Birds of the World*. New York: Doubleday, 1958. P

Many species of hawk and owl require dead standing trees as habitat. These birds devour tremendous numbers of small seed-eating rodents, as determined from examination of their pellets. It is therefore important to leave snags in place in order to encourage these birds, who will in turn control the rodent population and permit natural reforestation, a very important phenomenon.

101 Scott, Virgil E., and David R. Patton. *Cavity-Nesting Birds of Arizona and New Mexico Forests*. General Technical Report RM-10. Department of Agriculture, Forest Service, 1975. S

Reduction of bird populations within a forest could result in harmful increases in insect populations. Cavity-nesting birds depend on dead and unmerchantable trees for nesting and roosting. These trees are considered a fire hazard and a physical hazard in intensively used areas and are removed by loggers in the West. Because of the economic and aesthetic value of cavity-nesting birds, their habitat requirements must be considered in management plans. There are forty-one species of cavity-nesting birds in the forests of Arizona and New Mexico.

102 Scott, Virgil E., and David R. Patton. *Cavity-Nesting Birds of Arizona and New Mexico Forests*. General Technical Report RM-10. Department of Agriculture, Forest Service, 1975. S

Bird: *Ash-Throated Flycatcher*
Food: 92 percent animal material (beetles, bees, wasps, bugs, flies, caterpillars, moths, grasshoppers, spiders, etc.), and 8 percent vegetable material (berries, mistletoe, etc.).
Nest: Woodpecker holes and natural cavities, but also pipes, knotholes, and nest boxes.
Range: Central Washington (breeds), northern Utah, and west-central Texas south and west through northern Mexico to the Pacific.

103 Scott, Virgil E., and David R. Patton. *Cavity-Nesting Birds of Arizona and New Mexico Forests*. General Technical Report RM-10. Department of Agriculture, Forest Service, 1975. S

Bird: *Spotted Owl*
Food: Various forest rodents and a few birds.
Nest: Usually large tree cavities, but will nest in holes in shaded rock gorges.
Range: Coastal forest from southern British Columbia to California; mountains of California, New Mexico, Arizona, and western Texas south into central and western Mexico.

104 Scott, Virgil E., and David R. Patton. *Cavity-Nesting Birds of Arizona and New Mexico Forests.* General Technical Report RM-10. Department of Agriculture, Forest Service, 1975. **S**

Bird: *Northern Three-Toed Woodpecker*
Food: This is one of the most beneficial woodpeckers; more than 75 percent of its diet consists of destructive, wood-boring larvae of beetles and grubs; also spruce bark beetle.
Nest: Dead pine tree cavities 7 to 60 feet above the ground; also dead spruce and aspen.
Range: North to tree limit in North America, Europe, and Asia. South to northern New Hampshire, northern Michigan, northern Minnesota, in mountains to southwestern Oregon and Arizona.

105 Scott, Virgil E., and David R. Patton. *Cavity-Nesting Birds of Arizona and New Mexico Forests.* General Technical Report RM-10. Department of Agriculture, Forest Service, 1975. **S**

Bird: *Flammulated Owl*
Food: Insects such as beetles, moths, grasshoppers, crickets, and ants.
Nest: Flicker and other woodpecker holes in dead pine, ash, and aspen trees.
Range: Breeds in forests of ponderosa pine from the Rocky Mountains west to the Pacific Coast and from British Columbia to Guatemala.

106 Scott, Virgil E., and David R. Patton. *Cavity-Nesting Birds of Arizona and New Mexico Forests.* General Technical Report RM-10. Department of Agriculture, Forest Service, 1975. **S**

Bird: *Pygmy Owl*
Food: Mostly mice (rodents are considered to be a threat to tree regeneration by eating seeds) and larger insects such as grasshoppers.
Nest: Usually old woodpecker holes.
Range: Western North America from Alaska to Guatemala, at 5,000 to 10,000 feet (resident).

107 Scott, Virgil E., and David R. Patton. *Cavity-Nesting Birds of Arizona and New Mexico Forests.* General Technical Report RM-10. Department of Agriculture, Forest Service, 1975. **S**

Bird: *Whiskered Owl*
Food: Principal diet consists of insects.
Nest: Natural cavities and old flicker holes, mostly in white oak between 4,000 and 6,500 feet.
Range: Southern Arizona and southern New Mexico to El Salvador.

108 Scott, Virgil E., and David R. Patton. *Cavity-Nesting Birds of Arizona and New Mexico Forests.* General Technical Report RM-10. Department of Agriculture, Forest Service, 1975. **S**

Bird: *American Kestrel*

Food: Meadow mice, deer mice (rodents are considered to be a threat to tree regeneration by eating seeds) and house sparrows make up about 96 percent of the volume. Insects are 80 percent of the prey and 4 percent of the volume.

Nest: Usually natural cavities or old woodpecker holes, mostly in dead trees; also lightning scars of live trees.

Range: From southeastern Alaska to South America.

109 Scott, Virgil E., and David R. Patton. *Cavity-Nesting Birds of Arizona and New Mexico Forests.* General Technical Report RM-10. Department of Agriculture, Forest Service, 1975. **S**

Bird: *White-Breasted Nuthatch*

Food: In spring and summer, much animal material (beetles, spiders, caterpillars, true bugs, ants, flies, grasshoppers, moths, and millipedes), though nearly all winter food is mast. Insects include such pests as nut weevils, locust seed weevils, roundheaded wood borers, leaf beetles, treehoppers, psyllids, and scale insects.

Nest: Natural cavities or old woodpecker holes, in decayed trees (dead aspen and dead portions—lightning strikes—of live ponderosa pine).

Range: Southern Quebec, central Ontario, southern Manitoba, and southern British Columbia to Florida, the Gulf Coast, and southern Mexico.

110 Scott, Virgil E., and David R. Patton. *Cavity-Nesting Birds of Arizona and New Mexico Forests.* General Technical Report RM-10. Department of Agriculture, Forest Service, 1975. **S**

Bird: *Pygmy Nuthatch*

Food: 80 percent animal material (wasps and spittle insects, with some ants, beetles, and caterpillars); balance conifer seeds.

Nest: 8 to 60 feet above the ground in cavities of pine or dead remains of pine trees excavated by the birds.

Range: Pine forests of western North America from southern British Columbia and northern Idaho south to northern Lower California and southeastern Mexico.

111 Scott, Virgil E., and David R. Patton. *Cavity-Nesting Birds of Arizona and New Mexico Forests.* General Technical Report RM-10. Department of Agriculture, Forest Service, 1975. **S**

Bird: *Tree Swallow*

Food: 80 percent animal material (beetles, ants, flies, grasshoppers, dragonflies, spiders); balance fruits (bayberry).

Nest: Natural cavities and old woodpecker holes, but will utilize nest boxes.

Range: Breeds from Newfoundland, northern Manitoba, Mackenzie, and northern Alaska to Maryland, north-central Louisiaina, Colorado, and southwestern California. Winters from North Carolina Gulf Coast, northern Mexico, and southern California through Cuba and Guatemala.

112 Scott, Virgil E., and David R. Patton. *Cavity-Nesting Birds of Arizona and New Mexico Forests.* General Technical Report RM-10. Department of Agriculture, Forest Service, 1975. **S**

Bird: *Violet-Green Swallow*
Food: Insects on the wing exclusively (leafhoppers, leaf bugs, flies, and flying ants and some wasps, bees, and beetles).
Nest: Holes, cavities, and crevices ranging 30 to 70 feet above the ground; practically any available cavity.
Range: Breeds from central Alaska and central Alberta south to northern Mexico and east to western South Dakota and western Nebraska. Winters from Mexico, occasionally southern California, to Costa Rica.

113 Scott, Virgil E., and David R. Patton. *Cavity-Nesting Birds of Arizona and New Mexico Forests.* General Technical Report RM-10. Department of Agriculture, Forest Service, 1975. **S**

Bird: *Screech Owl*
Food: Major items are mice (rodents are considered to be a threat to tree regeneration by eating seeds) and insects in equal volume. Birds and other rodents are also part of the diet.
Nest: Natural cavities and flicker holes in apple, pine, poplar, and sycamore trees.
Range: Throughout the continental United States, southern Canada, and southeastern Alaska.

114 Scott, Virgil E., and David R. Patton. *Cavity-Nesting Birds of Arizona and New Mexico Forests.* General Technical Report RM-10. Department of Agriculture, Forest Service, 1975. **S**

Bird: *Downy Woodpecker*
Food: Nearly all insects eaten are economically harmful (e.g., beetles, most wood-boring larvae, ants, weevils).
Nest: Makes its own nest holes in branches or stubs 8 to 50 feet above the ground, mostly in dead or dying wood.
Range: Newfoundland, Ontario, southern Manitoba, southwestern Mackenzie, and northwestern Alaska south to southern Florida, the Gulf Coast, Texas, southern Mexico, and southern California.

115 Anderson, Walter C. "Southern Forestry Investments in an Era of Environmental Concern." *Forest Products Journal* 22 (1972): 14–16. **P**

Some sportsmen advise halting the removal of den- and mast-bearing snags, which are important to wildlife, during timber stand improvement. These trees are the prime targets for removal, but they cause substantial loss of timber production only when they are very large or numerous.

116 Swank, Wayne T., and James E. Douglass. "Stream Flow Greatly Reduced by Converting Deciduous Hardwood Stands to Pine." *Science* 185 (1974): 857–859. **S**

Conversion of hardwood forest to pine can result in heavy losses of water. Fifteen years after conversion of deciduous hardwood stands to white pine in North Carolina, annual stream flow was 8 inches (20 centimeters), or 20 percent below that from adjoining watershed left in hardwood for control. Causes of this loss were as follows:

1. Interception of rain by pine leaves (hardwoods are deciduous).
2. Transpiration of pine during periods when hardwoods are dormant.

Note: This water loss amounts to 90 million acre-feet when applied to the 130 million acres of converted eastern hardwood forest. Assuming an average fall of 500 feet, this would be enough water to generate 45 million megawatts. (One acre-foot dropping 1 foot equals 1 kilowatt-hour.)

117 Haupt, Harold F. *The Release of Water from Forest Snowpacks During Winter.* Research Paper INT-114. Department of Agriculture, Forest Service, 1972. **S**

Snowpack accumulates less under timber stands than in clearcut or naturally bare areas because snowfall accumulates in the crowns of trees. This subsequently melts, drips through snow on the ground, and percolates into the soil. Thus the soil under timber is provided with water during the winter periods when soil on bare areas remains dry. At the end of winter, more snow remains on bare areas.

Note: Although snowpack under timber is less in the spring, this does not mean that seasonal input of water into the soil is less. The charge that snow caught in tree crowns evaporates has not been proved by measuring snowpack depth at the end of winter, nor has it been disproved.

118 Brown, George. "Temperature, Sediment and Streamflow—Alsea Watershed Case Study." *Proceedings of a Symposium, Forest Land Uses and Stream Environment,* p. 244. J. T. Krygier and J. D. Hall, editors. Corvallis, OR: Oregon State University, School of Forestry and Department of Fisheries and Wildlife, 1971. **P**

In a study of Alsea Creek, Oregon, where 12 percent of the watershed was roaded and 42 percent was clearcut, the peak discharge increased by 28 percent after road building and by 43 percent following logging. Where 3.1 percent was roaded and 20 percent was clearcut, there was no change in peak discharge.

119 Rothacher, Jack. "Regimes of Streamflow and Their Modification by Logging." *Proceedings of a Symposium, Forest Land Uses and Stream Environment,* p. 53. J. T. Krygier and J. D. Hall, editors. Corvallis, OR: Oregon State University, School of Forestry and Department of Fisheries and Wildlife, 1971. **Q**

"It is doubtful if removal of 20 percent or less of the forest cover would result in a detectable change in streamflow. Rapid expansion of root systems and crowns of trees left after partial cutting or thinning would be expected to quickly reduce any changes in streamflow that did result from this type of logging."

120 Rothacher, Jack. "Regimes of Streamflow and Their Modification by Logging." *Proceedings of a Symposium, Forest Land Uses and Stream Environment*, p. 43. J. T. Krygier and J. D. Hall, editors. Corvallis, OR: Oregon State University, School of Forestry and Department of Fisheries and Wildlife, 1971. **Q**

". . . Experimental watersheds throughout the country [United States] show a pronounced increase in annual streamflow after clearcutting."*

121 Fredriksen, R. L. "Comparative Water Quality—Natural and Disturbed Streams Following Logging and Slash Burning." *Proceedings of a Symposium, Forest Land Uses and Stream Environment*, p. 125. J. T. Krygier and J. D. Hall, editors. Corvallis, OR: Oregon State University, School of Forestry and Department of Fisheries and Wildlife, 1971. **Q**

"The loss of nutrients from an old growth Douglas fir forest was measured in the streams of experimental watersheds. Following timber harvest and slash burning, loss of nutrients cations increased 1.6 to 3.0 times the loss from the undisturbed watershed. A surge of nutrients that followed broadcast burning contained concentrations of ammonia and manganese that exceeded Federal water quality standards for a period of 12 days. Annual nitrogen loss following burning averaged 4.6 pounds per acre; 53 percent of this was organic nitrogen contained in sediment. Inorganic nitrogen, dissolved in the stream, made up the remaining part. Annual loss of nitrogen from the undisturbed forest was very small—.16 pound per acre."

122 Fredriksen, R. L. "Comparative Water Quality—Natural and Disturbed Streams Following Logging and Slash Burning." *Proceedings of a Symposium, Forest Land Uses and Stream Environment*, p. 127. J. T. Krygier and J. D. Hall, editors. Corvallis, OR: Oregon State University, School of Forestry and Department of Fisheries and Wildlife, 1971. **P**

Clearcutting disrupts the nutrient cycle, because trees no longer take up nutrients and slash increases forest litter. Increased water content and soil temperature resulting from clearcutting accelerate the activity of microorganisms that decompose forest litter. Respiration is greatly increased, which raises the bicarbonate anion level and increases leaching loss of cations from the forest soil. Where nitrate is not used by returning vegetation, substantial nitrogen loss may occur, as in the Hubbard Brook Forest."†

123 Fredriksen, R. L. "Comparative Water Quality—Natural and Disturbed Streams Following Logging and Slash Burning." *Proceedings of a Symposium,*

---

*A. R. Hibbert, "Forest Treatment Effects on Water Yield," in *International Symposium on Forest Hydrology*, ed. W. E. Sopper and H. W. Lull (New York: Pergamon Press), 527–543.
†G. E. Likens et al., "Effects of Forest Cutting and Herbicide Treatment on Nutrient Budgets in the Hubbard Brook Watershed Ecosystem," *Ecology Monographs* 40 (1970): 23–47.

Forest Land Uses and Stream Environment, p. 130. J. T. Krygier and J. D. Hall, editors. Corvallis, OR: Oregon State University, School of Forestry and Department of Fisheries and Wildlife, 1971. Q

TABLE 3 *Total Annual Dissolved Chemical Loss in Streams Draining Clearcut and Control Watersheds (pounds per acre)*

	Logging Only 1966 Clearcut/Control		Following Slash Burning 1967 Clearcut/Control		1968 Clearcut/Control	
Chemicals						
NH3N	00.0	00.0	1.34	.025	.010	.000
NO3N	.23	.07	.62	.025	2.15	.007
Na	30.8	18.6	31.7	16.8	—	—
K	4.8	3.0	5.4	2.8	3.1	1.6
Ca	54.3	23.6	72.7	23.5	54.7	21.4
Mg	14.0	5.0	23.4	6.7	14.3	4.3
PO4P	.27	.19	.49	.13	—	—
HCO3C	51.3	25.0	64.0	31.0	35.5	20.7

124 Fredriksen, R. L. "Comparative Water Quality—Natural and Disturbed Streams Following Logging and Slash Burning." *Proceedings of a Symposium, Forest Land Uses and Stream Environment*, p. 134. J. T. Krygier and J. D. Hall, editors. Corvallis, OR: Oregon State University, School of Forestry and Department of Fisheries and Wildlife, 1971. Q

TABLE 4 *Annual Loss of Chemical Constituents Adsorbed on Mineral Sediment Plus That Contained in Suspended Organic Material (pounds per acre)*

	Following Slash Burning 1967 Clearcut/Control		1968 Clearcut/Control	
Chemicals				
Organic N	3.4	.14	1.7	.14
K	1.1	.023	.7	.022
Ca	2.8	.2	1.4	.4
Mg	1.7	.027	1.0	.027
Mn	1.4	.02	.7	.02

125 DeByle, Norbert, and Paul E. Packer. "Plant Nutrient and Soil Losses in Overland Flow from Burned Forest Clearcuts." *Proceedings of a Symposium on "Watersheds in Transition,"* p. 296. Department of Agriculture, Forest Service, Fort Collins, CO, 1972. Q

"In the white pine forests of the northern Rocky Mountains, research has revealed that four inches more water from snow alone must be handled by the soil mantle and substrate in clearcut areas than where a full forest canopy exists.

"Evapotranspirational loss is less from clearcuts than under mature timber, too. Thus, more water is made available for streamflow. Added to a soil mantle already taxed during spring periods of rapid snowmelt, often accompanied by rain, the additional water may create overland flow as well as rapid subsurface seepage flow, thus aggravating runoff peaks and soil erosion."

126 DeByle, Norbert, and Paul E. Packer. "Plant Nutrient and Soil Losses in Overland Flow from Burned Forest Clearcuts." *Proceedings of a Symposium on "Watersheds in Transition,"* pp. 296–307. Department of Agriculture, Forest Service, Fort Collins, CO, 1972. **S**

Large areas were clearcut and burned in old-growth Douglas-fir forests near Olney, Montana. Soils were relatively stable, derived from Belt Series rocks. Slopes averaged 24 percent in one study area and 55 percent in another; plots were located so as not to be influenced by roads and firebreaks. Erosion from control plots was nil. In the first year after clearcutting, erosion totaled 207 pounds per acre in the first area and 1,556 pounds per acre in the second area, which had steeper slopes. Most was due to summer storms. In the second year, erosion was 188 pounds per acre in the first area and lower in the second, although no figures are given. After 4 years, the rate of erosion in the first area leveled off at 15 pounds per acre.

127 Halls, Lowell K., and John J. Stransky. *Atlas of Southern Forest Game.* Unnumbered publication. Department of Agriculture, Forest Service (Southern Forest Experiment Station), 1971. **S**

The South is the wintering ground for woodcocks (*Philohela minor*). Their preferred range is wet areas (streams, bayous, marshes) bordered by southern pines or hardwoods. Small clearings, important for mating rituals, should be near feeding areas and brushy nesting cover.

128 Halls, Lowell K., and John J. Stransky. *Atlas of Southern Forest Game,* p. 16. Unnumbered publication. Department of Agriculture, Forest Service (Southern Forest Experiment Station), 1971. **S, Q**

The eastern bobwhite lives in the South. "During the early 1900's a combination of small patch farming, timber clearing, and field burning produced population highs that are unlikely to be equalled again. Since 1939, mechanized agriculture, reforestation, limited fire use, and conversion of cropland to improved pasture have caused quail to decline." Being seed-eating birds, the quail naturally decline as forest cover returns.

129 Halls, Lowell K., and John J. Stransky. *Atlas of Southern Forest Game,* p. 17. Unnumbered publication. Department of Agriculture, Forest Service (Southern Forest Experiment Station), 1971. **Q, P**

"Prime habitat [of the ruffled grouse] is found in extensive forests with a wide variety of cover types including hardwoods and conifers. Access to drumming logs is essential. Small openings are needed to provide edge and to furnish browse, other green vegetation and fruits for food." The heaviest populations of ruffled grouse are found in and around national forests in Virginia, Tennessee, and North Carolina.

130   Halls, Lowell K., and John J. Stransky. *Atlas of Southern Forest Game*, p. 22.
          Unnumbered publication. Department of Agriculture, Forest Service
          (Southern Forest Experiment Station), 1971. **Q, S**

"The eastern wild turkey (*Meleagris gallopave*) . . . was once abundant in
mature virgin forests, but as these forests were cut the turkey experienced hard
times."

Bottomland hardwood forests are considered prime habitat for turkeys, and
conversion of these forests to cropland causes them serious hardship.

"The best habitat comprises stands of mixed hardwoods, groups of conifers,
relatively open understories, scattered clearings, well-distributed water, and reasonable freedom from disturbance."

131   Grantham, John B. et al. *Energy and Raw Material Potentials of Wood Residue
          in the Pacific Coast States—A Summary of a Preliminary Feasibility Investiga-
          tion*, p. 21. General Technical Report PNW-18. Department of Agriculture,
          Forest Service, 1974. **Q**

" . . . The equivalent of almost 50 million Btu is required per ton of paper produced. Twenty percent of this gross energy demand is used as electrical energy.
The rest of the demand, or about 40 million Btu, is used to make process steam
for the pulping and papermaking operations."

132   Fellin, David G. *Weevils Attracted to Thinned Lodgepole Pine Stands in Mon-
          tana*. Research Paper INT-136. Department of Agriculture, Forest Service,
          1973. **S**

Weevils (*Magdalis gentilis*) damage recently thinned lodgepole pine stands in
the northern Rockies when the stands are thinned before late July. Opening of
the stand is correlated to an upsurge in the weevil population, but only when
done early in the growing season. Stands can be thinned later in the year with no
ensuing weevil damage. However, if stands are thinned so late in the season that
fresh slash is covered by snow, that slash will cause a weevil population buildup
in the spring, which may then attack trees. Thus, lodgepole pine stands should
be thinned between mid-August and the end of September.

133   Brink, David L., and Michael M. Merriman. "Influence of Young-growth
          on Characteristics and Utilization of Fiber." *Proceedings of a Conference
          on Young-Growth Forest Management in California*, p. 20. Berkeley, CA: Uni-
          versity of California, Department of Forest and Resource Management,
          1967. **Q**

"Young growth usually is fast growing with wide growth rings and a large
proportion of earlywood having thin-walled short fibers. This wood is of lower
specific gravity than mature wood. Chemically young-wood fibers have higher
hemicellulose and lignin contents and lower cellulose content. These characteristics will produce lower pulp yields and more dense paper with better tensile
properties—that is, breaking strength and burst factor, and poorer shearing
strength than would be produced from mature wood."

134   McGee, Charles, and Ralph Hooper. *Regeneration after Clearcutting in the Southern Appalachians*, p. 7.   Research Paper SE-70. Department of Agriculture, Forest Service, 1970. **S, Q**

This report's summary states that very favorable regeneration occurred after clearcutting, but details within the report indicate that many problems developed.

"The more than 700 desirable seedlings and sprouts per acre that were free to grow provide the study area with an adequate source of regeneration. However, the presence of many undesirable sprout clumps may affect the species composition and distribution of the stand. At best, undesirable sprout clumps will continue to occupy considerable area and will provide competition to the desirable crop trees for some time to come.

"There were over 500 sprout clumps over 4 1/2 feet tall per acre in the 5-year-old stand. Some of these clumps contain desirable stems, but over half are of undesirable species. One of the greatest threats to the favorable development of this area is the presence of red maple sprout clumps on 28 plots."

135   Bruce, David, and Arnold Comt. "Trees for the Aleutians." *Geographical Review* 35 (1945): 421. **Q**

"Evidence of a slow outward spread of the limit of trees is to be found on Kodiak. . . . Trees dead of old age are found only in areas with several younger generations present. None of these dead trees, all about 300 years old, can be found closer than three miles to the present forest edge, indicating an advance of about a mile in 100 years or 50 feet a year."

136   Baker, F. S. *Principles of Silviculture*. New York: McGraw-Hill, 1950. **S**

A pure forest may be riddled with insect damage, disease, or storm damage, or beneath its canopy such unsatisfactory soil conditions may develop that trees can be made to reproduce only at great expense. In Europe, the theorists, at least, tend to advocate the mixed forest, and the timberland owners continue to raise pure stands wherever they dare.

Some species occur naturally in pure stands and apparently have no difficulties on that account—notably ponderosa pine, lodgepole pine, and Douglas-fir.

Nevertheless, the natural weaknesses of widespread pure forests are not to be dismissed as theoretical; they have much basis in reality.

137   Plass, William T., and Willis G. Vogel. *Chemical Properties and Particle-size Distribution of 39 Surface-mine Spoils in Southern West Virginia*. Research Paper NE-276. Department of Agriculture, Forest Service, 1973. **S**

A comparison of spoils from strip mining in West Virginia with natural soils of the same area showed that pH was about the same in both (+ or - 5), but the strip-mining spoils had a much smaller proportion of small particles and a serious lack of nutrients.

Soil	pH	Particle Size	Phosphorus
Natural	4.0–5.5	80% under 2 mm; some under 50 mm	Sufficient, but not stated
Spoils	4.5–5.7	Only 37% under 2 mm	1.8–8.0 ppm

138 Bormann, F. Herbert, and Gene E. Likens. "The Nutrient Cycles of an Eco-system." *Scientific American* 223 (1970): 92–101. **S, C**

Serious nutrient losses may occur where clearcutting and reforestation are supplemented by control of competing vegetation with biocides. At Hubbard Brook in New Hampshire, a watershed was clearcut, the timber was left lying on the ground, and the area was sprayed with biocides. The purpose of the study was to determine the effect of herbicide spraying where soil was not disturbed but trees were no longer taking up nutrients. Nutrient losses for three subsequent years were as follows:

- Nitrates   40 times normal runoff
- Potassium   21 times normal runoff
- Calcium   10 times normal runoff
- Magnesium   7 times normal runoff

Note: This experiment has been used as an argument against clearcutting, but the argument has been rebutted on the grounds that it was not typical because biocides were used to prevent nutrient takeup.

139 Resch, Helmuth. "Considering the Physical Properties of Wood in Managing Forest Trees." *Proceedings of a Conference on Young-Growth Forest Management in California*, p. 26. Berkeley, CA: University of California, Department of Forest and Resource Management, 1967. **Q**

"Probably the greatest disadvantage of growing conifers in wide open stands is the long persistence of branches along the merchantable bole."

140 Resch, Helmuth. "Considering the Physical Properties of Wood in Managing Forest Trees." *Proceedings of a Conference on Young-Growth Forest Management in California*, p. 26. Berkeley, CA: University of California, Department of Forest and Resource Management, 1967. **Q**

"The suitability of second-growth Douglas fir veneer is greatly diminished, because it is not only undesirable for veneer faces, but also veneer cuts are rough, the numerous knots tend to chip the knife although the lathe settings are no more crucial than in old-growth."

141 Resch, Helmuth. "Considering the Physical Properties of Wood in Managing Forest Trees." *Proceedings of a Conference on Young-Growth Forest Management in California*, p. 26. Berkeley, CA: University of California, Department of Forest and Resource Management, 1967. **Q**

"If lumber is produced, the yield of high-grade material [from second-growth Douglas fir] is lower than from old-growth trees."

142 Switzer, George. Talk presented at Sierra Club Conference on Forest Management, Tuscaloosa, AL, January 31–February 1, 1967. **P**

Removing even-aged stands of loblolly pine on old fields before they reach 60 years of age removes more nutrients than the trees have developed. Practicing even-aged management in stands of loblolly pine on old fields with less than a 60-year rotation is not good husbandry of the land.

143 Stottlmeyer, J. Robert, and Charles W. Ralston. "Nutrient Balance Relationships for Watersheds of the Fraser Experimental Forest." *Tree Growth and Soils: Proceedings of the Third North American Forest Soils Conference*, pp. 359–382. Corvallis, OR: Oregon State University Press, 1970. **S**

Harvesting and burning of slash in areas where natural productivity is low may cause decreases in soil fertility and appreciable reductions in timber yields.

144 Urie, Dean H. *Ground Water Differences on Pine and Hardwood Forests on the Udell Experimental Forest in Michigan*, p. 12. Research Paper NC-145, Department of Agriculture, Forest Service, 1977. **S**

Groundwater recharge under hardwood and pine forests was measured between 1962 and 1971 in the Udell Experimental Forest in Michigan. Hardwood forests produced more net groundwater than pine forests by an average of 50 and 100 millimeters (2 and 4 inches) per year, using two methods of analysis. Shallow-water-table lands yield 80 to 100 millimeters (3 to 4 inches) less water per year than do deep, well-drained sands. Water yield decreased the most between drainage classifications of pine plantations.

145 Haupt, Harold F. *The Release of Water from Forest Snowpacks During Winter*, p. 1. Research Paper INT-114. Department of Agriculture, Forest Service, 1972. **Q**

"Processes affecting the amount of snowfall that penetrates the canopy of coniferous forests and reaches the ground surface are largely unknown to snow hydrologists. Comparisons of the amounts of snow on the ground almost invariably show less snow under the crowns than in the adjacent opening; but according to Hoover* this leaves unanswered the following questions:

(A) Is the deficiency of accumulated snow in the forest a result of evaporation of snow from tree crowns?

(B) Was intercepted snow blown off the tree crowns and redeposited into the opening?

(C) Or did the wind eddies caused by the surrounding tree crowns deposit excess snow in the opening and, conversely, deposit less in the forest?

"Surprisingly, after one hundred years of research, there remains a deficiency of basic data to answer these questions and a lack of suitable instruments for resolving the problem.†"

*M. D. Hoover, "Water Action and Water Movement in the Forest," in *Forest Influences*, Forest and Forest Products Study 15 (United Nations, Food and Agriculture Organization, 1967), 31–80, 282–289.

†D. H. Miller, *Transport of Intercepted Snow from Trees During Snow Storms*, Research Paper PSW-33 (Department of Agriculture, Forest Service, 1966).

146 Youngberg, Chester, and A. G. Wollum II. "Nonleguminous Symbiotic Nitrogen Fixation." *Tree Growth and Soils: Proceedings of the Third North American Forest Soils Conference*, p. 385. Corvallis, OR: Oregon State University Press, 1970. Q, P

The following species are important nitrogen fixers in the West: "Snowbrush (*Ceanothus velutinus* Dougl.) and bitterbrush (*Purshia tridentata* (Pursh) D.C.) are dominant understory plants in open Ponderosa pine (*Pinus ponderosa* Laws) stands in the Northwest. Canadian buffalo berry (*Shepherdia canadensis* Nutt.) occupies a similar position in Ponderosa pine stands in the Rocky Mountains. Red and White alder (*Alnus rubra* Bong. and *A. rhombifolia* Nutt.) as well as the shrubby species occur as dominant species along stream banks. Many of the *Ceanothus* species occur as dominant components of the chaparral vegetation in California."

147 Youngberg, Chester, and A. G. Wollum II. "Nonleguminous Symbiotic Nitrogen Fixation." *Tree Growth and Soils: Proceedings of the Third North American Forest Soils Conference*, p. 386. Corvallis, OR: Oregon State University Press, 1970. Q

Table 1 *Occurrence of Nodulation in Nonleguminous Angiosperms in North America*

Family	Genus	Number of Known Nodulated Species
Betulaceae	*Alnus*	10
Cactaceae	*Opuntia*	1
Compositae	*Artemisia*	1
Eleagnaceae	*Shepherdia*	3
Ericaceae	*Arctostaphylos*	1
Myricaceae	*Myrica*	4
Rhamnaceae	*Ceanothus*	30
Rosaceae	*Dryas*	3
	Purshia	1
	Cercocarpus	2

148 Youngberg, Chester, and A. G. Wollum II. "Nonleguminous Symbiotic Nitrogen Fixation." *Tree Growth and Soils: Proceedings of the Third North American Forest Soils Conference*, p. 383. Corvallis, OR: Oregon State University Press, 1970. P, S

The amount of combined nitrogen in the soil of "Douglas fir . . . ecosystems may vary from 3,000 kg/ha in one meter of gravelly soil near Puget Sound to 14,000 kg/ha in 1.5 meters of soil in the Oregon Coast range. . . . It is probable that the main source of soil nitrogen is the atmosphere."

The amount added from precipitation annually in North America varies from 1 to 19 kilograms per hectare, with most observations between 4 to 7 kilograms per hectare.

149   Youngberg, Chester, and A. G. Wollum II. "Nonleguminous Symbiotic Nitrogen Fixation." *Tree Growth and Soils: Proceedings of the Third North American Forest Soils Conference*, p. 384. Corvallis, OR: Oregon State University Press, 1970. **S**

Two free-living bacteria present in forest soils in North America are *Azotobacter* (aerobic) and *Clostridium* (anaerobic). Most forest soils are too acid for much nitrogen fixation by *Azotobacter*. Fixation of 50 kilograms of nitrogen per hectare per year has been reported for these organisms, but about 5 kilograms per hectare per year may be a more reasonable level.

150   Worthington, Norman, Robert Ruth, and Elmer Matson. *Red Alder—Its Management and Utilization*, p. 6. Miscellaneous Publication 881. Department of Agriculture, Forest Service, 1962. **Q**

"Alder contributes both to physical and chemical improvement of soil. Its litter decomposes rapidly, forming a mull humus layer, with subsequent improvement in soil structure."

151   Pessin, L. J. "Forest Associations in the Uplands of the Lower Gulf Coastal Plain (Longleaf Pine Belt)." *Ecology* 14 (1933): 1–14. **P**

Myrica caroliniensis is common in the lower Gulf Coastal Plain and may well produce nitrogen, as do other species of this genus. *Sarracenia* species (pitcher plants) are also common and put nitrogen into the soil by digesting insects.

152   Wilhite, Lawrence P., and Thomas H. Ripley. *Important Understory Plants of the Slash-Longleaf Flatwoods*. Georgia Forest Research Paper 29. Georgia Forest Research Council, 1965. **P**

Legumes and wax myrtle (*Myrica cerifera*) were frequent members of slash–longleaf pine flatwoods in southeastern Georgia and northeastern Florida. These species fix nitrogen.

153   Aho, Paul E. et al. "Distribution, Enumeration and Identification of Nitrogen-fixing Bacteria Associated with Decay in Living White Fir Trees." *Phytopathology* 64 (1974): 1413–1420. **S**

Bacteria associated with wood decay fungi are usually capable of fixing atmospheric nitrogen. Nitrogen-fixing bacteria are associated with the major decay fungi in white fir, *Echinodontium tinctorum, Philiota adiposa, Phillinus chrysolama,* and *Hericium abeitis*. These fungi probably are responsible for more than 90 percent of all decay in living white firs.

154   Li, C. Y. et al. "Separation of Phenolic Compounds in Alkali Hydrolysates of a Forest Soil by Thin-layer Chromatography." *Canadian Journal of Soil Science* 50 (1970): 458–460. **S**

Phenolic compounds produced by red alder inhibit *Poria weirii* and other fungi that cause root rot of Douglas-fir. A new technique for determining the presence of such compounds in forest soils has been developed to evaluate this possible mechanism of biological control of root diseases.

155 Stephens, F. R., C. R. Gass, and R. F. Billings. *Soils and Site Index in Southeast Alaska.* Unnumbered publication. Department of Agriculture, Forest Service (Alaska region), 1968. **S**

The factor most limiting to tree growth in Alaska is the amount of nitrates present. These accumulate best in deep soils.

The removal of duff (decaying organic matter) introduces an alder cycle in deep soils. This frequently occurs during logging.

Nutrients are made available for tree growth by decomposition of organic matter. The rate of decomposition is dependent on temperature, and duff is the warmest soil type during the growing season.

Obviously, therefore, openings from logging should be large enough to permit warming the duff, but care must be taken not to remove it.

156 Rothacher, Jack, C. T. Dyrness, and Richard L. Fredriksen. *Hydrologic and Related Characteristics of Three Small Watersheds in the Oregon Cascades,* p. 35. PNW-Unnumbered publication. Department of Agriculture, Forest Service, 1967. **Q**

"Dense vegetation and a relatively stable soil combine to give water of high purity. Sedimentation occurs in a cyclical manner both on an annual and on a storm basis. Under undisturbed forest conditions, even storms exceeding 135 cubic feet per second per square mile* seldom produce more than 200 parts per million of suspended sediment. Sediment load peaks rapidly during storms and recedes soon afterwards to modest concentrations. Concentrations exceeding 10 parts per million occur for only 1 to 2 percent of the time during a typical winter."

157 Campbell, Homer. "Economic and Social Significance of Upstream Aquatic Resources on the West Coast." *Proceedings of a Symposium, Forest Land Uses and Stream Environment,* p. 14. J. T. Krygier and J. D. Hall, editors. Corvallis, OR: Oregon State University, School of Forestry and Department of Fisheries and Wildlife, 1971. **Q**

"The connection between upstream activity and resulting economic loss in some other part of the watershed is strikingly seen when a slide on the Fraser River, occurring during railroad construction in 1913 at Hells Gate, stopped migratory fish runs. The estimate of direct economic loss occurring before a ladder could be installed was one billion dollars. Miniature models of this disaster have often happened on West Coast streams when slides and [logging] debris jams blocked salmon runs."

158 Rice, R. M., J. S. Rothacher, and W. F. Megahan. "Erosional Consequences of Timber Harvesting: An Appraisal." *Proceedings of a Symposium on "Watersheds in Transition,"* p. 328. Department of Agriculture, Forest Service, Fort Collins, CO, 1972. **Q**

"Accelerated erosion is a possible undesirable side effect of use of fire following a timber harvest. The effects of fire are most harmful on steep slopes, where

*Equivalent of 26 inches per minute. Refers to extreme runoff resulting from rain on snow.

it induces dry ravelling, and on coarse-textured soils, where it can—by the creation of a water repellent layer—increase overland flow and retard the regrowth of the forest."

159 Rice, R. M., J. S. Rothacher, and W. F. Megahan. "Erosional Consequences of Timber Harvesting: An Appraisal." *Proceedings of a Symposium on "Watersheds in Transition,"* p. 321. Department of Agriculture, Forest Service, Fort Collins, CO, 1972. **Q, C**

"This paper summarizes our current understanding of the effects of timber harvesting on erosion. Rates of erosion on mountain watersheds vary widely but the relative importance of different types of erosion and the consequences of disturbances remain fairly consistent. Therefore these conclusions seem to be valid for most circumstances: Most of man's activities will increase erosion to some extent in forested watersheds; erosion rarely occurs uniformly; sediment production declines rapidly following disturbance; landslides and creep are the chief forms of natural erosion in mountainous regions; cutting of trees does not significantly increase erosion, but clearcutting on steep unstable slopes may lead to increased mass erosion; accelerated erosion is a possible undesirable side effect of use of fire in conjunction with logging; the road system built for timber harvesting far overshadows logging or fire as a cause of increased erosion; and potentially hazardous areas can be identified in advance of the timber harvest."

Note: This article presents a general summary of what *may* happen, but the disparity between experimental conditions and common logging practice is not emphasized.

160 Rice, R. M., J. S. Rothacher, and W. F. Megahan. "Erosional Consequences of Timber Harvesting: An Appraisal." *Proceedings of a Symposium on "Watersheds in Transition,"* p. 322. Department of Agriculture, Forest Service, Fort Collins, CO, 1972. **Q**

"Certainly, bare and compacted soils resulting from logging disturbances are potential sites for erosion and surface runoff. However, because these areas are often not contiguous, eroded soils may come to rest on intervening undisturbed ground rather than move out of the watershed."

161 Megahan, W. F., and Delbert C. Molitor. "Erosional Effects of Wildfire and Logging in Idaho." *Proceedings of a Symposium on Watershed Management,* p. 442. New York: American Society of Civil Engineers, 1975. **P, Q**

Soil losses on a clearcut area in the Salmon River drainage of Idaho "probably caused some reduction in on-site productivity, at least on areas where losses [of soil] occurred. This was countered somewhat by deposition of eroded material at other locations on the watershed. However, considering that there was a net soil loss and that most deposition occurred where soils were deep, it is likely there was a net reduction in productivity."

162 Bethlahmy, Nedavia. *Effect of Exposure and Logging on Runoff and Erosion.* Research Note INT-61. Department of Agriculture, Forest Service, 1967. **S**

Erosion can be expressed as a logarithmic function: $\log_e E = 1.35R - 0.77$ (where E is erosion in grams and R is runoff in centimeters).

The equation is highly significant, since a slight increase in 30-minute runoff, as from 1 centimeter to 2 centimeters, results in almost a fourfold increase in erosion, from 1.8 grams to 6.9 grams. Thus, any land management practice that increases runoff may bring about a very large increase in erosion.

163   Rice, R. M., J. S. Rothacher, and W. F. Megahan. "Erosional Consequences of Timber Harvesting: An Appraisal." *Proceedings of a Symposium on "Watersheds in Transition,"* pp. 321–329. Department of Agriculture, Forest Service, Fort Collins, CO, 1972. **S**

In various steep, mountainous areas subject to severe storms, a large percentage of mass failure was associated with roads. Seventy-two percent of the landslides in the H. J. Andrews Experimental Forest were associated with roads, although the roads occupied only 1.8 percent of the area. In the Zena Creek area in southern Idaho, 90 percent of the mass failures were associated with roads. During the storm that caused these failures, mass failures were reported on roads that had been stable for 10 years. This seems to refute the argument that the erosion problems associated with road building are usually short term. In unstable terrain, such as the Idaho batholith, roads stable for 10 to 20 years are still prone to mass failure and add considerably to the sediment production of the watershed.

164   Larse, Robert. "Prevention and Control of Erosion and Stream Sedimentation from Forest Roads." *Proceedings of a Symposium, Forest Land Uses and Stream Environment,* p. 76. J. T. Krygier and J. D. Hall, editors. Corvallis, OR: Oregon State University, School of Forestry and Department of Fisheries and Wildlife, 1971. **Q**

"To minimize erosion and resultant stream sedimentation, prevention and control measures must be given consideration in every aspect of road planning, design, construction and maintenance. In mountainous terrain the forest land manager must establish specific objectives and prescriptions to guide road network construction and utilize the combined professional skills of the forester, engineer, geologist, biologist, and others to set standards for the protection of watershed values, identify alternatives, and offer solutions to specific problems.

"The decision to road an area should only be made after the resource-serving benefits have been carefully weighed against the cost and effect of roading on the watershed. The decision not-to-road and to accept other alternatives for land-use management must be strongly considered when the probability of lasting damage to soil, water and other ecological values is recognized."

165   Larse, Robert. "Prevention and Control of Erosion and Stream Sedimentation from Forest Roads." *Proceedings of a Symposium, Forest Land Uses and Stream Environment,* p. 78. J. T. Krygier and J. D. Hall, editors. Corvallis, OR: Oregon State University, School of Forestry and Department of Fisheries and Wildlife, 1971. **Q**

"In mountainous terrain, with complex drainage features, the higher precision of road engineering is usually necessary to insure that excavation is minimized, earthwork properly utilized, and drainage requirements are satisfied without creating the potential for road failure and erosion."

166 Phillips, Robert W. "Effects of Sediment on the Gravel Environment and Fish Production." *Proceedings of a Symposium, Forest Land Uses and Stream Environment*, p. 64. J. T. Krygier and J. D. Hall, editors. Corvallis, OR: Oregon State University, School of Forestry and Department of Fisheries and Wildlife, 1971. Q

"Only 10 to 30 percent of the total number of eggs deposited by spawning trout and salmon survives to emerge from the gravel. . . . Such low survival occurs naturally without any influence of man. When man's activities adversely affect the habitat, even lower survival results."

167 Narver, David. "Effects of Logging Debris on Fish Production." *Proceedings of a Symposium, Forest Land Uses and Stream Environment*, p. 102. J. T. Krygier and J. D. Hall, editors. Corvallis, OR: Oregon State University, School of Forestry and Department of Fisheries and Wildlife, 1971. Q

"Stream salmonids require cover in the form of undercut banks, logs, rubble, substrate, turbulence, overhanging streamside vegetation and deep pools. Such cover is used by juveniles for feeding stations, food source and refuges for escape and wintering. . . . Adult salmonids use such cover for resting and escape."

168 Narver, David. "Effects of Logging Debris on Fish Production." *Proceedings of a Symposium, Forest Land Uses and Stream Environment*, pp. 100–111. J. T. Krygier and J. D. Hall, editors. Corvallis, OR: Oregon State University, School of Forestry and Department of Fisheries and Wildlife, 1971. S

Salmonid fish require access to spawning and nursery areas; stream flow without extreme fluctuations; and clean, stable substrate for reproduction and benthos production. Logjams resulting from logging debris can block or delay upstream migration, and smaller jams and stranded logs cause erosion of the streambed due to repositioning with every freshet. Shifting of gravel after a jam breaks results in increased embryo and alevin mortality.

169 Lantz, Richard. "Influence of Water Temperature on Fish Survival, Growth and Behavior." *Proceedings of a Symposium, Forest Land Uses and Stream Environment*, p. 182.. J. T. Krygier and J. D. Hall, editors. Corvallis, OR: Oregon State University, School of Forestry and Department of Fisheries and Wildlife, 1971. Q

"In the Pacific Northwest, extremely small streams are essential to the production of salmonids, our most important group of fish. . . . On the Rogue River system in Oregon most of the spawning tributaries used by summer steelhead during the fall and winter are dry in the summer. . . . Young fish leave these streams in the spring, after emerging from the gravel, and move downstream. Such tributaries are essential to this important sport fish as spawning areas and should be protected."

170 Lantz, Richard. "Influence of Water Temperature on Fish Survival, Growth and Behavior." *Proceedings of a Symposium, Forest Land Uses and Stream Environment*, p. 182.. J. T. Krygier and J. D. Hall, editors. Corvallis, OR: Oregon State University, School of Forestry and Department of Fisheries and Wildlife, 1971. Q

"The U.S. Fish and Wildlife Service has recommended the following general-
ized optimum temperature ranges for salmonids:

- Migration: 45–60 degrees F.
- Spawning: 45–55 degrees F.
- Rearing: 50–60 degrees F."

171 Lantz, Richard. "Influence of Water Temperature on Fish Survival,
Growth and Behavior." *Proceedings of a Symposium, Forest Land Uses and
Stream Environment*, p. 182.. J. T. Krygier and J. D. Hall, editors. Corvallis,
OR: Oregon State University, School of Forestry and Department of Fisher-
ies and Wildlife, 1971. **P, C**

During April and May, juvenile coho salmon required twice as much food to
initiate growth at 63 degrees Fahrenheit than they needed at 41 degrees Fahrenheit. Later in the year, the same relationship was found, but more food was
needed to achieve growth.

Note: Therefore, temperature increases associated with logging may reduce
growth even if they are not lethal.

172 Lantz, Richard. "Influence of Water Temperature on Fish Survival,
Growth and Behavior." *Proceedings of a Symposium, Forest Land Uses and
Stream Environment*, p. 182. J. T. Krygier and J. D. Hall, editors. Corvallis,
OR: Oregon State University, School of Forestry and Department of Fisher-
ies and Wildlife, 1971. **P**

Migratory behavior of adult sockeye salmon is timed so that they arrive at the
spawning grounds when temperatures are between 45 and 55 degrees Fahrenheit. Temperature changes can influence both this migratory behavior and the
downstream migratory behavior of juveniles. In the past, migrations have been
blocked due to high water temperatures.

173 Lantz, Richard. "Influence of Water Temperature on Fish Survival,
Growth and Behavior." *Proceedings of a Symposium, Forest Land Uses and
Stream Environment*, p. 185. J. T. Krygier and J. D. Hall, editors. Corvallis,
OR: Oregon State University, School of Forestry and Department of Fisher-
ies and Wildlife, 1971. **P, Q**

Specific factors such as water temperature, sediment levels, and chemical pollutants may have a synergistic* effect on fish in some conditions. There is little
attempt to look at the total effect of all the factors influencing an organism because the impact is "too complex to comprehend."

174 Reynolds, Hudson G. *Aspen Grove Use by Deer, Elk and Cattle in Southwestern Coniferous Forests*, p. 4. Research Note RM-138. Department of Agriculture, Forest Service, 1969. **Q**

"Deer and cattle use, but not elk use, was greater within natural aspen groves
[than within thinned aspen groves] as measured by accumulated pellet group
counts.

*The simultaneous action of the separate factors taken together may have a greater total
impact than the sum of their individual effects.

"Fallen timber in the thinned aspen plots prevented deer, elk and cattle from completely utilizing the more abundant forage therein."

175 Reynolds, Hudson G. *Aspen Grove Use by Deer, Elk and Cattle in Southwestern Coniferous Forests*, p. 4. Research Note RM-138. Department of Agriculture, Forest Service, 1969. **Q**

"Preserving or providing for an interspersion of aspen groves in a mixed conifer forest and encouraging existing aspen groves in Ponderosa pine forests should effectively improve habitat for deer."

176 Reynolds, Hudson G. "Improvement of Deer Habitat on Southwestern Forest Lands." *Journal of Forestry* 67 (1969): 804. **Q, C**

"In denser stands of mature trees deer pellet groups were almost proportional to abundance of understory vegetation. In immature groups, however, the relation between deer use and understory vegetation was less striking, particularly above 160 square feet per acre basal area."

Note: Therefore, the assumption that an increase in understory vegetation on regenerating forest plots increases deer use is not necessarily valid.

177 Reynolds, Hudson G. "Improvement of Deer Habitat on Southwestern Forest Lands." *Journal of Forestry* 67 (1969): 804. **Q, C**

"Natural forest openings proved to be important habitat for both deer and cattle. Numbers of deer pellet groups in natural openings and adjacent forests were about the same. . . ."

Note: In an undisturbed situation, deer are not more abundant in openings than in the forest. What are the consequences of creating an unnatural situation in which they are more abundant in the openings? This seems to be the goal of many forest management plans.

178 Reynolds, Hudson G. "Improvement of Deer Habitat on Southwestern Forest Lands." *Journal of Forestry* 67 (1969): 804. **Q**

"The border zone along the forest edge in both openings and forest received heaviest use by deer; use decreased on either side of this border zone. There was some deer use at greatest distances measured into forests; there was no use at comparable distances into openings. In Ponderosa pine forests pellet groups of deer were found out to 1,200 feet from the forest edge into openings. In spruce-fir forests, there was no use by deer beyond 600 feet from the forest edge."

179 Reynolds, Hudson G. "Improvement of Deer Habitat on Southwestern Forest Lands." *Journal of Forestry* 67 (1969): 805. **Q, C**

"Deer use was confined to perimeters of circular openings of no more than 20 acres in spruce-fir habitat (or strip more than 1,050 feet across)."

Note: This suggests that openings of more than 20 acres are disadvantageous to deer.

180 Reynolds, Hudson G. "Improvement of Deer Habitat on Southwestern Forest Lands." *Journal of Forestry* 67 (1969): 805. **Q**

"In Ponderosa pine forests on the Kaibab Plateau, deer preferred areas where logging slash was undisturbed."

181 Halls, Lowell K., and John J. Stransky. *Atlas of Southern Forest Game.* Unnumbered publication. Department of Agriculture, Forest Service (Southern Forest Experiment Station), 1971. S

The white-tailed deer inhabits mainly bottomland hardwood forests but also loblolly pine–shortleaf pine–hardwood forests and to some extent oak–pine forests and longleaf pine–slash pine forests. The deer's home range extends within 1/2 to 1 mile of its birthplace. Timber management determines whether cover and food will be adequate for year-round survival. The best habitat occurs in forests with many small, well-dispersed openings within the deer's range and in areas where timber thinnings are frequent and heavy. In pinelands, a favorable habitat is one in which trees are at least 12 to 15 feet tall; prescribed burns are recommended every 3 to 5 years to improve quantity and quality of forage and to increase growth of legumes. These forest types are not common in all national forests.

182 Skovlin, Jon M., and Robert W. Harris. "Management of Conifer Woodland Grazing Resources for Cattle, Deer and Elk." *Proceedings of the XIth International Grassland Congress* (Australia), p. 77. Department of Agriculture, Forest Service, 1970. Q

"As cattle stocking increased, use by elk decreased. Elk use was significantly greater in game-only ranges than in the dual-use ranges."

183 Halls, Lowell K., and John J. Stransky. *Atlas of Southern Forest Game.* Unnumbered publication. Department of Agriculture, Forest Service (Southern Forest Experiment Station), 1971. S

Only 9,000 black bears live in the South; they are found mainly in areas of national forests, principally George Washington, Chattahoochee, Nantahala, Cherokee, and Osceola. Since the bear requires extensive undisturbed forests, it is now confined to less accessible forested mountains, thickets along river bottoms, and large swamps. Areas managed for bears should be kept remote by limiting the extent of year-round roads.

184 Halls, Lowell K., and John J. Stransky. *Atlas of Southern Forest Game,* p. 14. Unnumbered publication. Department of Agriculture, Forest Service (Southern Forest Experiment Station), 1971. Q

"Raccoons inhabit primarily the hardwood forests along rivers, small streams, and swamps. They are also found in mixed pine-hardwood forests, but seldom far from water. . . . Lack of den trees may limit populations."

185 Trevis, Lloyd, Jr. "Responses of Small Mammal Populations to Logging of Douglas Fir." *Journal of Mammalogy* 37 (1956): 195. Q

"Logging of the forest causes an increase in numbers of white-footed and big-eared mice, Townsend chipmunks, dusky-footed wood rats, digger squirrels, chickarees, gray squirrels and brush rabbits. It caused a decrease in number of Trow-bridge shrews, red-backed mice, flying squirrels and shrew-moles."

186   Atkinson, William. "Economics of Young-growth Management." *Proceedings of a Conference on Young-Growth Forest Management in California*, pp. 65–74. Berkeley, CA: University of California, Department of Forest and Resource Management, 1967. **P**

In addition to felling, yarding, and loading, the cost of hauling second-growth logs varies inversely with the size of the log. A load of smaller logs, containing less volume than a load of large logs but weighing the same, travels the same distance. But for small-log loads, the delivery costs are higher per thousand board feet. A similar trend is experienced in other second-growth operations. Fixed costs, overhead, road maintenance, and other aspects remain constant, even though volume harvested decreases. As log size and volume decrease, the logging cost per thousand board feet keeps going up.

187   Payne, Brian. *Accelerated Roadbuilding in the North Umpqua—An Economic Analysis*, p. 17. Research Paper PNW-137. Department of Agriculture, Forest Service, 1972. **Q**

"Accelerated roadbuilding does not appear economically justified on the North Umpqua, neither for timber access nor for multiple use management. Although this conclusion is based on conditions as of 1966, changes in harvesting technology, stumpage prices and roadbuilding costs since that time only strengthen this finding."

188   McDonald, Philip M. *Logging Costs and Production Rates for the Group Selection Cutting Method*, p. 1. Research Paper PSW-59. Department of Agriculture, Forest Service, 1965. **S, Q**

The size of clearcut opening and the silvicultural method employed have no practical bearing on the cost of logging in second-growth mixed conifer stands in California.

"Young-growth mixed-conifer stands were logged by a group selection method designed to create openings 30, 60 and 90 feet in diameter. Total costs for felling, limbing, bucking and skidding on these openings ranged from $7.04 to $7.99 per thousand board feet. Cost differences were not statistically significant. Logging costs for group selection compared favorably with those previously reported for seed-tree and selection harvest cuts; $8.20 and $8.39 per thousand board feet respectively."

189   Boyce, J. S. *Forest Pathology*, p. 514. New York: McGraw-Hill, 1961. Reproduced with permission. **Q, C**

"Conditions in natural stands point strongly to the fact that there is no factor more important in relation to disease than tree vigor. Stands on good sites are generally not damaged significantly by native diseases, but those on poor sites often suffer severely."

Note: Therefore, logging practices that reduce site quality will lead to trouble with tree diseases.

190   Keen, F. P. *Insect Enemies of Western Forests*, pp. 13–14. Miscellaneous Publication 273 (revised edition). Department of Agriculture, Forest Service, 1952. **Q**

"Before observed damage is charged to insects, other possible causes should be investigated. Often several agents, such as fire, insects, fungi, and physiological injuries, are so closely associated or interrelated that it is difficult to determine the primary cause of the injury.

"Mechanical and physiological injuries are frequently the primary cause of sickliness, weakness, or death of forest trees. The insects that invade the wood after such injuries have occurred are usually only secondary enemies, and cannot be charged with primary responsibility.

"Usually insect damage is readily apparent from the very start, but it is well to make certain whether other conditions are partly responsible before taking steps to control the insect pests. If they are not the primary cause, little benefit can be expected from the effort to control them."

191 Yerkes, Vern P. *Occurrence of Shrubs and Herbaceous Vegetation after Clearcutting Old-Growth Douglas fir in the Oregon Cascades*, p. 7. Research Paper PNW-34. Department of Agriculture, Forest Service, 1960. **P, Q**

The following changes were noted after clearcutting old-growth Douglas-fir in Oregon:

- *"Woody survivors* increased slowly in frequency;
- *Herbaceous survivors* formed a relatively unimportant part of the vegetative cover;
- *Woody invaders* increased more slowly in frequency than did woody survivors;
- *Herbaceous invaders (annuals)* exhibited a high frequency the first 2 years, then declined;
- *Herbaceous invaders (perennials)* exhibited a generally rapid rise in frequency for the first 4 or 5 years, then increased more slowly."

192 Godman, Richard M., and Carl H. Tubbs. Establishing Even-age Northern Hardwood Regeneration by the Shelterwood Method—A Preliminary Guide, p. 4. Research Paper NC-99. Department of Agriculture, Forest Service, 1973. **Q**

"Grass and shrubs commonly invade heavily cut hardwood stands. In some cases these species appear to retard tree production for lengthy periods. Both intensity of cut and season of logging appear related to invasions by grass and shrubs. Site and geographic location are also factors."

193 Swanston, Douglas. "Principal Mass Movement Processes Influenced by Logging, Road Building, and Fire." *Proceedings of a Symposium, Forest Land Uses and Stream Environment*, p. 36a. J. T. Krygier and J. D. Hall, editors. Corvallis, OR: Oregon State University, School of Forestry and Department of Fisheries and Wildlife, 1971. **Q**

"Destruction of vegetation by fire can also lead to progressive deterioration of the mechanically stabilizing root systems, a factor which Croft and Adams consider important, along with logging, to reduction of soil strength and resultant increase in soil mass movements in the Wasatch Mountains."*

194   Krinard, R. M., and R. L. Johnson. *Ten-year Results in a Cottonwood Planta-tion Spacing Study*, p. 1. Research Paper 50-106. Department of Agricul-ture, Forest Service, 1975. **S, Q**

Thinning treatments did not increase yields in two basal-area-controlled thin-ning experiments in a cottonwood plantation spacing study.

"During the first 10 years, unthinned cottonwood planted at four spacings grew from 2.8 to 3.4 cords per acre per year in trees 5.0 inches in diameter breast height and larger. Two basal area controlled thinning treatments did not in-crease yields. Initial spacings were 4 x 9, 8 x 9, 12 x 12 and 16 x 18 feet. Only trees at the widest spacing averaged an inch in diameter growth annually for the 10 years."

195   Parmeter, John R., and Fields W. Cobb, Jr. "Diseases and the Management of Young-growth Stands in California." *Proceedings of a Conference on Young-Growth Forest Managment in California*, p. 125. Berkeley; CA: Uni-versity of California, Department of Forest and Resource Management, 1967. **Q**

"The more frequent cutting which accompanies intensive management will in itself create disease problems. Scarring of residual trees during cutting, particu-larly in non-resinous species, will lead to decay and stem defects. Stumps left af-ter thinning (or final cutting) provide entrance for root disease fungi. . . . Physio-logical disturbances associated with stand opening may also lead to greater sus-ceptibility to diseases."

196   Miller, R. E., and L. V. Pienaar. *Seven-year Response of 35-year-old Douglas fir to Nitrogen Fertilizer*. Research Paper PNW-165. Department of Agricul-ture, Forest Service, 1973. **S**

In a young Douglas-fir forest in western Washington and Oregon, application of 280 and 420 pounds of nitrogen per acre over a period of 7 years resulted in increased winter breakage, primarily in smaller trees, and at least doubled the number and cubic volume of trees lost to mortality. This was probably due more to increased length and amount of foliage than to reduced wood strength accom-panying rapid growth. Whatever the reason, heavy fertilization resulted in in-creased snow breakage.

197   Pritchett, W. L., and W. H. Smith. "Fertilizing Slash Pine on Sandy Soils of the Lower Coastal Plain." *Tree Growth and Soils: Proceedings of the Third North American Forest Soils Conference*, p. 36. Corvallis, OR: Oregon State University Press, 1970. **Q**

"Not all attempts at forest fertilization in the Lower Coastal Plain have been successful. Many soils are adequately supplied with nutrients for the rate of growth expected under present management conditions and, in some cases,

---

*A. R. Croft and J. A. Adams, *Landslides and Sedimentation in the North Fork of Ogden River*, May 1949, Research Paper INT-21 (Department of Agriculture, Forest Service, 1950).

other factors may be more limiting than nutrients. For example, the principal reason that Slash pine responds so poorly to fertilizers on deep sands—even though the sands are deficient in nutrients—is probably the lack of adequate soil moisture during much of the year."

198 Pritchett, W. L., and W. H. Smith. "Fertilizing Slash Pine on Sandy Soils of the Lower Coastal Plain." *Tree Growth and Soils: Proceedings of the Third North American Forest Soils Conference*, p. 23. Corvallis, OR: Oregon State University Press, 1970. **Q**

"In several experiments, fertilizer applications, particularly nitrogen, have adversely affected Slash pine growth. Since impaired mycotrophy is suggested as a cause for reduced growth, the effects of ferti salts on fungal association should be considered in fertilizer trials."

199 Resch, Helmuth. "Considering the Physical Properties of Wood in Managing Forest Trees." *Proceedings of a Conference on Young-Growth Forest Management in California*, p. 27. Berkeley, CA: University of California, Department of Forest and Resource Management, 1967. **Q**

"Fertilization, in some instances, increases ring width and decreases latewood percent and density, but may in other cases, especially when combined with thinning, increase the growth rate without adversely affecting the wood density."

200 Graham, S. A., and F. B. Knight. *Principles of Forest Entomology*, p. 208. New York: McGraw-Hill, 1965. Reproduced with permission. **Q**

" . . .In the carefully managed forest favored nesting sites for certain birds are often incidentally eliminated, especially those that nest in the hollows or holes of tree trunks. . . . In some European forests, the provision of nesting boxes for hole-inhabiting birds is common and is said to pay a high return for the investment."

201 Trappe, James M. "Biological Control—Forest Diseases." *Proceedings of an Annual Meeting of [the] Western Forest Pest Committee*, pp. 16–19. Portland, OR: Western Forestry and Conservation Association, 1971. **S**

All Pinaceae are susceptible to *Poria*, but especially *Abies, Pseudotsuga,* and *Tsuga heterophylla; Pinus* is much less so; *Thuja* is resistant, as are all hardwoods, notably *Alnus rubra* (red alder). Two modes of combating *Poria* are noted for alder: alder's roots produce *Poria*-inhibiting phenolic compounds and long-chain fatty acids, and its nitrogen-fixing root nodules encourage the growth of bacteria and fungi that compete successfully with *Poria*. Culture of alder in mixture with Douglas-fir thus combats *Poria* spread in the above ways as well as by physical separation of susceptible roots, as *Poria* can only spread through contiguous roots, not through the soil. However, inoculum can remain virulent in rotting roots for decades even after all forest has been cleared away. Addition of resistant *Thuja* to a mix of *Alnus* and *Pseudotsuga* is an interesting possibility.

202 Graham, S. A., and F. B. Knight. *Principles of Forest Entomology*, pp. 44, 49, 50, 51, 52. New York: McGraw-Hill, 1965. Reproduced with permission. **Q, P**

"One of the most important physical factors regulating insect activity is temperature. Each species of insect has a definite range of temperatures within which it is able to live. . . .

"Both the number of generations and the time of emergence are correlated with temperature conditions. . . .

"With moisture, as well as with temperature, each species has definite requirements. . . .

"Barkbeetles are definitely limited by moisture conditions in the phloem region. . . .

"Weather influences the abundance of insects and the rate of development from year to year and from season to season in every locality." The effect may be favorable or unfavorable.

203 Graham, S. A., and F. B. Knight. *Principles of Forest Entomology*, pp. 222–230. New York: McGraw-Hill, 1965. P

Except at high elevations, where temperature is a limiting factor, moisture is the most important factor determining which sites will be attacked by bark beetles. During a drought, though, good sites are more severely affected, since the trees on those sites aren't "used" to water stress.

Some logging practices, such as full-length skidding and use of heavy tractors, may increase basal scarring, leading to increased populations of black turpentine beetles and other pests. These practices may also break the roots of remaining trees, leaving the trees more susceptible to root disease and root-feeding weevils.

204 Mitchell, R. G. "Insects in the Young Stand of Douglas-fir and Hemlock." *Proceedings of a Symposium on Management of Young Growth Douglas-Fir and Western Hemlock*, p. 50. Corvallis, OR: Oregon State University Press, 1968. Q

"[One] type of insect pest outbreak is more often caused by man than not and is often permanent. It results from moving the mean density [of pest population] curve upwards, thus increasing the risks that peak populations will reach the level of economic damage. This happens when you plant pure stands where mixed stands ought to be, when the gene pool in a plantation is very limited. It can happen when cultural techniques cause untoward losses of soil depth or fertility. It can happen when the water table is drastically changed. It can happen when you introduce a pest."

205 Mitchell, R. G. "Insects in the Young Stand of Douglas-fir and Hemlock." *Proceedings of a Symposium on Management of Young Growth Douglas-Fir and Western Hemlock*, p. 47. Corvallis, OR: Oregon State University Press, 1968. Q

"New problems undoubtedly will arise in managing young-growth timber. We have only to look at the experience in the East to see this. Many of their most important insect problems are recent in origin; they generally did not appear until intensive management became common. Pales weevil, Saratoga spittlebug, and the Nantucket pin tip moth are examples. All are serious pests now, yet 20 years ago they were little more than entomological curiosities."

206 Tubbs, Carl H. *Effect of Sugar Maple Root Exudate on Seedlings of Northern Conifer Species.* Research Note NC-213. Department of Agriculture, Forest Service, 1976. **S**

Sugar maple roots exude a substance that inhibits growth of competing vegetation.

207 Speers, Charles F. *Ips Bark Beetles in the South*, p. 6. Forest Pest Leaflet 129 (revised). Department of Agriculture, Forest Service, 1971. **P, Q**

Ips beetle populations are generally kept in partial control by predators, parasites, birds, and natural mortality.

"Fresh cuttings or damaged trees attract large numbers of beetles. The insects may then attack standing trees as well as slash."

208 *Final Environmental Statement and Renewable Resource Program—1977 to 2020*, p. 369. Department of Agriculture, Forest Service, 1976. **Q**

TABLE 66   *Logging Costs (Stump to Truck) for National Forest Timber Production by Cutting Methods and Species Type Group* [a]

Forest Species Group	Dollars per Thousand Cubic Feet				
	Single-Tree Selection	Group Selection Cutting	Shelter-wood Cutting[b]	Shelter-wood Cutting	Clearcut Seed-Tree Cutting
Spruce-fir	106.26	106.26	107.46	105.34	99.79
	19.32[c]	19.32[c]	19.53[c]	19.15[c]	18.14[c]
Hemlock-spruce	173.19	173.19	175.15	171.68	162.65
	31.49[c]	31.48[c]	31.85[c]	31.21[c]	29.57[c]
Northern hardwoods	91.43	91.43	92.46	90.63	85.86
	16.62[c]	16.62[c]	16.81[c]	16.48[c]	15.61[c]
Ponderosa pine	121.44	121.44	122.81	120.38	114.05
	22.08[c]	22.08[c]	22.83[c]	21.89[c]	20.74[c]
Douglas-fir	146.63	146.63	148.28	145.35	137.70
	26.66[c]	26.66[c]	26.96[c]	26.43[c]	25.04[c]
Oak	91.43	91.43	92.46	90.63	85.86
	16.62[c]	16.62[c]	16.81[c]	16.48[c]	15.61[c]
Southern pine	63.83	63.83	64.55	63.27	59.94
	11.61[c]	11.61[c]	11.74[c]	11.50[c]	10.90[c]
Lodgepole pine	94.45	94.45	95.52	93.63	88.70
	17.17[c]	17.17[c]	17.37[c]	17.02[c]	16.13[c]
Aspen-birch & alder	50.03	50.03	50.59	49.59	46.98
	9.10[c]	9.10[c]	9.10[c]	9.02[c]	8.54[c]

[a]FSH 2409.22, *Timber Appraisal Handbook*
[b]Modified for esthetic purposes
[c]Converted to board feet by ratio of 5.5:1 (Gordon Robinson)

209   Swanston, D. N. "Principal Mass Movement Processes Influenced by Logging, Road Building, and Fire." *Proceedings of a Symposium, Forest Land Uses and Stream Environment.* J. T. Krygier and J. D. Hall, editors. Corvallis, OR: Oregon State University, School of Forestry and Department of Fisheries and Wildlife, 1971. **Q**

"Dominant natural soil mass movement processes active on watersheds of the western United States include:

1. debris avalanches, debris flows and debris torrents;
2. slumps and earth flows;
3. deep-seated soil creep; and
4. dry creep and sliding.

"A dominant characteristic of each is steep slope occurrence, frequently in excess of the angle of stability of the soil. All but dry creep and sliding occur under high soil moisture conditions and usually develop or are accelerated during periods of abnormally high rainfall. Further, all are encouraged or accelerated by destruction of natural mechanical support on the slopes. Logging, road building, and fire play an important part in initiation and acceleration of these soil mass movements. Road building stands out at the present time as the most damaging activity, with soil failures resulting largely from slope loading, back-slope cutting, and inadequate slope drainage. Logging and fire affect stability primarily through destruction of natural mechanical support for the soils, removal of surface cover, and obstruction of main drainage channels by debris."

210   Ruth, Robert H. "Silviculture of the Coastal Sitka Spruce—Western Hemlock Type." *Proceedings, Society of American Foresters.* Denver, CO, 1964. **Q**

"The shelterwood system of harvest cutting is receiving increased attention in the spruce-hemlock type. It has the advantage of getting the new crop established before the preceding one is harvested and has the potential for preventing encroachment by relatively intolerant red alder."

211   Dyrness, C. T. "Erodibility and Erosion Potential of Forest Watershed." Reprinted with permission from *International Symposium on Forest Hydrology, Pennsylvania State University, Pennsylvania; August 29–September 10, 1965.* New York: Pergamon Press, 1967. **Q**

"That logging generally results in increased soil erosion and stream sedimentation in undeniable. However, it is important to realize it is not the tree removal itself which causes increased overland flow and surface erosion. This fact was borne out at Coweeta Lab. In one forested watershed, all vegetation was cut and left where it fell. The result was no increase in overland flow and no increase in stream sedimentation. Studies have generally indicated that the factors contributing most to increased soil erosion following logging are exposure of bare mineral soil and surface soil compaction from mechanical disturbance."

212   Stephens, F. R. *Conifer Mortality on a Mineral Seedbed.* Department of Agriculture, Forest Service, 1968. **Q, S**

"Spruce and hemlock regeneration, according to observations by myself and others, is generally good on duff and very poor on exposed mineral soil.

"Foresters tend to assume that mineral seedbeds are best from experience in other regions and other species. For the shallow-rooted Sitka spruce and western hemlock in southeast Alaska, however, mineral soil is a very poor seedbed. One major reason for this is frost heaving."

In a controlled experiment, on a mineral seedbed, 100 percent of the hemlock seedlings and 92 percent of spruce seedlings were uprooted by frost during the winter of 1967–1968. But on an organic seedbed that winter, only 7 percent of the hemlock and 20 percent of the spruce were uprooted. About 400,000 seedlings were involved in the experiment.

213 Brown, William M. III, and John R. Ritter. *Sediment Transport and Turbidity in the Eel River Basin, California.* U.S. Geological Survey Water Supply Paper 1986. U.S. Geological Survey, 1970. **Q, C**

"The Eel River has the highest recorded average annual suspended sediment yield per square mile of drainage area of any river of its size or larger in the United States."

This creates a major watershed problem.

"The combination of geology, soil types, steep slopes, and heavy precipitation produces slumps and landslides which contribute heavily to the sediment yield of the basin."

214 Klock, Glen O. "Snowmelt Temperature Influence on Infiltration and Soil Water Retention." *Journal of Soil and Water Conservation* 27, no. 1 (1972). **C, S**

It is extremely important to maintain ground cover and to practice uneven-aged management—if, indeed, any logging at all—with subalpine and alpine species and on steep terrain in snow country.

Snowmelt caused by rain falling on a snowpack and/or by chinook winds is frequently associated with floods and mudslides.

Water near snowmelt temperature has twice the viscosity of water at 25 degrees Celsius, a normal summer temperature. (Viscosity is 1.8 at 0 degrees Celsius and 0.9 at 25 degrees Celsius.)

215 Packer, P. E. and W. A. Laycock. "Watershed Management in the United States: Concepts and Principles." *Proceedings of a Symposium on Watershed Management.* Lincoln, IL: Lincoln College, 1969. **Q**

"History abounds with accounts of man's failures to recognize, control and conquer the devastating effects of floods, soil erosion and sediments from steep mountainous lands. Learned men mostly agree that the tragic downfall of highly developed civilizations was not conquest of the land by invaders nor the loss of fertile fields but rather the relentless encroachment of sediment from the mountain watersheds down the rivers into the canals and ditches."

216 Dyrness, C. T. "Erodibility and Erosion Potential of Forest Watershed." Reprinted with permission from *International Symposium on Forest*

Hydrology, Pennsylvania State University, Pennsylvania; August 29–September 10, 1965. New York: Pergamon Press, 1967. **Q**

"Type of logging has a tremendous influence on soil stability, as does the intensity of cut—whether the area has been clearcut or selectively logged."

217   *Timber Management Plan, Tongass National Forest,* p. 27. Department of Agriculture, Forest Service, 1958. **Q**

"Generally, in Southeast Alaska with the exception of valley floors, soil is thin and unstable. . . .

"Soil erosion has two serious damaging effects. First, the fertile layer of top soil, of which there is little enough already, is lost with a consequent reduction in site quality. Sometimes a severe loss of productive site occurs over substantial areas. Second, the eroded soil is carried into the streams resulting in damage to salmon spawning areas, downstream developments and navigation. With large scale logging, damage potentials are great.

"Past cutting in a number of cases has resulted in excessive and unnecessary erosion damage. . . .

"Areas where serious erosion damage is likely to occur in spite of all practical preventive measures will be excluded from timber sales."

218   Woodmansee, Robert, and George S. Innis. "Nutrient Dynamics Model of a Lodgepole Pine Forest." *North American Forest Biology Workshop Program Abstracts.* Corvallis, OR: Oregon State University and Society of American Foresters, 1972. **P, Q**

A computer-simulated model of a typical stand of lodgepole pine in the Colorado Front Range showed significant nutrient losses at the end of three cutting cycles. The researchers first created a hypothetical system that was balanced for nutrient flow over a 70-year fire/growth cycle, then simulated clearcutting.

"This balanced system was then perturbed by two different clearcutting practice simulations. One practice simulated removal of the boles of trees and the scattering of slash, which was left to decompose as litter. At the end of three cutting cycles, or 210 years, total biomass of trees was 13 percent smaller than the comparable stage in the fire-maintained system. Potassium losses from the system were 15 to 20 percent of the total nutrient capital. The other practice simulated bole removal and complete removal of slash to insure optimal seedbed conditions. This exercise of the model resulted in a 20 percent reduction in total biomass of trees and a 42 percent decrease in the potassium capital of the system."

219   Knight, Herbert. *A Preview of Florida's Timber, 1970.* Research Note SE-136. Department of Agriculture, Forest Service, 1970. **P**

In Florida, nearly 2.7 million acres classified in 1959 as commercial forestland have been reclassified as natural rangeland or unproductive forest. Inclusion of these marginal lands in the timber base has distorted the timber supply picture. (Perhaps there are many more examples of such misclassification of commercial forestland.)

220 Quarterman, Elsie and Catherine Keever. "Southern Mixed Hardwood Forest: Climax in the Southeastern Coastal Plain, U.S.A." *Ecological Monographs* 32 (1962): n. 2 **P**

Cercis canadensis (redbud) is a common leguminous shrub in old stands. *Myrica cerifera*, a nonleguminous nitrogen fixer, is also present in these stands.

221 Harrar, Ellwood, and George Harrar. *Guide to Southern Trees*, p. 113. New York: Dover Publications, 1962. **P**

Myrica cerifera (southern bayberry or wax myrtle) is a nonleguminous nitrogen fixer, and its waxy fruit is used in making bayberry candles. It is widely distributed in the South.

222 Bolsinger, Charles L. *Changes in Commercial Forest Area in Oregon and Washington 1945–1970*. Resource Bulletin PNW-46. Department of Agriculture, Forest Service, 1973. **S**

Much of the objection to wilderness classification of public land comes from people in the forest industries; they see it as a withdrawal of valuable natural resources from legitimate enterprise. However, forest proposed for wilderness is mostly in high mountains, where growing seasons are short and soils are shallow and rocky. An acre of well-stocked forest in the high mountains grows less than can be grown on a third of an acre at lower elevations. Once logged, these high mountain sites may be difficult or impossible to reforest. It was probably an error to ever class them as commercial forestland.

223 Worthington, Norman, Robert Ruth, and Elmer Matson. *Red Alder—Its Management and Utilization*, p. 6. Miscellaneous Publication 881. Department of Agriculture, Forest Service, 1962. **Q**

"Alder is useful for erosion control on steep slopes or where soil has been disturbed, especially along roadbanks. The heavy cover, including the litter layer that is created within 3 to 5 years, effectively protects the soil."

224 Grigsby, Roy C. *Exotic Trees Unsatisfactory for Forestry in Southern Arkansas and Northern Louisiana*. Research Note SO-92. Department of Agriculture, Forest Service, 1969. **S**

One hundred and forty species, mainly pine and eucalyptus, were tried in southern Arkansas and northern Louisiana. The best growth was obtained in slash, pond and Virginia pine, but none grew as large as native loblolly after 9 to 12 years. This experiment strongly supports the well-known principle of silviculture that one is safest with natural regeneration, or at least with perpetuation of indigenous species.

225 DeBano, L. F. and R. M. Rice. "Water-repellent Soils: Their Implications in Forestry." *Journal of Forestry* 71 (1973): 220–223. **S**

Water-repellent organic substances produced by both higher plants and soil microorganisms may mix among or coat soil particles and diminish or preclude the soil's capacity to absorb moisture. In chaparral, a water-repellent (hydrophobic) layer forms directly beneath the litter layer. Fire causes this layer to volatilize and move downward into the soil. After the fire, the nonwettable layer lies several centimeters below the surface. It usually dissipates within 5 to 10 years, but it can cause serious erosion before that when soil and ash above the layer become saturated and flow. Forest soils react similarly, but arid, sandy soils are most seriously affected.

Repellency is not a problem before fire because vegetation and litter slow precipitation reaching the soil, allowing the soil to gradually moisten. The wetter the repellent soil, the less marked is the repellency. Additionally, litter and vegetation serve as a mechanical barrier to erosion.

A "cool" fire is not significant in forming a hydrophobic layer, but intense fire is. Piling and burning of slash may cause a localized erosion or revegetation problem, but this may be preferable to the problem resulting from an intense broadcast burn. A sheepsfoot roller may break up a hydrophobic layer, as may a seed drill.

226 Conkle, M. Thompson. *Forest Tree Improvement in California,* p. 4. Research Note PSW-275. Department of Agriculture, Forest Service, 1972. **S**

Direct seeding presents two problems:

1. Control of stocking is difficult, and stand improvement costs for replanting or thinning may outweigh the reduced cost of seeding.
2. The quantity of seed required is great (1/2 to 1 pound per acre). As a result, seed may be spread too thin or acquired from sources outside the suitable range.

Ecological studies are scarce, and knowledge of genetic variability is weak or nonexistent for some of the most important species. Consequences of using non-local seed are unknown. Information is lacking on management of California species with regard to stocking levels, young-growth management practices, and stand improvement techniques.

227 Gordon, Donald T. *Shade Improves Survival Rate of Outplanted 2-0 Red Fir Seedlings.* Research Note PSW-210. Department of Agriculture, Forest Service, 1970. **S**

Shading significantly increased survival of 2-0 red fir seedlings in the California Sierra. The use of artificial shade was particularly worthwhile on high-elevation sites where red fir regeneration had previously been difficult.

228 Kennedy, Patrick, and David Fellin. *Insects Affecting Western White Pine Following Direct Seeding in Northern Idaho.* Research Note INT-106. Department of Agriculture, Forest Service, 1969. **P**

Despite the use of pesticides, insects were discovered to be a potentially limiting factor in the regeneration of western white pine by direct seeding. Ground beetles (*Amara erratica*) damaged and consumed seeds; species of cutworms (*Lepidoptera* and *Phalaenidae*) and grasshoppers (*Orthoptera, Acrididae,* and *Tettigoniidae*) damaged seedlings on direct-seeded clearcuts.

229 Zavitkovski, J., and David H. Dawson. *Structure and Biomass Production of 1- to 7-year-old Intensively Cultured Jack Pine Plantation in Wisconsin.*

Research Paper NC-157. Department of Agriculture, Forest Service, 1978. **P, Q**

In a study in Wisconsin, the maximum production of wood fiber in jack pine (dry weight) was achieved from trees spaced 9 inches apart and grown on a 5-year rotation.

"Spacing and rotation length effects were studied for 7 years in intensively cultured jack pine stands. Production culminated at age 5 in the densest planting and progressively later in more open spacing. Biomass production was two to several times higher than in jack pine plantations grown under traditional silvicultural systems."

230 Larse, Robert. "Prevention and Control of Erosion and Stream Sedimentation from Forest Roads." *Proceedings of a Symposium, Forest Land Uses and Stream Environment*, p. 83. J. T. Krygier and J. D. Hall, editors. Corvallis, OR: Oregon State University, School of Forestry and Department of Fisheries and Wildlife, 1971. **Q**

"The days are long past when we can build roads by traditional 'bulldozer' methods. The public, rightfully concerned with a natural or carefully manipulated forest environment, will not accept it. The public and private forest manager must resist political and economic factors that produce an imbalance between resource utilization and protection. In many situations, it may be necessary to forego harvesting forest lands until these opposing values can be brought into the proper perspective through new and different ways of doing business."

231 Knutson, Donald M., and Jay W. Toevs. "Dwarf Mistletoe Reduces Root Growth of Ponderosa Pine Seedlings." *Forest Science* 18 (1972): 323–324. **S**

Dwarf mistletoe (*Arceuthobium campylopodum*) in ponderosa pine has long been known to cause reduced growth in volume and height, fewer and shorter terminal buds, shorter needles, and a smaller crown. Indications have been that mistletoe also causes a shortage of food materials stored in roots and general root suppression. This paper describes a laboratory experiment that supports the hypothesis that mistletoe-infested trees are at a disadvantage in competing for water and nutrients and that they lack adequate storage capacity for carbohydrates.

232 Johnson, R. L., and R. C. Biesterfeldt. "Reforestation of Hardwoods." *Forest Farmer* 30 (1970): 15, 36–38. **S**

1. Native hardwood timber of high grades is being cut 50 percent faster than it is growing. This is supposedly due to undermanagement rather than overcutting.
2. The authors advocate a complete clearcut for achieving best results in regeneration. If large numbers of smaller trees are left, they will dominate the new stand and prevent desirable trees from developing. Openings should be at least 1/2 acre in size. When these methods are used, natural regeneration produces satisfactory results. (The clearcut need not be large.)

233 Miller, J. M., and F. P. Keen. *Biology and Control of the Western Pine Beetle*, pp. 164, 169. Department of Agriculture, Forest Service, 1960. **Q**

"Fungi, disease, and other pathological agents that affect trees can in many cases increase the trees' susceptibility to insect attack.

"Trees injured by lightning, fires, top-killing insects, girdling, or mechanical bark injuries, are frequently attacked by the Western Pine Beetle."

234 Mitchell, R. G. "Insects in the Young Stand of Douglas-fir and Hemlock." *Proceedings of a Symposium on Management of Young Growth Douglas-Fir and Western Hemlock*, p. 47. Corvallis, OR: Oregon State University Press, 1968. **Q**

. . . [This] expresses our situation with regard to insects in young-growth stands—we're not exactly sure where we're going, but we're getting there awfully fast. We have little experience in dealing with problems in young stands; indications are that the problems of the future will be quite different from those experienced in the past. And intensively managed stands will be particularly vexatious."

235 Smith, R. H., and R. E. Lee III. *Black Turpentine Beetle*. Forest Pest Leaflet 12. Department of Agriculture, Forest Service, 1972. **P**

The black turpentine beetle (*Dendroctonus terebrans*) affects all southern pines but is most severe in slash and loblolly. It may kill 25 percent of a stand in a single season; freshly cut stumps are usually preferred for breeding. It prefers weakened trees damaged by fire, worked for naval stores (products such as turpentine, pitch, and rosin), or infested by other beetles, but it may attack normal, healthy trees. Rarely does the beetle persist for more than a year or two, except where naval stores are harvested—there, for 3 to 5 years.

Woodpeckers are of no help in controlling the beetle, and nematodes and mites are not known to be effective. However, the feeding activities of other insects, such as the *Ips* pine borers, weevils, and termites, cause considerable mortality of larvae, probably through competition for food.

236 Smith, Clarence F., and S. E. Aldous. "The Influence of Mammals and Birds in Retarding Artificial and Natural Reseeding of Coniferous Forests in the United States." *Journal of Forestry* 45 (1947): 367. **Q**

"Many factors have been involved in the failures of reseeding operations, highly important among them being the destructive work of rodents and seed-eating birds. A total of 44 small mammal and 37 bird species have been found to eat coniferous seeds. The animals vary with the part of the country and the type of habitat involved."

237 Smith, Clarence F., and S. E. Aldous. "The Influence of Mammals and Birds in Retarding Artificial and Natural Reseeding of Coniferous Forests in the United States." *Journal of Forestry* 45 (1947): 361–369. **S**

After clearcutting, the only effective way to prevent rodents and seed-eating birds from retarding natural and artificial reseeding is to keep the openings small. Use of diseases, trapping, shooting, repellents, mulches, screens, cultural control, and predator control has met with only limited success.

238 Wikstrom, J. H, and Blair S. Hutchison. *Stratification of Forest Land for Timber Management Planning of the Western National Forests,* p. 4. Research Paper INT-108. Department of Agriculture, Forest Service, 1971. **Q**

"Former timber inventories on the six National Forests that were analyzed indicate an aggregate timber growing base of 4.1 million acres. However, this timber growing base is reduced to 3.2 million acres when careful account is taken of soil-slope conditions, land productivity, and land use. In other words, the area suitable and available for growing tree crops on these six National Forests is 22 percent less than had been previously estimated."

239 Worthington, Norman, Robert Ruth, and Elmer Matson. *Red Alder—Its Management and Utilization,* p, 1. Miscellaneous Publication 881. Department of Agriculture, Forest Service, 1962. **Q**

"Several factors have prompted an accelerating industrial demand for red alder: (1) technological advances in alder pulping, chiefly over the past 10 years, have expanded this use to the point of exceeding all other uses combined; (2) a decline in hardwood quality on the national scale, particularly in the East and South, has stimulated a growing recognition of alder as a wood possessing both high quality and value; (3) expansion of local markets on the West Coast, particularly in California, has substantially favored locally grown hardwoods in railroad shipping costs; (4) long recognized as a versatile wood in furniture manufacture, red alder has continued to meet the expanding requirements of the furniture industry; and (5) effective promotion by an association of hardwood producers and landowners, both in establishing new markets and further exploiting current manufacturing outlets, has stressed the species' desirable qualities."

240 *Final Environmental Statement and Renewable Resource Program—1977 to 2020,* p. 351. Department of Agriculture, Forest Service, 1976. **Q**

"Soil compaction during logging affects site productivity reducing soil pore [or air] space which can adversely affect tree growth. The timber required for recovery depends upon climate, soil type, and degree of compaction. In areas where soil freezing and thawing occur recovery normally takes from three to ten years; where freezing does not occur it takes longer."

241 *Final Environmental Statement and Renewable Resource Program—1977 to 2020,* p. 352. Department of Agriculture, Forest Service, 1976. **Q**

"The amount of nutrients lost after cutting varies greatly among cutting methods. Losses are not increased significantly by partial cuttings or even by such modified clearcutting as alternate strip cutting. Extensive clearcutting does accelerate loss, but only until regeneration has become established, usually one to ten years. Under shelterwood cuttings, nutrient losses should increase only slightly because the regeneration is already established before the final cut."

242 *Final Environmental Statement and Renewable Resource Program—1977 to 2020,* p. 353. Department of Agriculture, Forest Service, 1976. **Q**

"Stream water temperature is important to fisheries. Temperature rises when most or all of the trees are cut along the borders of the stream so that the water is warmed by exposure to direct sunlight. Increases of 10 to 15 degrees Fahrenheit have been reported after clearcutting."

243 *Final Environmental Statement and Renewable Resource Program—1977 to 2020*, p. 358. Department of Agriculture, Forest Service, 1976. **Q**

"To provide stable habitat there must be a proper mix of all stages of stand development within the home range of the wildlife species to be favored. This may require additional planning effort and regulation for sustained yield on smaller units of land than required for timber production alone. The optimum size opening for wildlife cannot be precisely specified, but openings of 5 to 10 acres are generally considered about right."

244 *Final Environmental Statement and Renewable Resource Program—1977 to 2020*, p. 359. Department of Agriculture, Forest Service, 1976. **Q**

"The greatest impact of logging on fisheries occurs when large amounts of organic material are added directly to streams and lakes as slash or other logging debris, or when sedimentation is increased by improper logging or road building practices. Organic debris causes oxygen deficiencies to develop, creates barriers to fish migration, and traps silt. Sedimentation of stream bottoms reduces the number and diversity of stream bottom organisms, reduces the suitability of stream bottoms for spawning areas, reduces light penetration and therefore the efficiency of site feeding fish such as bass and trout, and kills young fish by abrasive and smothering action."

245 *Final Environmental Statement and Renewable Resource Program—1977 to 2020*, p. 361. Department of Agriculture, Forest Service, 1976. **Q**

"Of all cutting methods, clearcutting creates the strongest contrast with natural appearance. Clearcuts create contrast of form, line, color and texture that are difficult to blend with natural landscape patterns. In addition, clearcuts generate the heaviest concentrations of slash and debris which gives the appearance of forest devastation and represents the most objectionable visual effect of forest harvesting."

246 *Final Environmental Statement and Renewable Resource Program—1977 to 2020*, p. 369. Department of Agriculture, Forest Service, 1976. **Q**

"Table 66 indicates the difference per thousand feet in the cost of logging between single tree selection, group selection, shelterwood, and clearcutting. It costs only $6 to $8 more per thousand cubic feet to log selectively than to clearcut. When converted to board feet, which is the more common unit of measure, the differential is seen to be less than $1 per thousand board feet, an item so small as to be negligible when one considers that purchasers bid up to $150 a thousand board feet for stumpage [standing trees], and wholesale lumber prices range in the vicinity of $300."

247 *Final Environmental Statement and Renewable Resource Program—1977 to 2020*, p. 371. Department of Agriculture, Forest Service, 1976. **Q**

"Rapidly increasing costs of fertilizer may prevent increases in forest fertilization."

248 *Final Environmental Statement and Renewable Resource Program—1977 to 2020*, p. 372. Department of Agriculture, Forest Service, 1976. **Q**

"The impacts of site preparation on soil productivity depend primarily on the amount of land surface distributed, kind of equipment used, soil type, and topography. Techniques that remove topsoil will reduce soil productivity; those that bare the surface will increase the potential for soil erosion; drainage and bedding may modify site quality and use of some types of equipment may compact the soil."

249 *Final Environmental Statement and Renewable Resource Program—1977 to 2020*, p. 372. Department of Agriculture, Forest Service, 1976. **Q**

"Impacts of site preparation on water quality depend on the potential for erosion. Intensive site preparation that bares the soil can cause short term increased runoff and erosion. Where soils erode readily losses can be severe."

250 *Final Environmental Statement and Renewable Resource Program—1977 to 2020*, p. 372. Department of Agriculture, Forest Service, 1976. **Q, C**

"Establishing or re-establishing forest cover reduces soil movement, decreases the sediment moving from the land into the streams and reduces runoff. Planting made on middle and upper coastal plain eroded sites have reduced sediment production from gullied land to insignificant amounts within two decades."
Note: It takes a long time for reforestation to stop erosion.

251 *Final Environmental Statement and Renewable Resource Program—1977 to 2020*, p. 373. Department of Agriculture, Forest Service, 1976. **Q**

"Site preparation that leaves the soil bare can increase runoff, particularly peak discharge rates. Where revegetation promptly follows site preparation, the increase in runoff and peak discharges are short term. On less productive sites, where revegetation is slow, the impacts of site preparation on timing of flow may be long term."

252 *Final Environmental Statement and Renewable Resource Program—1977 to 2020*, p. 375. Department of Agriculture, Forest Service, 1976. **Q**

"The greatest diversity of wildlife species occurs with a variety of tree species, brush, forbs, and numerous openings."

253 Anonymous. *Factors for Pacific North West Forest Products*. Seattle, WA: Institute of Forest Products, 1957. **P**

1,000 board feet log scale yields:

        1,000 board feet of lumber plus 0.5 unit chips, or

        2,300 square feet of 3/8-inch plywood plus 0.5 unit chips, or

        1 ton of paper

1 unit of chips = 20 cubic feet

        weighs 4,000 pounds when green (uncompacted)

        weighs 2,200 pounds when air dry

weighs 2,000 pounds when bone dry

produces 900 pounds of dry pulp

1,000 cubic feet of solid wood yields 14 units of chips

1 cord = a compact pile 8 feet by 4 feet by 4 feet

1 cord of round wood yields 1 unit of chips

254 Morgan, Paul D. "This Mushroom Loves Fire." This article first appeared in *Pacific Search* magazine (February 1973). **P, Q**

Rhizina undulata is a fungus posing a serious threat to young conifer seedlings planted on slash burn sites in the Pacific Northwest.

"A root parasite of conifer trees, it attacks the root tissue, eventually killing the tree. The disease problem starts with the necessary removal of slash by burning to permit planting. Paradoxically, the burning not only facilitates immediate planting, but also initiates the development of this root parasite in the soil. Once established in the soil, the fungus awaits the planting of young seedlings, which it quickly parasitizes and kills. Without a very selective diet, it attacks all varieties of conifers, including our common species—Douglas fir, Western hemlock, Grand fir, and Noble fir."

255 Aweeka, Charles. "Regeneration of State's Forests Is Endangered by Tree Disease." *Seattle Times* 1 April 1973. **P, Q**

Rhizina undulata is spreading at alarming rates in plantations and clearcut lands in the Pacific Northwest. Because of this, Paul D. Morgan, a forest pathologist, states: "The establishment and growth of our second forest is not proceeding as well as some private forestry officials have indicated, and the guaranteed flow of logs is not as secure as originally believed. In fact, I have found that in some regions of Washington the failure to obtain adequate regeneration is disturbingly common. . . . Plantations are being annihilated; on some plantations there's not a tree left."

256 Massey, C. L. and N. D. Wygant. *Biology and Control of the Engelmann Spruce Beetle in Colorado.* Department of Agriculture, Forest Service (Rocky Mountain Experiment Station), 1954. **P**

Woodpeckers are the most important predators of the Engelmann spruce beetle. In some areas, they have destroyed as much as 75 percent of the beetle population.

Three species of woodpecker are abundant where infestations of the beetle occur in Colorado: the Alpine three-toed, the Rocky Mountain hairy, and the downy. The hairy and three-toed woodpeckers work over infested trees in pairs. In one study, trees moderately worked by woodpeckers, the beetle population was reduced by nearly half, but in trees heavily worked, the beetles were almost completely destroyed.

257 Fitzgerrell, Jenny. May 9,1973. **O**

Some weeds in southern pine plantations seem to hold down insect populations. Weyerhaeuser's Norman Johnson of Hot Springs, Arkansas, observes that suppression of weeds is followed by insect problems. Research is needed.

258 Dahlsten, D. L.. and S. G. Herman. "Birds as Predators of Destructive Forest Insects." *California Agriculture* (September 1965). **P, Q**

Chickadees, grosbeaks, and woodpeckers are important predators of lodgepole needle miners, sawfly larvae, and pine beetles, respectively, in California forests.

"It is hoped that through study the more effective predators will be determined; and that means of environmental manipulation can be found to increase populations of these birds. It is also vital to avoid indiscriminate use of insecticides that may seriously hamper populations of these birds."

259 *Fireline Notebook.* Department of Agriculture, Forest Service, 1973. **S**

Fire Hazard of Fuel Types, California Region

Rate of Spread (feet per hour or chains per hour*)	Fuel Type
100	Mature timber, woodland
200	Mixed Douglas-fir and white fir with brush and reproduction, also pole stands
300	Open, patchy brush; medium timber with reproduction and brush
400	Heavy brush; medium brush on cutover or previously burned site
600	Slash on cutover land; brush with sage, bear clover, chamise
800	Grass; grass with sage

*A chain is a measure of distance commonly used by foresters. One chain equals 66 feet; there are 80 chains per mile and 10 square chains per acre.

260 Koerber, Thomas W. *Young-growth Forest Management in California.* Department of Agriculture, Forest Service (Pacific Southwest Forestry and Research Station), 1967. **S**

Plantations of young pine in California are being invaded by a variety of little-known insects, some indigenous, some imported. They damage young stands in various ways:

1. *By slowing growth.* Defoliation and sap sucking by insects and aphids reduce growth, lead to deer damage, stretch out rotation, and reduce both height and diameter growth.

2. *By deforming or causing defects in the stem.* Insects kill tops, leaders, or terminal buds, causing crooked or forked stems. Dead stubs provide an entry for heart rot. At best, such attacks will cause loss of a year's growth; at worst, entire stands may be rendered unmerchantable.
3. *By killing trees outright.* At minimum, this reduces stocking so that the site is not fully utilized and trees are open grown, reducing their quality. At times, virtually all trees in a young stand are killed. The pine reproduction weevil and our more familiar bark beetles are principal agents of destruction in young stands.

261   Keen, F. P. *Insect Enemies of Western Forests.* Miscellaneous Publication 273. Department of Agriculture, Forest Service, 1952. **Q**

"In epidemics *Dendroctonus monticolae* (pine beetle) frequently will kill all the Lodgepole trees down to a 3 inch diameter."

262   Anonymous. "Mendocino Forest May Be Contaminated." *The Press Democrat* (Santa Rosa, CA) 27 September 1975. **Q, S**

"Venison may be unfit for human consumption if the deer have eaten vegetation which was sprayed with herbicides, the Environmental Protection Center warns."

More than 1,600 acres in the Mendocino National Forest were sprayed with 2,4-D and 2,4-DP in June 1975. The phenoxy herbicides may be present in plant leaves for as long as a year after spraying; groundwater may be contaminated for years. Deformed deer have been observed after the weed and brush killers were sprayed. When sprayed vegetation is eaten by the deer, their flesh may become contaminated.

263   Library of Congress. Unpublished information, 1973. **S**

Toxin	Lethal Dose in Lab Animals	Lethal Dose in Humans
Botulinum toxin	2 parts per 100 billion (mice)	1 drop will kill 50,000 men
Dioxin	6 parts per 10 million (guinea pig)	1 drop will kill 1,200 men
VX (standard V-type nerve agent)	8 parts per 100 million	1 drop will kill 8 men
Parathion	1.7 ppm (male rat) 30 ppm (female rat)	2 drops
Sarin (standard G-type nerve agent)	24 ppm	34 drops
2,4,5-T		1 teaspoonful
Cyclamates		1 pint to 1 quart
Amitrole		1 pint
DDT		1 pint

264 Sears, Howard, and William Meehan. "Short Term Effects of 2,4-D on Aquatic Organisms in the Nakwasina River Watershed, Southeastern Alaska." *Pesticide Monitoring Journal* (September 1971). **S**

Six percent of the fish (juvenile coho salmon and Dolly Varden trout) and 26 percent of the aquatic insects in the Nakwasina River watershed died one week after spraying with 2,4-D, compared with no deaths of insects or fish in an unsprayed control stream. The watershed was sprayed to eliminate red alder. Studies were inconclusive due to pretest conditions, such as handling and storage of organisms. The tests also did not evaluate the long-term effects of 2,4-D.

265 *Forest Statistics for the United States, by State and Region.* Department of Agriculture, Forest Service 1970. **Q**

Cut and Growth of Softwood Sawtimber on Commercial Forestland in USA, in Billions of Board Feet

	1976 Cut	1976 Growth	1970 Cut	1970 Growth	1962 Cut	1962 Growth	1952 Cut	1952 Growth
All ownerships	51.7	49.2	47.7	40.3	37.7	34.7	39.2	29.5
National forest	12.0	11.1	12.7	8.6	10.6	8.1	5.8	6.9
Other public	5.1	4.7	4.2	4.0	3.2	3.4	2.3	3.0
Forest industry	19.3	11.3	16.3	10.0	12.5	8.8	15.6	7.8
Farm & miscellaneous	15.3	22.1	14.4	17.7	11.3	14.3	15.4	11.8

266 Norris, Logan A., and Richard A. Miller. *The Toxicity of 2,3,7,8-Tetrachlorodibenzo-p-dioxin (TCDD) in Guppies.* Bulletin of Environmental Contamination and Toxicology 12, no. 1. Department of Agriculture, Forest Service (Pacific Northwest Experiment Station), 1974. **Q, C**

"Exposure of guppies to 0.1, 1.0 or 10.0 ppb TCDD (dioxin) for 120 hours caused complete mortality in the next 32, 21, and 30 days respectively correlated with body length. The concentrations of TCDD used in these tests were considerably greater than expected to occur in forest streams after aerial application of 2,4,5,-T. The threshold response level for TCDD in fish has not been reported."

Note: TCDD is a contaminant of commercially produced 2,4,5-T. It is immobile and only slowly degraded in soils, not readily taken up by plants, subject to photo decomposition, and low in water solubility. It is highly toxic and teratogenic (causing developmental malformations and monstrosities) in mammals.

267 Thut, Rudolph, and Eugene Haydu (Weyerhaeuser scientists). "Effects of Forest Chemicals on Aquatic Life." *Proceedings of a Symposium, Forest Land Uses and Stream Environment.* J. T. Krygier and J. D. Hall, editors.

Corvallis, OR: Oregon State University Press, School of Forestry and Department of Fisheries and Wildlife, 1971. **Q, P**

"If we were to accept the assumptions of the National Technical Advisory Committee regarding bioassays and application factors, it becomes apparent that the 'safe' amount of pesticide which enters a stream or lake would have to be very small, indeed, in some cases. A 'safe' concentration of Endrin would be in the range of 0.001 to 0.01 ppb; of the other chlorinated hydrocarbons and Malathion in the range 0.01 to 0.1 ppb. The 'safe' concentrations of most of the formulations of 2,4-D and 2,4,5-T would be quite high (50 to 500 ppb). . . ."

"Safe" concentrations of picloram and isocotyl esters of 2,4-D and 2,4,5-T range from 500 to 5,000 parts per billion; "safe" concentrations of amitrole and amine salt formulations of 2,4-D and 2,4,5-T range from 5,000 to 50,000 parts per billion.

268 Miller, Richard A., Logan A. Norris, and Clifford L. Hawkes. *Toxicity of 2,3,7,8-Tetrachlorodibenzo-p-dioxin (TCDD) in Aquatic Organisms: Environmental Health Perspectives*. Technical Paper 3624. Corvallis, OR: Oregon Agricultural Experiment Station, 1973. **S**

Dioxin, the ubiquitous contaminant of 2,4,5-T, is lethal to guppies, young coho salmon, rainbow trout, snails, and earthworms, but apparently not to mosquito larvae.

Death upon exposure appears to be certain, the variables being only amount of exposure and size of the animal—the larger the animal and the smaller the exposure, the longer it takes for death to occur.

269 *Forest Statistics for the United States, by State and Region*. Department of Agriculture, Forest Service, 1977 **Q**

Cut and Growth of Softwood Sawtimber on Commercial Forestland in Pacific Northwest, in Billions of Board Feet

	1976 Cut	Growth	1970 Cut	Growth	1962 Cut	Growth	1952 Cut	Growth
All ownerships	15.6	7.8	15.1	7.0	12.5	6.1	12.9	5.4
National forest	3.4	1.3	3.5	1.4	3.7	1.1	2.4	1.0
Other public	3.1	1.8	2.4	1.8	1.8	1.6	1.1	1.4
Forest industry	7.6	2.8	7.8	2.1	5.8	1.9	7.7	1.7
Farm & miscellaneous	1.4	1.9	1.4	1.7	1.1	1.4	1.7	1.2

270 Josephson, H. R. (Director of Forest Economy, USDA). *"Substitution—A Problem for Wood?"* Speech given in Washington, DC, December 1969. **S**

Rising lumber and plywood prices during the second half of 1968 precipitated an accelerated search for wood substitutes. Unless supplies of wood are greatly increased during the next decade or two, the forest industries will not share in the industrial growth anticipated to meet the needs of our expanding population. Substitutes are steel framing; precast and prestressed concrete (used for bridge beams, floor-roof-wall panels, beams, slabs, joists, window frames, pilings, and poles); carpeting; aluminum and fiberboard siding; honeycomb paper panels; high-density urethane structural parts; and plastics.

Wood has been able to hold its own fairly well in competition with other building materials because of research and development of wood substitutes for other products. The Forest Service does most of this research.

271   Sartwell, Charles. *"IPS Pini" Attack Density in Ponderosa Pine Thinning Slash as Related to Felling Date in Eastern Oregon*, p. 8. Research Note PNW-131. Department of Agriculture, Forest Service, 1968. **S**

The *Ips* pine beetle attacked 86 percent of ponderosa pine thinning slash felled during 3 years near Burns, Oregon. Density of attack averaged 10.8 penetration by egg-laying adult females per square feet of bark surface and varied slightly with felling date.

Conclusion: Dense attack in slash ordinarily should be expected following precommercial thinnings in eastern Oregon.

272   *Forest Statistics for the United States, by State and Region.* Department of Agriculture, Forest Service, 1970. **Q**

Cut and Growth of Softwood Sawtimber on Commercial Forestland in Pacific Southwest, in Billions of Board Feet

	1976 Cut	1976 Growth	1970 Cut	1970 Growth	1962 Cut	1962 Growth	1952 Cut	1952 Growth
All ownerships	5.9	3.9	5.6	3.8	6.0	2.1	6.9	2.0
National forest	2.0	1.9	2.5	1.7	1.8	.8	.8	.7
Other public	.2	.09	.2	.09	.1	.06	.03	.06
Forest industry	2.5	.8	1.8	.8	2.6	.5	2.7	.4
Farm & miscellaneous	1.1	1.1	1.1	1.2	1.7	.8	3.4	.8

273   Silen, Roy R. "Lethal Surface Temperatures and Their Interpretation for Douglas-fir." *Abstracts* 21, no. 3 (1960): 404. **Q**

"Douglas fir seedling mortality is usually caused by heat injury and drought (among other factors). Surface soil temperatures over 125 degrees F may cause heat lesions on the stems of newly germinated seedlings. Regeneration is generally most successful on shaded northerly aspects. On southern exposure some shade is essential to protect newly germinated seedlings. New seedlings need light shade."

274   Isaac, Leo A. *Reproductive Habits of Douglas Fir.* Washington, DC: Charles Lathrop Pack Foundation, 1943. **Q**

"Moisture requirements [for Douglas-fir regeneration] are high but the soil must be well drained. On good seedbeds, a large number of viable seed will normally germinate, but about three-fourths of the seedlings usually die during the first year or two."

275   Dennison, William C. "Life in Tall Trees." *Scientific American* (June 1973). Copyright ©1973 by Scientific American, Inc. All rights reserved. **P, Q, S**

Trees are inhabited by a great variety of plant and animal life. "The plants that grow on tree trunks, branches, and foliage include bacteria, algae, fungi, mosses, lichens, and ferns. (In warm climates, even advanced species of plants, such as orchids, are epiphytes.) The animals that live out their lives in trees show a similar range in size and diversity: protozoans, nematodes, higher invertebrates such as arthropods and mollusks, and various vertebrates (including primates, in warm climates)."

One hundred and twenty-one different species of lichens have already been identified in treetops, and a type of succession in flora and fauna occurs as a twig grows into a branch. Old-growth forest floors are typically poor in nitrogen fixers. *Lobaria oregana,* by far the most abundant epiphyte, is a nitrogen fixer. The author calculates that this lichen contributes between 1.8 and 10.0 pounds of nitrogen per acre per year to the forest ecosystem. Atmospheric pollution is particularly damaging to epiphytic lichens in treetops. These lichens may be the *main* source of nitrogen in old-growth Douglas-fir ecosystems.

276   Bennet, William H. "Silvicultural Techniques Will Help Control Bark Beetles." *Proceedings from [the] 1971 Southern Regional Technical Conference,* pp. 289–295. New Orleans: Society of American Foresters, 1971. **Q, S**

"Site disturbances in hill country are greatest when sawtimber is removed full-length. Pines left for growing stock inadvertently are skinned by tractors and many of the largest and best are girdled and killed by cable winching. The logging machinery also causes considerable rutting and root damage, and most important, substantial loosening of topsoil which generally is followed by severe erosion."

In these cutover forests, bark beetles first are attracted to stumps, slash, and injured trees and later spread through the residual stands.

Road construction also causes severe site disturbance, enhancing beetle activity. Excellent breeding places are found in the uprooted and broken trees. Additionally, when logging roads have inadequate culvert systems, water gets trapped between roads. The most persistent beetle infestations occur in these undrained areas. Flooding resulting from reservoir construction on forestlands also aggravates the beetle problem. Expansion of development around these reservoirs aggravates a critical situation.

"Stands are under so much stress that even the nailing of signs to pines at development sites or along roadsides results in beetle attack."

277 Tackle, David. "A Preliminary Stand Classification for Lodgepole Pine in the Intermountain Region." *Journal of Forestry* 53, no. 8 (1955): 556–559. **P**

Lodgepole occurs in a variety of age classes and in both even-aged and all-aged stands.

278 Trappe and Harris. Lodgepole Pine in the Blue Mountains of Northeastern Oregon, p. 19. Research Paper 30. Department of Agriculture, Forest Service (Pacific Northwest Forest and Research Station), 1958. **Q**

"Lodgepole pine in the Blue Mountains [Eastern Oregon] exhibits the same general characteristics found in most other regions. Pure stands originate primarily after fire. Cone crops are produced almost every year, with large crops occurring at frequent intervals. Stands may vary from even-aged to all-aged, depending on their development history."

279 Powers, H. R. Jr., and C. S. Hodges, Jr. *Annosus Root Rot in Eastern Pines.* Forest Pest Leaflet 76. Department of Agriculture, Forest Service, 1970. **Q**

"The highest losses from *Fomes annosus* occur in plantations subjected to thinnings. The fact that a large proportion of the tremendous acreages planted to pines in the East and South is just reaching thinning age makes this threat especially serious.

"When residual pines or other conifers die within a few years after thinning, *annosus* is suspected. . . .

"The primary means of entrance into a healthy stand is through infection of freshly cut stumps by airborne spores. It spreads from there by root grafts. Further spread by root contact usually results in a circular infection involving 50 trees or more. Killing may occur within as little as 1 year after thinning. . . .

"Plantations were much more severely attacked than natural stands, sometimes with 30% killed within a year after thinning. Loblolly had [the] highest incidence. . . .

"Two most significant findings were very low mortality of natural stands compared with plantations, and the low level of damage in stands on land continually forested in comparison to those on former cropland. "

Note: Control by silvicultural measures includes planting pines in mixtures with hardwoods and using wide spacing.

280 Collingwood. *Knowing Your Trees.* Washington, DC: American Forestry Association, 1933. **S**

The following are characteristics of the various southern pines:

- *Pinus palustris* (longleaf pine). This is the largest and originally the most common southern pine. The longleaf grows 100 to 120 feet tall and 2 to 3 feet in diameter.
- *Pinus taeda* (loblolly pine). The loblolly is the most common southern pine today. It attains a height of 90 to 120 feet in 150 years, but few now exist taller than 100 feet. The loblolly grows faster over a longer period than

do other southern pines. Trees have attained 170 feet in height and 6 feet in diamter.

- *Pinus echinata* (shortleaf pine). This pine matures at 120 years and may reach 300 years of age. It grows on well-drained sites, in contrast with the above two species, and withstands cold better than others. Trees reach 80 to 100 feet in height and 2 to 3 feet in diameter. Trees 120 feet tall and 4 feet in diameter have been recorded.
- *Pinus caribea* (slash pine). Slash pine grows in swamps. Trees can grow 150 feet tall but average 80 to 100 feet in height and 15 inches in diameter in 50 years, 45 feet in height and 6 inches in diameter in 25 years.
- *Pinus rigida* (pitch pine). Range is from upland northern Georgia to Maine. Pitch pine is rugged and has few enemies but is not very important commercially.

281   Anderson, Henry W., and Robert L. Hobba. "Forests and Floods in the Northwestern United States." *Symposium Hannoversch-munden* (September 1959). **Q**

"1. In northwestern United States clearcutting of forests and forest fires have increased floods from watersheds for both rain-snowmelt floods and snowmelt floods.

2. Where stocking of the forest has recovered with time in a watershed, the flood peak discharges have again decreased.

3. For watersheds with geology of marine sediments and for those with volcanic rocks the forest effects on floods were the same.

4. For great storms and small storms the effects of forest cutting on floods were the same.

5. For rain-snow floods, forest effects on floods were greatest in the zone below the snowmelt line in a given storm and watershed."

282   Hallin, William E. *The Application of Unit Area Control.* Technical Bulletin 1191. Department of Agriculture, Forest Service, 1959. **S**

Logging costs per thousand board feet do not vary enough with volume per acre to justify clearcutting in preference to selective logging.

Logging Costs: Clearcutting Versus Selection Cutting

	Man-Minutes per Thousand Board Feet	Volume per Acre (thousands of board feet)
Clearcutting	133	17.3
Heavy selection cutting	118	13.0
Moderate selection cutting	113	9.2
Sanitation-salvage cutting	119	2.8

283 Ashe, W. W. "The Forests of the Future." *Southern Lumberman* (5 August 1916). Q

"The cost of operating hardwood trees below 15" dbh is out of all proportion to the value of the lumber which they will yield. The cost per [thousand board feet] of felling, bucking and mill-sawing trees between 14" and 15" is more than double that for trees 20" +. The cost of skidding is more than triple. For trees smaller than 12" the relative cost per [thousand board feet is] about 5 times as high as for trees 20" plus.

"In most operations in virgin stands, where clearcutting is practiced, the larger timber is paying in large part for the cost of operating the smaller. Much of the small timber is cut at a loss, notwithstanding that it contributes proportionately to reducing the charges per [thousand board feet] due to mill construction, transportation construction, and overhead."

284 Barrett, John W. *Regional Silviculture of the United States*, p. 454. New York: The Ronald Press, 1962. Q

"Where one 24-inch tree yielded 1,000 board feet and 175 cubic feet of slash, six 12-inch trees yielded the same amount of lumber but 400 cubic feet of slash."

285 Minore, Don. "Shade Benefits Douglas Fir in Southeastern Oregon Cutover Area." *Tree Planter's Notes* 22, no. 1 (n.d.). S, Q

Dead shade (shade from nonliving things) has long been recognized as a beneficial influence on survival of Douglas-fir seedlings on hot, dry sites, and now live shade (such as that provided by a currant bush) seems to be about as good.

"Shade as such, live or dead, was essential to Douglas fir seedling survival on this hot, dry site [an area east of Ashland, Oregon, where Douglas-fir plantations have repeatedly failed]."

286 Zak, B. "Characterization and Identification of Douglas-fir Mycorrhizae." *Proceedings of the First North American Conference on Mycorrhizae*. Miscellaneous Publication 1189 (Forest Service Separate No. FS-284). Department of Agriculture, Forest Service, 1969. Q, C

"Despite the many advances in mycotrophy of forest trees during the past 50 years, we still are unable, with few exceptions, to differentiate the types of natural ectomychorrhizae. We are unable to define and identify each mycorrhiza as a function of both a known tree species and known fungus. In fact, we are yet unable to simply recognize distinctive mycorrhizae, regardless of fungal partner identities, in the forest and nursery. To both the mycorrhiza worker and the forester, the kinds of mycorrhiza remain a confusion of colors, sizes, and shapes."

Note: In spite of the fact that trees require symbionts to grow properly, little is known about these associations. This raises questions about type conversion, clearcutting, and fertilization as well as compaction and other rough treatment of forest soils.

287 Wikstrom, J. H., and S. Blair Hutchison. *Stratification of Forest Land for Timber Management Planning on the Western National Forests*. Research Paper INT-108. Department of Agriculture, Forest Service, 1971. Q

"There is a premium on 'in-place' information for National Forest planning. Unless mapping is used, it is impossible to relate sample plot information about the timber-to-land capability, land use plans, and other pertinent characteristics that are area related."

288   Collins, Charles. "North Umpqua Case Study—An Introduction." *Proceedings of a Conference on Forest Land Uses and Stream Environment.* J. T. Krygier and J. D. Hall, editors. Corvallis, OR: Oregon State University, School of Forestry and Department of Fisheries and Wildlife, 1971. **Q**

"It is in this kind of country [with heavy annual precipitation on thin soils and sparse vegetation] that forest management often fails to cooperate with the handbook and the school solution. We have not seen many of the Weyerhaeuser or Georgia Pacific photographers taking reproduction photos for the slick paper magazines. There are logged areas where some natural reproduction seems assured. There are others where five or six attempts at seeding or replanting are enough of the latter to conclude that the 70-year cutting cycle is not realistic."

289   Resch, Helmuth. "Considering the Physical Properties of Wood in Managing Forest Trees." *Proceedings of a Conference on Young-Growth Forest Management in California.* Berkeley, CA: University of California, Department of Forest and Resource Management, 1967. **Q**

"Densely grown trees show a fast recession of the crown which in turn is related to rapid transition from juvenile to mature wood and an earlier increase in the formation of a larger proportion of latewood. Variations in the wood structure between different crown classes are being reported. Dominant Douglas fir trees tend to have lower density wood than co-dominants or intermediates at any one height level. Likewise Douglas firs grown on good sites tend to be less dense than those grown on average sites. An increase in site quality also tends to result in greater ring width and lower latewood per cent. On the other hand, site index is reported to have no significant correlation with specific gravity in California Red fir (a tolerant species)."

290   Resch, Helmuth. "Considering the Physical Properties of Wood in Managing Forest Trees." *Proceedings of a Conference on Young-Growth Forest Management in California.* Berkeley, CA: University of California, Department of Forest and Resource Management, 1967. **Q**

"A greater amount of sapwood is generally found in young-growth than in old-growth trees, and a relationship exists between the proportion of the heartwood and the diameter of the tree section."

291   Robinson, Gordon. 1968. **O**

Culmination of mean annual growth is generally regarded as technical maturity. Rotation age varies with site and with criteria. The lower the site, the longer the rotation, and the more selective the criteria, the longer the rotation. For example, cubic volume culminates before board-foot volume; total fiber, before length of fiber; total board feet, before clear board feet; total board-foot volume, before heartwood board-foot volume. I know of no thorough studies testing out these variables to determine ideal rotations for various sites and species. With the computer science at our disposal, this should be done. Until it is done, however, it is safe to say that rotations worked out on the basis of quality will be very long.

292 Mason, David T. "Ad Valorem Taxation of Forest Land in Oregon." Paper presented at Yale School of Forestry and at Oregon State College, School of Forestry, Corvallis, OR, January 16–17, 1961. Q.

"One sometimes hears it stated that sustained yield can be practiced only on very large forest units. This is untrue, for such practice is possible under suitable conditions on areas of any size down to a single forty-acre subdivision."

293 Brink, David L., and Michael M. Merriman. "Influence of Young-growth on Characteristics and Utilization of Fiber." *Proceedings of a Conference on Young-Growth Forest Management in California*. Berkeley, CA: University of California, Department of Forest and Resource Management, 1967. S

The length of fibers laid down in new growth of conifers increases with the age of the tree. Length varies from 1 millimeter at age 1 to about 4 millimeters at age 70, after which it remains constant.

294 Rice, Ray, and J. S. Krammes. "Mass-wasting Processes in Watershed Management." *Proceedings of the Symposium on Interdisciplinary Aspects of Watershed Management*, pp. 231–259. New York: American Society of Civil Engineers; 1970. Q

"Erosion by mass-wasting processes is often underestimated because some processes, such as soil creep, are unspectacular and others, landslides, occur infrequently. Actually in mountainous regions, these forms of erosion make up a large proportion of the total erosion. Mass movements are especially sensitive to disturbance by man such as roadbuilding, logging, and vegetative manipulation.

"Recently logged areas have only become unstable when the roots have begun to decay. In some areas (California) this decay takes up to 30 years. After this period, landslides can become prevalent and increasing erosion is noticeable. Also, cutting reduces the transpiration of the ecosystem thereby increasing the soil water content. The increased weight of the soil will increase the instability of the slope with regard to mass-wasting.

"Natural slopes are in long term equilibrium and changes such as logging or brush conversion will disrupt the ground water regime, changing seepage and runoff. These changes will affect the local regime of the stream bed. Increased scouring, flow, and meandering will tend to undercut toe slopes thus causing slope instability."

295 Reynolds, Richard T. Letter from Department of Fisheries and Wildlife Research, Oregon State University, Corvallis, OR, 25 May 1973. Q

"The following species require old-growth timber for nesting and forage: Goshawk, Spotted Owl, Vaux's Swift, Townsends Warbler, Pine Marten.

"Other species whose centers of abundance [most viable populations] are in mature forests in Oregon: Olive-sided Flycatcher, Blue Grouse, Northern Three-Toed Woodpecker, Black-Backed Woodpecker, Pileated Woodpecker, Williamson's Sapsucker, White-Headed Woodpecker, Varied Thrush, Gray Jay,

Clark's Nutcracker, Sharp-shinned Hawk, Pacific Salamander, Tailed Frog, Oregon Slender Salamander."

296 Reukema, Donald. Telephone conversation, 22 January 1974. **S**

Donald L. Reukema, silviculturist with the Pacific Northwest Experiment Station, Olympia Branch, said that Douglas-fir trees in thinned stands grow more in diameter and less in height than do those in unthinned stands.

After questioning, he said there is no evidence that thinning changes form factor. (Form factor means the ratio of the volume of a tree to a cylinder of tree height and basal area.) This probably means there is no research on this topic, because it is obvious that if a tree grows relatively more in breast-height diameter than in height as a result of thinning, form factor is decreased by buttressing.

If the same volume tables are used for measuring thinned and unthinned stands (form factor not considered), estimates of increased growth due to thinning may be exaggerated.

297 Paul, B. H. *U.S. Forest Products Laboratory Report No. 2094.* Department of Agriculture, Forest Service, 1957. **S**

The density of fiber, and therefore its strength, increases with the age of a tree. In most trees, the densest fiber is found near the surface and within the first 10 feet of height. Suppressed trees, however, tend to have dense fiber in the crown as well. Correlations with age are lacking.

298 Robinson, Gordon. Calculations made using information contained in *Pulp Manufacturing Information.* (Department of Agriculture, Forest Service, Madison, WI, 1972). **S**

Paper manufacturing requires from 35,000 to 100,000 gallons of water per ton of paper, or 20 to 60 gallons per pound of paper. Paper milk cartons, for example, weigh as follows:

	Flat Tops	Gable Tops
Half-pints	17 g	14 g
Quarts	39 g	32 g

Therefore, the paper in a quart milk carton weighs about 1/15 pound; manufacture of quart milk cartons requires about 1.3 to 4.0 gallons of water per carton.

299 Atkinson, William. "Economics of Young-growth Management." *Proceedings of a Conference on Young-Growth Forest Management in California.* Berkeley, CA: University of California, Department of Forest and Resource Management, 1967. **S**

Felling time and costs vary inversely with tree size:

Diameter Inside Bark at Breast Height (inches)	Felling	Limbing	Bucking and Lopping	Travel and Delay	Total	Cost (@$.371 per man-minute)
12–16	15.4	11.4	12.4	10.3	49.5	$ 18.36
17–20	7.0	10.0	8.2	10.3	35.5	13.17
21–24	5.4	8.7	6.3	10.3	30.7	11.39
25–28	4.4	6.0	4.8	10.3	25.5	9.46
29–32	3.3	6.1	3.5	10.3	23.2	8.61
33–36	3.2	5.3	3.4	10.3	22.2	8.24
37–40	3.2	4.0	2.5	10.3	20.0	7.42
41–44	3.8	3.7	2.3	10.3	20.1	7.46
45–48	3.1	3.8	2.3	10.3	19.5	7.23

Time (man-minutes per thousand board feet)

300 Atkinson, William. "Economics of Young-growth Management." *Proceedings of a Conference on Young-Growth Forest Management in California.* Berkeley, CA: University of California, Department of Forest and Resource Management, 1967. **S**

Skidding and loading time varies inversely with log diameter, thus greatly increasing the cost of handling small timber:

Average Diameter Inside Bark at Small End of Log (inches)	Skidding	Loading	Total
12	18.4	6.4	24.8
14	16.0	4.9	20.9
16	14.3	4.0	18.3
18	12.7	3.5	16.2
20	11.7	3.0	14.7
22	10.8	2.8	13.6
24	10.2	2.6	12.8
26	9.7	2.5	12.2
28	9.4	2.5	11.9
30	9.2	2.5	11.7

Time (man-minutes per thousand board feet)

301 Thomas, William A. "Accumulation and Cycling of Calcium by Dogwood Trees." *Ecological Monographs* 39, no. 2 (n.d.). **Q, P**

"Dogwood trees function as 'pumps' which keep calcium in circulation through the biologically active upper layers of soil. . . .

"Calcium is the element removed in greatest quantity when timber is logged . . . .

"Flowering dogwood (*Cornus florida*) has been acknowledged as a nutritionally beneficial understory species due to accumulation of calcium in its leaves and rapid decomposition of its litter, thus releasing calcium for use by other species."

The calcium pumping efficiency of trees, expressed as a percentage, is calculated as the amount of calcium in leaves divided by the amount in the rest of the tree, multiplied by 100. In dogwood, the figure is 71 percent, which surpasses that of other species.

302   Swank, W. T., and N. H. Miner. "Conversion of Hardwood-Covered Watersheds to White Pine Reduces Water Yield." *Water Resources Research* 4, no. 5 (1968). **S, Q**

Conversion of mature mixed hardwood forest to white pine (*Pinus strobus*) resulted in a sharp reduction of water yield. When pines were 10 years old, water yield was 3.7 inches less than before conversion.* Loss is expected to increase as pines mature due to increased interception.† Stream flow is particularly affected during the dormant season.

303   Stein, William. "Some Lessons in Artificial Regeneration from Southwestern Oregon." *Northwest Science* 29, no. 1 (1955): 10–22. **Q**

"Artificial reproduction of Douglas-fir has not been fully satisfactory by any method. On national forests, Douglas-fir plantings of several thousand acres, survival has averaged less than 50 per cent. Survival in research installations was only 16 per cent for seedlings in K-screens (two tests) and for nursery stock (one test).

304   Halls, Lowell K., and John J. Stransky. *Atlas of Southern Forest Game.* Department of Agriculture, Forest Service (Southern Forest Experiment Station), 1971. **S**

Squirrel hunting reaches its peak of popularity in the South. Both gray and fox squirrels are having a hard time. Eradication of upland hardwoods, removal of den trees, shortening of timber rotations, conversion of bottomland forests to cropland and pasture, and construction of large reservoirs restrict squirrel habitat more each year.

305   Gilliard, E. Thomas. *Living Birds of the World.* New York: American Museum of Natural History, 1958. **P**

While foresters frequently insist on the felling of all dead trees during logging operations for fire suppression, it is frequently overlooked that these very trees are required habitat for many birds who perform great service in controlling our forests' insect enemies. These birds include woodpeckers, chickadees, titmice, nuthatches, creepers, the mountain bluebird, and the violet-green swallow.

---

*Water yield is measured as stream flow but is expressed as "depth of water" over the entire watershed.

†"Helvey's (1967) interception work . . . shows an average annual interception difference of 9 inches between 60- and 10-year-old white pine stands."

306   Brown, Claire. *Wildflowers of Louisiana and Adjoining States*, pp. xxiv–xxvi. Louisiana State University Press, 1972. **P**

The conversion of many acres of old-growth and second-growth forests to even-aged stands has destroyed many rare and interesting native plants. In addition, weed killers, other pesticides, and fertilizers have taken a substantial toll. Draining of wetlands has also destroyed rare plants.

307   Robinson, Gordon. 1968. **O**

In view of all factors relating to fiber quality, such as rate of growth and age of trees, it is clear that the highest-quality fiber comes from trees more than 70 years old and from slowly grown and suppressed trees. This implies that chips for pulp should ideally come from slabs of old trees, particularly the butt logs, and from the tops of slowly grown or suppressed trees. This class of material is the product of trees grown on a long rotation, more than 70 years at least, and trees grown in partial shade, characteristic of selection forests.

308   Collins, Charles. "North Umpqua Case Study." *Proceedings of a Symposium, Forest Land Uses and Stream Environment*. J. T. Krygier and J. D. Hall, editors. Corvallis, OR: Oregon State University, School of Forestry and Department of Fisheries and Wildlife, 1971. **P, Q**

The present 70-year rotation in the Umpqua National Forest is not realistic due to lack of regeneration following five or six attempts at seeding or planting.

". . . We must resist the political pressure to cut more and more timber for housing needs, to stimulate a sagging economy or for any other reason. In fact, we had better begin to scale down annual cuts in line with what we now know about reproduction and of areas where landscape cutting will be a necessity. It will be much better to maintain a modest cut than to one day face a protracted timber scarcity so severe that we must lose most of our timber manufacturing capacity."

309   Kruse, William. *Effects of Wildfire on Elk and Deer Use of a Ponderosa Pine Forest*. Research Note RM-226. Department of Agriculture, Forest Service, 1972. **Q**

"In the Wild Bill Range Study area, wildlife preferred an area burned by wildfire to areas thinned, clearcut, or clearcut and seeded. Elk use was declining on the clearcuts. Deer use declined on all the logged areas and continues to decrease. The deer use increased on the area burned by wildfire."

310   Jensen, Frank, and Larry Finn. *Hydrologic Analysis Report of the Zena Creek Logging Study Area*. Department of Agriculture, Forest Service (Intermountain Region, Payette National Forest, Ogden, UT), 1966. **P, Q**

In the Zena Creek Logging Study Area, 10 percent of the winter range for big game has been altered by logging activity. "This could have an adverse effect on the big game population and adjoining winter ranges.

"Fishery habitat has been altered severely by timber sale activities. Zena Creek is filling with sediment, which in turn is smothering out the aquatic life and native cutthroat fishery."

311   Gebhardt, Gerald L. (plant engineer, Evans Products Co.). "Simple Conservation Measure Cut Plywood Energy Costs 50%." *Forest Industries* (March 1976): 52. **S**

A plywood mill's total energy use was averaging 60 therms (1 therm = 10^5 Btu) per thousand 3/8-inch panels in 1974 *but* was reduced to 30 therms when energy became scarce. Actual peak figures were 62.9 therms in August 1974 and 29.4 therms in September 1975. These figures may not be valid for other mills, since approximately 15 percent of the energy went into an overlay process completely separate from plywood manufacture.

312   Weibe, J. "The Correlation Between Stem Diameter/Height Ratio, Normal Form Factor and Crown Length Ratio in Norway Spruce Stands." *Forstarchiv* 48, no. 10 (1977): 200–203. **S**

Thinning of stands of Norway spruce (*Picea abies*) leads to a decrease in form factor. This was concluded from data gathered in 1959 from five stands 57 to 82 years old at different sites.

313   Morrow, R. R.   "Stem Form and Radial Growth of Red Pine After Thinning." *Northern Logger* 22, no. 10 (1974): 20–21, 44. **S**

Heavily thinned and normally thinned stands of red pine showed no change in height growth as compared with an unthinned stand. Form factor was not affected by normal thinning but was markedly reduced by heavy thinning.

314   DeBano, L. F., and R. M. Rice. "Fire in Vegetation Management: Its Effects on Soil," pp. 327–346. *Proceedings of the Symposium on Interdisciplinary Aspects of Watershed Management.* New York: American Society of Civil Engineers, 1970. **P, Q, C**

Chemical and physical properties of soils change dramatically after fire.

"Loss of organic material causes the soil structure to deteriorate, and both the water-storing and transmitting properties of the soil are reduced. The living tissues of microorganisms and plants can be damaged by fire if the temperatures are above 120 degrees F."

Oftentimes after a hot fire, a water-repellent layer forms several inches below the soil surface. In steep topography, the wettable soil layer can move down the slope, riding on the water-repellent layer. This can contribute large amounts of debris to channel bottoms. Water repellency following fire has been found to be highest under pine needle litter.

In one study, it was found that water repellency was distributed differently under four species. Under grass, the water-repellent layer occurred from the surface to a depth of about 2 centimeters. Under oak litter, the layer was located between 1 and 2 centimeters and between 2 and 3 centimeters below the surface. In chamise, the layer occurred between 1 and 2 centimeters below the surface. Under pine litter, however, the water-repellent layer was the thickest of the four species tested.

Note: Some implications can be drawn about the effect of fire on forested watersheds and about burning following type conversion and clearcut logging.

315 Youngberg, Chester, and A. G. Wollum II. "Nonleguminous Symbiotic Nitrogen Fixation." *Tree Growth and Soils: Proceedings of the Third North American Forest Soils Conference.* Corvallis, OR: Oregon State University Press, 1970. **Q**

"A number of CEANOTHUS species fix approximately 60 kg/ha/yr [of nitrogen]. Alnus rugosa fixed 84 to 160 kg/ha/yr."

316 Gray, Donald H. "Effects of Forest Clearcutting on the Stability of Natural Slopes." Ann Arbor, MI: University of Michigan, College of Engineering, 1969. **S**

It is fair to conclude from published literature that there exists a definite cause-and-effect relationship between clearcutting and mass movement of soil. Removal of forest cover affects deep-seated stability of a slope in two ways: by modifying the hydrologic regime in the soil mantle and by disrupting the mechanical reinforcement provided by the root system. The former is important only during the first year following clearcutting, before invading vegetation takes hold. The root system is far more important; gradual deterioration of tree roots leads to progressively greater slope instability.

317 Rothacher, Jack. "Regimes of Streamflow and Their Modification by Logging." *Proceedings of a Symposium, Forest Land Uses and Stream Environment,* p. 53. J. T. Krygier and J. D. Hall, editors. Corvallis, OR: Oregon State University Press, School of Forestry and Department of Fisheries and Wildlife, 1971. **P**

In one study, road construction that altered 4 percent of the drainage had little influence on peak flows, but when more than 12 percent of the drainage was covered by roads, storm flows increased significantly. When 72 percent of the drainage was logged, peak flows increased even further. Clearcut drainages produced peak flows as much as 33 percent higher in winter.*

On eastern slopes of the Pacific Northwest, the situation is different. Forest vegetation may greatly reduce flood flows under dry antecedent conditions. High-intensity summer storms on dry terrain often result in "gully-washers" that scour the streambeds.

318 Baker, F. S. *Principles of Silviculture.* New York: McGraw-Hill, 1950. **S**

Where large areas are clearcut in even-aged management, certain insects may breed in great numbers in the slash and stumps and later attack the young reproduction.

---

*D. J. Gilleran, "Rapid Calibration of Coastal Streams to Detect Effects of Road Building" (Master's thesis, Oregon State University, 1968); W. C. Harper, "Changes in Storm Hydrographs Due to Clearcut Logging" (Master's thesis, Oregon State University, 1969); F. S. Hsieh, "Storm Runoff Response from Road Building and Logging on Small Watersheds in the Oregon Coast Range" (Master's thesis, Oregon State University, 1970).

319 Baker, F. S. *Principles of Silviculture.* New York: McGraw-Hill, 1950. Reproduced with permission. **Q**

"The even-aged stand tends, like pure forests, to have certain practical advantages. The uneven-aged forests, like the mixed stand, tends to possess certain definite biological advantages. There is a very general correlation of even-aged form with pure composition and of mixed forests with an all-aged form, which tends to intensify the commercial and biological peculiarities that are involved in each case."

320 Hutchison, Keith. *Alaska's Forest Resource,* p. 12. Department of Agriculture, Forest Service (Institute of Northern Forestry, Juneau, AK). **Q**

"The stands of coastal Alaska are often described as mature or overmature, of declining quality, and suitable primarily for the manufacture of pulp. Much of this is true, but intermixed in these predominantly pulpwood stands there is presently a good supply of the finest quality Sitka spruce and Western hemlock to be found anywhere."

321 Cannon, W. A. "Studies on Roots." *Carnegie Institute Washington Yearbook (1925–1926)* 25 (1926): 317–325. **Q**

"Apparently redwoods have no root hairs. Consequently, redwood roots do not seem to function efficiently in extracting soil moisture. This fact may limit natural distribution to sites where favorable water relations result from high rainfall, humid air, moist soil, or low summer temperatures, or from various combinations of these conditions."

322 Lantz, Richard. "Influence of Water Temperature on Fish Survival, Growth and Behavior." *Proceedings of a Symposium, Forest Land Uses and Stream Environment.* J. T. Krygier and J. D. Hall, editors. Corvallis, OR: Oregon State University, School of Forestry and Department of Fisheries and Wildlife, 1971. **Q**

"Logging activities that increase water temperatures can be expected to have their greatest influence on juvenile salmonids rearing in small streams and on embryonic stages developing in streambed gravels. It is probable that effects during the time that juveniles are rearing in freshwater, in terms of lethal temperature changes, are the most significant. Temperature increases can also affect fish survival by increasing the virulence of many diseases and modifying the effects of toxic materials."

323 Lantz, Richard. "Influence of Water Temperature on Fish Survival, Growth and Behavior." *Proceedings of a Symposium, Forest Land Uses and Stream*

Environment, p. 184. J. T. Krygier and J. D. Hall, editors. Corvallis, OR: Oregon State University, School of Forestry and Department of Fisheries and Wildlife, 1971. **Q, P**

"A number of physical characteristics of fish can be modified by either high or low temperatures during the early stages of embryonic development."

These characteristics include numbers of vertebrae, fin rays, scales in the lateral line, pharyngeal teeth, and gill rakers. Temperature increases also cause supersaturation of water with nitrogen gas, which causes symptoms similar to the "bends" in man. The gas can destroy body tissues when it comes out of solution, and gas bubbles in the blood can clog the entrance to the heart. Also, oxygen dissolves less readily as water temperature rises, just when fish need more oxygen for respiration.

324 Lantz, Richard. "Fish Population Impacts—Alsea Watershed Case Study." *Proceedings of a Symposium, Forest Land Uses and Stream Environment*, pp. 246–248. J. T. Krygier and J. D. Hall, editors. Corvallis, OR: Oregon State University, School of Forestry and Department of Fisheries and Wildlife, 1971. **P**

In the Alsea watershed study in Oregon, a 175-acre watershed (Needle Branch) was completely clearcut, leaving no streamside buffer. The population of resident cutthroat trout declined significantly during the first year following logging, to 25 percent of the prelogging abundance, and declined to a lower level in 1970. Migratory cutthroat trout populations declined substantially during the first 2 years, then returned to previous levels. The coho salmon population was not significantly reduced, but there was a noticeable decline in the condition of the fish, and they began their migration to the ocean 2 months earlier than they had prior to logging.

325 Stephens, F. R. *Soil and Watershed Characteristics of Southeast Alaska and Some Western Oregon Drainages*, p. 10. Department of Agriculture, Forest Service (Alaska Region), 1966. **Q**

"Clay content influences sedimentation hazard in several ways. Because of their small size and colloidal and electrostatic properties, clay particles are the kind of sediment that would be most damaging to salmon eggs, alevins, and fry. Road cuts in soils of high clay content are more likely to fail and erode than those in soils of low clay content."

326 *The Demand and Price Situation for Forest Products, 1973–74.* Miscellaneous Publication 1292. (Figures for 1974–1980 are from Miscellaneous Publication 1442.) Department of Agriculture, Forest Service. **Q**

Softwood Lumber Production in the United States (billions of board feet)

1869	9.3	1916	28.6	1932	8.7	1948	29.0	1964	29.3
1879	13.3	1917	27.1	1933	11.9	1949	27.2	1965	29.3
1889	20.0	1918	24.1	1934	12.7	1950	31.5	1966	28.8
1899	26.2	1919	27.4	1935	16.2	1951	29.8	1967	27.3
1904	27.3	1920	24.3	1936	20.2	1952	30.2	1968	29.3
1905	24.9	1921	22.2	1937	21.6	1953	29.6	1969	28.3
1906	30.2	1922	26.6	1938	18.3	1954	29.3	1970	27.5
1907	31.0	1923	30.9	1939	21.4	1955	30.3	1971	30.0
1908	25.6	1924	29.4	1940	24.9	1956	30.7	1972	31.2
1909	33.9	1925	31.7	1941	28.0	1957	27.1	1973	31.5
1910	31.2	1926	30.5	1942	29.5	1958	27.4	1974	27.7
1911	28.9	1927	28.4	1943	26.9	1959	30.5	1975	26.7
1912	30.5	1928	28.3	1944	25.2	1960	26.7	1976	29.9
1913	30.3	1929	29.8	1945	21.1	1961	26.1	1977	31.2
1914	29.4	1930	21.3	1946	25.9	1962	26.8	1978	31.3
1915	25.4	1931	13.8	1947	27.9	1963	27.6	1979	30.4
								1980	25.3

327 Moore, Dwane. *Pesticides, Pest Control and Safety on Forest Range Lands: 1971 Proceedings, Short Course for Pesticide Applicators.* Joseph Capizzi and James M. Witt, editors. Corvallis, OR: Oregon State University, Continuing Education Publications, 1971. **P, Q**

In a chemical brush-control project in Oregon, herbicide concentration in streams was as follows:

TABLE 1   *Contamination in the Eddyville Unit* [a]

Sample Point 12			Sample Point 13	
Hours After Spraying	**2,4-D (ppb)**		**Hours After Spraying**	**2,4-D (ppb)**
0.83	33		1.33	62
1.83	13		2.3	71
2.8	13		3.3	58
54.0	9		4.3	44
115.0	0		54.0	25
			115.0	0

[a]Rate of application was 2.2–3.0 pounds per acre; 71 acres were treated.

Some of this contamination would have been avoided if live streams had not been included in the spraying project.

328 Jensen, Frank, and Larry Finn. *Hydrologic Analysis Report of the Zena Creek Logging Study Area*. Department of Agriculture, Forest Service (Intermountain Region, Payette National Forest), 1966. **P, Q**

In 1966, roads in the Zena Creek Logging Study Area of central Idaho were producing about 680 cubic yards of sediment per mile of road. This was several years after road construction. Roads in the decomposed granitic lands had "started an accelerated erosion cycle that cannot be stopped within the realm of realistic economics."

329 *Erosion Impact Evaluations, Magruder Corridor Resource Inventory Supplement*. Department of Agriculture, Forest Service (Bitterroot National Forest), 1971. **Q**

"Increased bedload sediment reduces deep water pool space important to overwinter survival of both anadromous and resident species, and reduces the food supply available to resident species. Anadromous spawners generally do not feed during the period that they are in fresh water. Increased bedload sediment also encumbers the spawning act by creating large amounts of sediment that must be removed from the redd to insure a good interchange of water.

"The increase in suspended sediment or turbidity can also delay the spawning act and cause increased mortalities. Resident salmonids are sight feeders, and an increase in suspended sediment or turbidity can alter the ecological food web to the point that growth and development are impaired."

330 Jensen, Frank, and Larry Finn. *Hydrologic Analysis Report of the Zena Creek Logging Study Area*. Department of Agriculture, Forest Service (Intermountain Region, Payette National Forest), 1966. **P**

Regeneration of clearcut areas remains a major problem in portions of the Zena Creek Logging Study Area in central Idaho. Reforestation of cut and fill slopes is practically impossible.

331 Norris, Logan. "Behavior of Chemicals in the Forest." *Pesticides, Pest Control and Safety on Forest Range Lands: 1971 Proceedings, Short Course for Pesticide Applicators*. Joseph Capizzi and James M. Witt, editors. Corvallis, OR: Oregon State University, Continuing Education Publications, 1971. **P, Q**

In eastern Oregon, two hundred and twenty acres of flat, marshy land with a high water table were treated with aerial spraying of herbicide. Some herbicide was sprayed directly on the stream.

TABLE 6   *Concentration of 2,4-D in Streams in Keeney-Clark Meadows* [a]

Hours After Spraying	2,4-D (ppb)
0.7	840
2.5	48
3.1	128
3.6	106
4.1	106
6.1	121
8.1	176
9.6	138
14.3	113
37.8	91
56.4	76
100.1	115
103.6	95
289.9	5
297.0	7

[a]Rate of application—2 lb/acre.

332   Smith, Clarence F., and S. E. Aldous. "The Influence of Mammals and Birds in Retarding Artificial and Natural Reseeding of Coniferous Forest in the United States." *Journal of Forestry* 45, no. 5 (n.d.): 361–369. **Q, C**

"Predators such as hawks, owls, and carnivorous mammals take small rodents wherever they are found, but rarely are the rodents controlled to the point where their influence on forest regeneration is completely removed. In general, the predator-prey relationship is somewhat stabilized, so that a rodent population adequate to maintain food for the predators is often times sufficient to exert serious pressure on the natural or artificial reseeding of forests."

Note: This is an indication of the severity of disturbance produced by clearcutting. The elements of the ecosystem that normally control balance are no longer effective.

333   Anderson, Walter. "Southern Forestry Investments in an Era of Environmental Concern." *Forest Products Journal* 22, no. 6 (1972). **P**

The vanishing red-cockaded woodpecker nests only in shortleaf or loblolly pines suffering from red-heart disease. Present timber-harvesting techniques have greatly diminished its nesting habitat. A major forest products firm is modifying its harvesting techniques to protect this woodpecker.

334   Evans, Lance S., and Paul R. Miller. "Ozone Damage to Ponderosa Pine: An Histological and Histochemical Appraisal." *American Journal of Botany* 59, no. 3 (1972). **Q**

"Wert conducted an aerial photographic survey of an oxidant-damaged mixed conifer forest, comprised mostly of ponderosa and Jeffrey pine (*Pinus ponderosa* Laws. and *Pinus jeffreyi* Grev. and Balf.), within the boundaries of the San

Bernardino National Forest.* On 160,950 acres an estimated 1,298,000 trees were affected by air pollutants: 82% moderately, 15% severely, and 3% dead."

335 Frischknect, Neil C., and Lorin E. Harris. "Sheep Can Control Sagebrush on Seeded Range If. . . " *Utah Science* (March 1973). **S**

A widespread practice in the Great Basin region is to eradicate sagebrush (*Artemisia tridentata*) and sow crested wheatgrass (*Agropyron desertorum*). This is a valuable practice, but continued spring cattle grazing reconverts the land back to brush. However, if sheep are placed on the range in the fall, they will hold the sage back, decrease its vigor, and minimize reproduction. Sheep only work on range that is relatively free of sage and will lose weight if the practice is tried on heavily infested range. Sheep can *control* sage if it is not too heavy, but they cannot convert sage to grass.

336 Reynolds, Hudson G. *Effect of Logging on Understory Vegetation and Deer Use in a Ponderosa Pine Forest of Arizona.* Research Note RM-80. Department of Agriculture, Forest Service, 1962. **Q**

"Selectively logged Ponderosa pine lands on the North Kaibab: Average production of understory vegetation . . . was slightly greater under residual stands [of mature forest] than under either small openings or stands of pole-sized timber. . . ."

337 Kelley, Charles D. Statement presented to Alabama Conservancy, Auburn University, Auburn, AL, February 26, 1972, quoted from a report by an unidentified state game biologist. **Q (indirect)**

"Immediate damage to all species of wildlife. Squirrel and turkey habitat lost permanently in areas planted to pines. After one to two years, deer, quail and rabbit habitat returns, then is again lost as pines mature and shade out other species of desirable plants. Long range damage affects all species of wildlife. Loss of mast restricts carrying capacity of most wildlife species. Erosion following clearcutting is detrimental to streams."

338 Wikstrom, H. H., and S. Blair Hutchison. *Stratification of Forest Timber Land for Timber Planning on the Western National Forests*, p. 1. Research Paper INT-108. Department of Agriculture, Forest Service, 1971. **Q**

"Between 1952 and 1969, total timber harvested in the West [annually] showed an increase of 35%. In this same period, timber cutting on the National Forests of the West showed a dramatic 154% increase, from 3,855 million board feet (per annum) to 9,798 million. From a significant, but somewhat secondary place in the Western Timber Supply, the National Forests have moved to a dominant role."

---

*S. L. Wert, "A System for Using Remote Sensing Techniques to Detect and Evaluate Air Pollution Effects on Forest Stands," in *Proceedings of the 6th International Symposium on Remote Sensing of Environment* (Ann Arbor, MI: University of Michigan Press, 1969), 1169–1178.

339 Wikstrom, H. H., and S. Blair Hutchison. *Stratification of Forest Timber Land for Timber Planning on the Western National Forests*. Research Paper INT-108. Department of Agriculture, Forest Service, 1971. **Q**

". . . Timber inventories and plans are not and cannot be independent entities but are subordinate aspects of a total multiple use planning process. Anything less than complete and definitive multiple use plans results in timber being cut where it shouldn't be cut and roads being built where they shouldn't be built on the one hand, and misguided reservations of timber on the other."

340 Wikstrom, H. H., and S. Blair Hutchison. *Stratification of Forest Timber Land for Timber Planning on the Western National Forests*. Research Paper INT-108. Department of Agriculture, Forest Service, 1971. **S**

Overestimation of the timber-growing land base of Western national forests is a result of inadequate productivity; slope stability; erosion potential; and ecological data. Often it has not been possible to identify areas that are not presently economically feasible to log or impossible to log with present technology. Multiple-use plans have lacked a clear sense of purpose.

341 Wikstrom, H. H., and S. Blair Hutchison. *Stratification of Forest Timber Land for Timber Planning on the Western National Forests*. Research Paper INT-108. Department of Agriculture, Forest Service, 1971. **S**

In addition to areas that cannot be normally stocked and hence do not produce the volume that might be expected from measuring height-age relationships and referring to a normal yield table, other classes of land formerly judged to be suitable for sustained-yield management were found to be submarginal. These lands were as follows:

1. Lands that are unstable but have a sustained-yield potential if harvesting technology is upgraded.
2. Lands permanently unavailable due to instability.
3. Patches and "stringers" of timber at both the arid and alpine forest fringes, which are not economically feasible to log or are too difficult to regenerate.
4. Lands on which the multiple-use mix does not call for the maximum sustainable yield of timber.

342 McKillop, William. "Future Demand and Value for Young-growth Species." *Proceedings of a Conference on Young-Growth Forest Management in California*. Berkeley, CA: University of California, Department of Forest and Resource Management, 1967. **P**

Young-growth stumpage prices are not likely to increase substantially over the next 25 to 30 years. Prices of higher-grade commodities will increase substantially, but these commodities cannot come from young growth.

There will be a great increase in the use of pulp, but the large quantities of young growth available will hold down prices. In pulp, however, quality of fiber will become an important factor. The forest manager must not be fooled into growing for quantity alone.

343 Fritz, Emanuel. "Redwood, the Extraordinary." *Timberman* 30, no. 7 (1929): 38–39, 77. **P**

Sprouts of redwood are commonly 24 to 36 inches high at the end of the first year of growth but often are taller. They may be more than 6 feet tall at 1 year of age.

344 Fritz, Emanuel. "Silviculture of Coast Redwoods." *Timber* 2, no. 10 (1958). **P**

Redwood seedlings on fully exposed soil can withstand considerable surface heat if their roots have reached an abundant permanent moisture supply. Otherwise, they die before soil surface temperatures reach 140 degrees Fahrenheit.

345 Fritz, Emanuel. "Redwood Forest Management for Utilization." *Mechanical Engineering* (1940): 859–863. **P**

Small redwood trees may be suppressed for over 400 years but still maintain a remarkable capacity to accelerate growth rates when released, if they are not injured seriously during logging or slash-burning operations.

346 Fritz, Emanuel. "Silviculture of Coast Redwoods." *Timber* 2, no. 10 (1958): 46, 53, 59, 60. **P**

New redwood seedlings require a greater supply of soil moisture for survival than do seedlings of most trees associated with redwood. Therefore, redwood generally requires shade for successful regeneration from seed.

347 Campbell, Robert. "Manipulating Biotic Factors in the Southern Forest." *The Ecology of Southern Forests.* Louisiana State University Press, 1969. **P**

A questioner reported that large numbers of quail and doves had died from eating treated pine seed on direct-seeded sites.

In rebuttal, it was stated that this was probably due to misapplication of the poison (brush-off).

348 Resch, Helmuth. "Considering the Physical Properties of Wood in Managing Forest Trees." *Proceedings of a Conference on Young-Growth Forest Management in California.* Berkeley, CA: University of California, Department of Forest and Resource Management, 1967. **Q**

"In many ways more important than age is the influence of growth conditions of a tree on the structure of its wood. For instance the specific gravity of young-growth Douglas fir was found comparable to that of old-growth trees with a growth rate of 15 rings per inch for both. . . . It is important to distinguish between young-growth grown in competition with other trees and those grown in open space."

349 Taylor, R. F. *First Records of Growth for Southeast Alaska's Young Stands.* Technical Note 1. Department of Agriculture, Forest Service, 1949; and Taylor, R. F. and R. M. Godman. "Increment and Mortality in South East Alaska's Second-Growth Stands." *Journal of Forestry* 48, no. 8 (1950): 329–341. **S**

A study of twenty-five plots of spruce-hemlock stands throughout southeastern Alaska 20 years after logging showed that on the average, actual growth was 10.8 percent less than predicted. The aggregate difference was 6.19 percent less than predicted.

350   Boe, Kenneth N. *Natural Seedlings and Sprouts after Regeneration Cuttings in Old-growth Redwood*, p. 17. Research Paper PSE-111. Department of Agriculture, Forest Service (Pacific Southwest Forestry Experiment Station), 1975. **Q**

"Three types of regeneration cuttings were investigated in old-growth redwood; small clearcutting, shelterwood, and selection. All provided satisfactory results—chiefly in redwood, but also Douglas fir and other conifers. Redwood sprouts added many potential crop trees. Of the two main seedbeds created by logging disturbance, the unburned mineral was more productive than burned mineral seedbed for all conifer species."

351   *Timber Management Plan, Tongass National Forest*, p. 20. Department of Agriculture, Forest Service, 1958. **Q**

"Several possible obstacles to natural regeneration must be carefully considered in developing logging and stand improvement plans. Major seed crops of both hemlock and spruce are erratic, occurring at intervals as long as five years. Residual brush may prevent or delay the establishment of seedlings by taking over some sites during poor seed years. Creek bottoms (best sites) often present a problem of brush competition. Excessive slash accumulations may also hinder the timely establishment of satisfactory stocking and distribution of reproduction."

352   Parmeter, J. R., and Fields W. Cobb, Jr. *Proceedings of a Conference on Young-Growth Management in California*. Berkeley, CA: University of California, Department of Forest and Resource Management, 1967. **P, C**

"While intensive management will magnify present losses and create conditions likely to lead to new kinds of losses [through diseases], it will also create new opportunities to reduce disease losses. Diseased and defective trees can be eliminated during thinnings. Pruning offers opportunity not only to improve quality of the first log, but the chance to remove diseased limbs, such as mistletoe infections, cankers, rust galls, etc."

Note: Selective logging has this same advantage, and we must not overlook the road systems developed for selective logging as access routes to dead and dying trees.

353   Harris, A. S. *Natural Reforestation on a Mile-square Clearcut in Southeast Alaska*, p. 10, Table 4. Department of Agriculture, Forest Service (Institute of Northern Forestry, Juneau, AK), 1976. **S, C**

Stocking in southern Alaska averages about 80 percent 8 years after logging in large clearcuts.

Inference: It seems reasonable, therefore, to discount yield table volumes by 20 percent to allow for understocking.

354 Roy, Douglass R. *Silvicultural Characteristics of Redwood.* Department of Agriculture, Forest Service (Pacific Southwest Forest and Range Experiment Station), 1966. Q

"Only one disease which is a potential killer [for redwood trees] is known. This is a twig and branch canker (CORYNEUM SP.) which has been observed on sprouts and plantation trees of seedling and sapling size. This canker, which girdles small stems and branches, could become damaging in plantations."

355 Roy, Douglass R. *Silvicultural Characteristics of Redwood.* Department of Agriculture, Forest Service (Pacific Southwest Experiment Station), 1966. Q

"The redwood forest is a climax type. When growing with other species redwood is always a dominant tree."

356 Tarrant, Robert, and James Trappe. "The Role of Alnus in Improving the Forest Environment." *Plant and Soil, Special Volume 1971,* pp. 335–348. The Hague: Martinus Nijhoff Publishers, 1971. Q

"Short rotations of small [red alder] trees with high total volume per acre would offer additional benefits of mechanical harvesting, short term investment and tax benefits, reduction of labor costs, and restoration to productivity of many thousands of hectares now cleared for uses such as powerline rights-of-way.

Another possibility for use of *A. rubra* to improve forest environments is creating mixed plantations of alder and other tree species. In the only *A. rubra*-Douglas-fir plantation known to exist, alder and fir at age 27 years were the same average diameter, and dominant Douglas-firs were significantly larger than those in an adjacent pure fir plantation. In addition, total wood volume in the mixed plantation was more than twice that of the pure Douglas-fir plantation."

357 Johnson, R. L. "Renewing Hardwood Stands on Bottomlands and Loess." *Silviculture and Management of Southern Hardwoods, Louisiana State University 19th Annual Forestry Symposium Proceedings,* pp.113–121. Louisiana State University, 1970. S

Natural regeneration may be the best way of renewing hardwood stands on bottomlands and loess. Before, these stands were high-graded and left alone, but this approach favors least favorable seedlings. As a result, many foresters have become wary of natural regeneration systems.

In natural stands, briars and annuals are helpful. The herbaceous cover serves as a nurse crop that prevents baking and puddling of the soil, and briars may protect trees from browsing by deer or cattle. Vines are the main problem with natural regeneration of hardwoods in this area. Other factors that favor natural regeneration over plantations include self-pruning due to dense stocking of natural stands, less susceptibility to insects and disease, better wildlife habitat, and a mixture of species, which provides more latitude in meeting unpredictable future market demands.

358 Tarrant, Robert, and James Trappe. "The Role of Alnus in Improving the Forest Environment." *Plant and Soil, Special Volume 1971,* pp. 335–348. The Hague: Martinus Nijhoff Publishers, 1971. Q

"Several possibilites for exploiting red alder in an enlightened forest management program are immediately evident. Enhancing the nitrogen capital of the forest ecosystem may be a paramount consideration under highly intensified forest management. . . .

"Alder rotations of 30 years or less would provide both the soil-improving effect and wood fiber. Wood of red alder is similar in properties to yellow-poplar or Ponderosa pine and is highly regarded for both pulp and furniture manufacture."

359	Daniel, T. W. "The Comparative Transpiration Rates of Several Western Conifers under Controlled Conditions." Ph.D. diss., University of California, Berkeley, 1942. **Q**

"Redwood seems capable of extremely high transpiration rates. Therefore, long periods of relatively low humidity, with resulting evaporational stress, could prevent redwood from maintaining its internal vapor pressure and desiccate the foliage."

360	Norris, Logan. "Behavior of Chemicals in the Forest." *Pesticides, Pest Control and Safety on Forest Range Lands: 1971 Proceedings, Short Course for Pesticide Applicators.* Joseph Capizzi and James M. Witt, editors. Corvallis, OR: Oregon State University, Continuing Education Publications, 1971. **P, Q**

In eastern Oregon, 600 acres of forestland, including live streams, were treated with aerial application of herbicide. (A live stream, as opposed to an intermittent stream, flows year round.) Concentrations of herbicide in streams were measured after spraying.

TABLE 4	*Concentration of 2,4-D in Myrtle Creek* [a]

| Sample Point 1 | | | Sample Point 2 [b] | |
Hours After Spraying	2,4-D (ppb)		Hours After Spraying	2,4-D (ppb)
1.7	132		2.0	T [trace]
3.7	61		3.9	T
4.7	85		5.0	T
6.0	10		6.2	2
7.0	26		7.2	7
8.0	75		8.2	8
9.0	59		9.2	13
13.9	51		14.1	14
26.9	3		17.0	7
37.9	9		38.0	6
78.0	8		77.8	9
80.8	1		81.0	9
1 week	T		104.8	3

[a] Rate of application—2 lb/acre.
[b] Sample point 2 is 1 mile downstream from sample point 1.

In another study, 300 acres were treated in eastern Oregon. Live streams were excluded from the treatment area.

TABLE 5   *Concentration of 2,4-D in Camp Creek*[a]

Hours After Spraying	2,4-D (ppb)
0.1	T
2.0	25
5.4	1
8.7	1
84.5	3
1 week	0

[a]Rate of application—2 lb/acre.

361   Worthington, Norman, Robert Ruth, and Elmer Matson. *Red Alder—Its Management and Utilization.* Miscellaneous Publication 881. Department of Agriculture, Forest Service, 1962. Q

"Yields of alder on average sites are normally less than those of conifers. . . . Alder increments are roughly one-half to three-fourths those of hemlock and Douglas-fir. Chief reasons for this are (1) alder has a much larger crown area per tree, hence the number of trees per acre is less; (2) alder has a shorter merchantable tree height—40 to 50 feet at 50 years, compared with 65 to 90 feet for conifers."

362   Sternitzke and Christopher. *Land Clearing in the Lower Mississippi Valley.* Department of Agriculture, Forest Service (Southern Forest Experiment Station), 1969. Q

"Between 1957 and 1967, 170,000 acres annually were removed from hardwood forest in Arkansas and Mississippi. Sweetgum-water oak stands were most heavily affected. This highly desirable type had occupied more than one-third of the cleared land. From mid-1930's to 1967, 3.7 million acres were cleared in Mississippi, Arkansas and Louisiana. Clearing is primarily to grow soybeans."

363   Pessin, L. J. "Forest Associations in the Uplands of the Lower Gulf Coastal Plain (Longleaf Pine Belt)." *Ecology* 14, no. 1 (1933). P, Q, C

The following species are found in the xerophytic deciduous forests of the longleaf pine belt:

Quercus catesbaei (turkey oak), *Quercus stelllata margaretta* (post oak), *Quercus cinerea* (blue jack oak), *Quercus virginiana* (live oak), *Pinus palustris* (longleaf pine), *pinus clausa* (sand pine), *Diospyros virginiana* (persimmon), *Clinopodium coccineum* (scarlet balm), *Crataegus panda* (haw), *Chrysobalanus oblongifolius* (gopher apple) and *Aristida purpurascens* (predominant grass).

Note: In successional stages, longleaf pine is the predominant tree species.

"Five species of legumes are always found on the sandy ridges. *Pitcheria galactoides* is particularly abundant."

Other species are *Cracca spicata* (devil's shoestring), *Cassia chamaecrista*, and *Morongia angustata*. *Eriogonum tomentosum* (not a legume) is abundant.

364 Swanston, Douglas. *Debris Avalanching in Thin Soils Derived from Bedrock.* Department of Agriculture, Forest Service (Institute of Northern Forestry, Juneau, AK), 1967. **Q**

"On slopes steeper than the internal angle of friction and in the absence of a well-developed, cohesive soil, landslides must be considered a natural erosion process. . . . They are an inevitable result of any occurrence which tends to reduce the resistance of a slope to sliding. Many of these slopes remain stable for years despite [logging]. . . . Present indications are that [delayed action following logging] is produced by tree rooting through the soil and into cracks in underlying bedrock. Destruction of this rooting system would greatly increase susceptibility of the slope to slide."

365 Swanston, Douglas. *Mass Wasting in Coastal Alaska.* Research Note PNW-83. Department of Agriculture, Forest Service (Pacific Northwest Experiment Station), 1969. **Q, P**

"Sections of almost every timbered slope [in coastal Alaska] exceed the natural angle of stability of the soil on them."

Root systems anchor the thin soil of this region to the underlying fractured bedrock or glacial till. Decay of these roots after cutting may substantially increase the potential for mass failures. A time delay of about 4 or 5 years has been observed between cutting and increased sliding. This corresponds to the time it takes for roots to begin to decay in this climate.

"Decay was apparent almost universally on samples from stumps older than 4 years. . . ."

Therefore, it is advised that no clearcutting or road building be permitted on slopes exceeding the lower limit of internal friction angle of 34 degrees.

366 U.S. Congress, House Committee on Banking and Currency. *Hearings on the Rising Cost of Housing.* 91st Cong., 1st sess., 1969. **Q**

"Significant reductions in annual inventory increases [in the South] between 1962 and 1968 emphasize the immediate need to concentrate on more timber production before annual cut exceeds growth and inventories start plunging."

367 Norris, Logan. "Degradation of Herbicides in the Forest Floor." *Tree Growth and Soils: Proceedings of the Third North American Forest Soils Conference.* Corvallis, OR: Oregon State University Press, 1970. **Q**

"Most studies of the behavior of herbicides in soil have been conducted with fairly pure chemicals applied alone. However, the growing intensity of forest management and the widespread use of pesticides indicate that multichemical residues will become more common. Nearly all pesticide residue monitoring programs now report finding several biologically active chemicals in many samples."

368 Wickman, Boyd, Richard R. Mason, and C. G. Thompson. *Major Outbreaks of the Douglas-fir Tussock Moth in Oregon and California.* General Technical Report PNW-5. Department of Agriculture, Forest Service, 1973. S, Q

This is *the* Forest Service publication on the tussock moth.

"1. Tussock moth populations can increase in a single year from relatively inconspicuous levels to numbers causing severe defoliation. Detection at low levels is difficult. [Detection seldom occurs until the second year of the outbreak when defoliation becomes noticeable.] Outbreaks can collapse naturally at the end of the second, or most commonly in the third year (declining phase). . . .

"2. . . . no significant spread of defoliation in subsequent years beyond the initial area of infestation. Local outbreaks apparently develop largely from resident populations which build up slowly over several years before entering the outbreak cycle. Although early instar larvae are easily dispersed by wind, they are not relocated in enough concentration to cause significant damage before the natural collapse of the outbreak.

"3. A nuclear polyhedrosis virus appears to be the major mortality factor causing population collapse in most tussock moth outbreaks. In natural virus epizootics, egg masses are usually contaminated by the beginning of the decline phase and disease-caused mortality occurs throughout the larval cycle. To prevent this defoliation and possible added tree mortality before population collapse, chemical control has often been applied, but always during the declining population phase. Thus, the actual effectiveness of control applied at that stage of an outbreak can be difficult to demonstrate. For example, limited comparisons in California of two chemically treated with two untreated areas showed no significant differences in total tree mortality.

"5. As much as one-third of the stand can be killed in large outbreaks, but aside from the patches of tree mortality, recovery of the other severely defoliated areas can be rapid. Two outbreaks suffering heavy tree mortality 33 and 25 years ago have shown such rapid growth in surviving trees that light, selective cuts have been made recently."

369 Swanston, Douglas. *Soil-Water Piezometry in a Southeast Alaska Landslide Area.* Research Note PNW-68. Department of Agriculture, Forest Service (Pacific Northwest Experiment Station), 1967. P

In southeastern Alaska, pore water pressures have been shown to increase toward the bottom of a slope and within drainage depressions. This means that shear strength in these areas rapidly decreases during a storm. Thus, landsliding is apt to begin in drainage depression areas and in the lower halves of steep slopes. Once a landslide has occurred in the lower portion of a slope, the resulting instability is apt to release slides farther up the slope.

370 Amman, Gene D. "Prey Consumption and Development of *Thanasimus undulatus,* a Predator of the Mountain Pine Beetle." *Environmental Entomology* 1, no. 4 (1972): 528–530. S, Q, C

Thanasimus undulatus (Coleoptera: Cleridae) larvae feed on the mountain pine beetle, *Dendroctonus ponderosae*.

"Realistically, a *T. undulatus* larva during development could be expected to consume between 18 and 43 *D. ponderosae* larvae, depending upon prey size and abundance."

Note: Use of biocides would kill the predator as well as the prey.

371 Mielke, Krebill, and Powers. *Comandra Blister Rust of Hard Pines*. Forest Pest Leaflet 62. Department of Agriculture, Forest Service, 1968. S, Q, C

Comandra blister rust is a disease common in lodgepole pine in the Rocky Mountains. It ranges from New Brunswick north to the Yukon and south to California and Alabama. The fungus has two alternate hosts, *Comandra umbellata* and *Geocaulon lividum*, both bastard toadflaxes. Control of the disease is impractical; however, timber cutting should be concentrated in heavily diseased stands.

"Maintaining large closed stands of trees and shrubs limits the potential habitat of *Comandra* and has been the best natural protection of pines in the West."

Research is directed at herbicides to eliminate *Comandra umbellata*.

Note: No *Comandra umbellata* occurs in undisturbed natural stands in the Northern Rockies, where *Comandra* blister rust is most common.*

372 Wickman, Boyd, Richard R. Mason, and C. G. Thompson. *Major Outbreaks of the Douglas-fir Tussock Moth in Oregon and California*, pp. 12–13, 16. General Technical Report PNW-5. Department of Agriculture, Forest Service, 1973. Q, P

"Outbreaks of forest defoliators can be viewed as going through three phases of population change: release, outbreak and decline. In outbreak cycles of the Douglas-fir tussock moth, all phases seem to be compressed into about 3 years. That is 1 year for release, 1 to 1 1/2 years of outbreak, and 1 1/2 to 1 year for decline. In the release phase, defoliating larval populations may multiply 5 to 10 times or more and, thus, increase from a relatively insignificant level to one of outbreak proportions in a single year. Several years of inconspicuous buildup are probably required to reach the level where quick release can occur. The second year, or the outbreak phase, is the period of most conspicuous tussock moth defoliation. This, of course, is the year when the 'blow up' is first recognized. Some outbreaks apparently collapse naturally at the end of this second year, but frequently a large number of eggs laid that fall indicated a further population increase the next year. However, the third season of the cycle inevitably spells a population decline, especially at high outbreak levels. If defoliation has been severe and egg masses are abundant, survival during the early larval instars is apt to be low. Trees may be defoliated of new needles again in the third year, but the population usually begins to collapse during the summer. Significant oviposition rarely occurs in the third year.

"Historically, there is no sound evidence to indicate that tussock moth outbreaks ever expand much beyond the boundaries of the initial infestation."

*Daubenmire and Jean B. Daubenmire, *Forest Vegetation of Eastern Washington and Northern Idaho* (Pullman, WA: Washington State University, College of Agriculture, 1968).

A nuclear polyhedrosis virus is almost totally responsible for the collapse of *epidemic* populations, but it is not detected in *endemic* populations, whose numbers are controlled by entomophagous (insect-eating) insects such as wasps.

Damaging defoliation occurs only during the moth's outbreak (second) phase. Although defoliation continues during the decline (third) phase, it is significantly associated only with trees that already have been damaged; that is, decline phase defoliation is "overkill." Most tree mortality actually occurs during the decline phase, as a result of defoliation during the outbreak phase. Bark beetle attack is associated with three-fourths of total merchantable volume mortality.

"As would be expected, the heaviest tree mortality occurs in patches coincident to the distribution of high population centers. These patches of killed trees amounted to almost half the total mortality in an outbreak area. . . . Treatment applied early enough to prevent these 'hot-spots' of tree mortality should be the primary objective in control considerations.

"Aside from the patches of tree mortality, recovery of moderately to severely defoliated stands can be rapid."

373 Speers, Charles F., and John L. Rauschenberger. Pest Leaflet 104. Department of Agriculture, Forest Service, 1971. **S**

The *pales weevil* is the most serious insect pest of reproducing pine in the eastern United States. This weevil has been considered a pest in the Northeast for the past 50 years. Since 1950, it has also become increasingly serious on cutover pine lands in the South.

374 Speers, Charles F. *Pales and Pitch-eating Weevils: Ratio and Period of Attack in the South.* Research Note SE-156. Department of Agriculture, Forest Service, 1971. **S**

Disking and burning of a Florida site in early November was followed by an immediate renewal of pales and pitch-eating weevil attraction, indicating that these measures probably increase rather than decrease the likelihood of additional weevil damage.

375 *Southwide Suppression Program for the Southern Pine Beetle.* Department of Agriculture, Forest Service, 1986. **Q**

"*Dendroctonus frontalis* (the southern pine beetle) is a native bark beetle that can destroy pines in the South. This pest is usually present in numbers too small to cause major problems. However, it periodically multiplies in vast numbers and attacks pine forests from Texas to Virginia. An outbreak began in East Texas in 1982. Since then, outbreaks have occurred in Arkansas, Louisiana, Mississippi and Alabama. In these states, the beetles have killed about 250,000 acres of southern pines which would have yielded 1.5 billion board feet of lumber."

376 Yates, Harry, and Raymond Beal. *Nantucket Pine Tip Moth.* Forest Pest Leaflet 70. Department of Agriculture, Forest Service, 1971. **S**

The Nantucket pine tip moth, an important forest pest, extends from Massachusetts into Florida and west into Texas. The moth's preference for large pine plantations poses an ever-increasing problem. In such areas, and where wild seedlings occupy open areas, the Nantucket pine tip moth may cause severe damage.

Control is often accomplished naturally, by thirty known parasites and by several predatory insects and birds. Close spacing of trees and planting under an overstory may also reduce moth populations.

377 Tarrant, Robert F., and James M. Trappe. "The Role of Alnus in Improving the Forest Environment." *Plant and Soil, Special Volume 1971,* pp. 335–348. The Hague: Martinus Nijhoff Publishers, 1971. **Q, S**

"Worldwide experience indicates that alder contributes significantly to the supply of nitrogen in the ecosystem. This contribution markedly benefits soil fertility. A definite potential exists for employing alder in forest management in much the same way that legumes are utilized in agriculture. Current research indicates also that *Alnus rubra* may play a significant role in controlling *Poria weirii,* a virulent root pathogen which causes extensive losses of commercial timber tree species in western North America and Japan."

Nitrogen-fixing bacteria were more numerous in alder-conifer forests than in pure conifer forests; transformation of nitrogen in soil organic matter was also greater. Under current practice in the Pacific Northwest, nitrogen is applied at a rate of 225 kilograms per hectare every 5 years. An alder forest adds a conservatively estimated 780 kilograms of nitrogen per acre every 5 years; this may be valued at nearly $100 per hectare per 5 years. Soil properties may also be improved, resulting in improved infiltration and better control of moisture for tree growth and dry-season water supply. Douglas-fir implanted with red alder produced larger trees with more cylindrical boles. Alder produces unusual amounts of phenolic and other organic compounds that affect soil organisms. Some of these successfully inhibit growth of root pathogens such as *Poria weirii* and *Fomes annosus.*

378 Keen, F. P. *Insect Enemies of Western Forests,* p. 16. Miscellaneous Publication 273. Department of Agriculture, Forest Service, 1938 (revised 1952). **Q**

"The insects most important to forestry are included in seven main . . . orders. . . .

- beetles (Coleoptera)
- butterflies and moths (Lepidoptera)
- wasps (Hymenoptera)
- flies (Diptera)
- scales and aphids (Homoptera)
- bugs (Hemiptera)
- and termites (Isoptera).

"The mites, belonging to the class Arachnida, are sometimes injurious to trees. The spiders, belonging to the same class, are predaceous and usually beneficial. Millipedes and centipedes, belonging to the classes Chilopoda and Diplopoda, are occasionally of importance in the forest."

379 *Southern Pine Beetle.* Forest Pest Leaflet 49. Department of Agriculture, Forest Service, 1971. **P, Q**

The following measures are recommended for control of the southern pine beetle (*Dendroctonus frontalis*):

"Logging should be planned to minimize damage to the site and to the remaining timber. Thinnings or other partial cuttings should be scheduled at intervals long enough to allow the stands to recover. Logging machinery should be operated carefully; heavy equipment is prone to compact the soil or crush tree roots, especially when the soil is wet. Roads and trails should be planned and built in ways that avoid causing erosion, floodings, or changes in the water table. Trees that are bruised or skinned by heavy equipment should be salvaged."

380 Schmid, J. M. "A Problem in the Front Range: Pine Beetles." *Colorado Outdoors* 21, no. 6 (1972): 37–39. Q

"Regulation of stand density may be a more promising method for long term stability of beetle populations. Research has indicated that stands become more susceptible to beetle outbreaks when the trees attain a certain size and density. . . . By periodically cutting some trees in the stand [thinning], we can lower the number of trees per acre and reduce susceptibility. In essence, this is what the beetles do when they infest areas but their habit of removing the trees in groups is not what we usually desire. . . .

"It is necessary to remove some large trees as well as smaller ones."

381 Schwab, J. W., "Mass Wasting: October–November 1978 Storm, Rennell Sound, Queen Charlotte Islands, British Columbia." Ministry of Forest Research Note 91. Province of British Columbia, 1983. S

The rate of soil transfer during a heavy, but not unusual, storm was forty-one times as great on clearcut land as on undisturbed old-growth forest and forty-six times as great where road failures occurred.

382 Steyermark, Julian A. *Vegetational History of the Ozark Forest*. University of Missouri Studies, vol. 31. Columbia, MO, 1959. S

Critical studies of accounts by early settlers, paleobotanists, and geologists and of records by U.S. government surveyors show that the forests of the Ozark and Ouachita mountains were of five types:

1. Sugar maple–bitternut hickory association, the final stage of a hydrarch development from a flood plain associated with the maturity of a stream.
2. Sugar maple–white oak association, the final stage of a zerarch development arising from a calcareous prairie limestone glade or limestone bluff.
3. Oak-hickory association, on the drier and more acid of the ridge tops and upper slopes, starting from acid rock exposures or acid prairie areas.
4. Oak-pine association occupying the less acid ridge tops.
5. White oak–red maple association, developing always where the soil is acid in draws or ravines, heads of tributaries of streams, and upper slopes of hills and ravines.

383 Cunningham, James B., Russell P. Balda, and William S. Gaud. *Selection and Use of Snags by Secondary Cavity-Nesting Birds of the Ponderosa Pine Forest*. Research Paper RM-222. Department of Agriculture, Forest Service, 1980. **P, Q**

The authors conducted exceedingly detailed studies of habitat requirements of secondary nesting birds. The studies took place over many years in eight areas of undisturbed pine forest in the Southwest.

"The results of this investigation indicate that snags are important as nest and roost sites; provide a large number of bird species with hawking, singing and drumming, or perching posts; and provide a feeding substrate for many species. The following guide to the characteristics of desirable snags is proposed:

1. Diameter of snags should be greater than 13 inches.
2. Total height of snags should be greater than 10 feet.
3. Percent bark cover should be greater than 40%.
4. Snags which have broken tops should be saved if they also fit the above criteria.
5. Ponderosa pine snags in the most frequently used age range of 5–29 years should be saved.
6. In areas where the available snags are below the size range stated above, the largest snags should be saved.
7. Snags with existing cavities should be given preference.
8. In areas where oaks are found and oak removal is to occur, those oaks with a diameter of 10 inches and greater should be saved as suitable nest sites.
9. Secondary cavity nesters such as the white-breasted nuthatch utilize the dead strips from lightning strikes. Since such trees are usually poor quality timber trees, they should be saved for immediate use by the birds and as a means of producing future snags.
10. Hard snags could be removed in preference to soft snags, if necessary, but, if possible, hard snags should be saved as territory and perching posts.
11. Those live ponderosa pines with dead tops should be left for nest and roost sites and for future snag replacement.
12. The density of snags should be 6.5 snags per ha [2 1/2 snags per acre] to maintain secondary cavity nesters at natural levels."

384 Maclean, Colin D., and Charles L. Bolsinger. *Estimating Productivity on Sites with a Low Stocking Capacity*. Research Paper PNW-152. Department of Agriculture, Forest Service, 1973. **Q, C**

"In most areas, normal yield tables are the only tools available for estimating timber productivity and establishing stocking standards. However, the stocking capacity of naturally sparse stands in the arid West is often lower than was found in the stands sampled by the makers of normal yield tables. . . .

"About half of the commercial forest land . . . in eastern Oregon and northern California appears unable to support normal yield table stocking levels."

Note: Disregard of this factor has undoubtedly led to serious overestimates of the sustained-yield capacity of many national forests.

One Way to Check Sustained Yield or Allowable Cut

Note Table A1 below. The Forest Service lists commercial forestland under three categories. The allowable cut is based on the *standard component*. *Special* lands include roadside strips, campgrounds, administrative sites, and so forth, lands generally not subject to even-aged management. *Marginal* lands may or may not be logged, depending on market conditions or acceptance of heroic logging methods. Marginal lands usually are composed of forest stocked with low-valued species, land having a very low capacity to grow timber, or land that is steep or unstable. Bear in mind that commercial *timber* consists of trees that can be profitably logged, but commercial *forestland* is land capable of returning a profit on investment in forestry comparable to other investment opportunities of equal risk. There is much commercial timber on noncommercial forestland. Logging such timber is timber mining and cannot be considered sustained-yield forestry.

Next, note Table A2. This table illustrates the current practice of classifying commercial forestland. Standard, special, and marginal lands are lumped together and called "available productive forestland." If the allowable cut is based on the standard component (now called some variation of "full timber production") but the forest plan provides statistics for the undifferentiated "available productive forestland," a grossly excessive allowable cut may appear to be reasonable or even conservative.

See Table A3, "Six Rivers National Forest—Standard Component, Commercial Forestland Silvicultural Classification." This table represents the land on which the allowable cut of that national forest is calculated. Obtain a table of this kind for any forest for which you are reviewing a plan. Then, simply divide the total amount of timber by the allowable cut to see whether there is enough timber in the forest to last out the rotation. Adjustments should be made for growth on the even-aged stands below rotation age, as explained in Chapter 7.

TABLE A1   *National Forest System Inventory and Management Summary, Based on Data Compiled for 1979 Assessment, as of January 1, 1977*

	Area (millions of acres)	Total Volume (billions of board feet)[a]	Total Potential Yield (billions of board feet)[b]	Pro- grammed Harvest, FY 77 (billions of board feet)[c]	Potential Productive Capacity (billions of board feet)[d]
Total national forest land	187.6	1,569	20.1	10.8	37.1
Productive deferred	4.5	64	0.9	—	1.7
Productive reserved	8.9	125	1.8	—	3.2
Commercial forestland					
Standard	50.8	711	12.4	9.4	18.4
Special	12.3	172	1.1	0.5	4.5
Marginal	19.2	269	2.7	0.4	6.9
Subtotal					
Regulated	82.3	1,152	16.2	10.3	29.8
Unregulated	6.7	94	1.2	0.5	2.4
Total commercial forestland	89.0	1,246	17.4	10.8	32.2
Other forest (nonproductive)	38.5	134[e]			
Annual net forest growth on commercial forestland			15.7		
Forest mortality on commercial forestland			5.1		

[a]Includes "growing stock," "salvable dead," "rough and rotten."
[b]From 1977 Potential Yield File Plus Yields attributed to reserved, deferred, and unregulated.
[c]From 1977 Programmed Harvest File.
[d]From Table 4, 1979 Assessment—Forest Survey Site Productivity Based on Culmination of Mean Annual Increment of Fully Stocked Stands.
[e]Based on 25 percent of commercial forestland (volume per acre). This is thought to be a conservative estimate. These lands have not been inventoried in the past but will be in the future. This estimate will be refined as new information becomes available.
SOURCE: *Forest Service Manual* (Department of Agriculture, Forest Service, 1980).

TABLE A2   *Region "Y" Inventory and Management Summary, Based on Data from 1979 Assessment*

	Area (thousands of acres)	Total Volume (millions of board feet)[a]	Full Potential Yield, Annual Basis (millions of board feet)[b]	1977 Annual Program (millions of board feet)	Productive Capacity, Annual Basis (millions of board feet)[c]
Total national forest land	20,000	102,480	1,579	410	2,987
Productive deferred	900	6,660	96	—	211
Productive reserved	800	5,920	86	—	188
Commercial forestland					
Standard[d]	4,200	32,600	620	340	987
Special[d]	900	6,520	90	50	211
Marginal[d]	2,900	22,820	420	10	682
Unregulated	2,500	19,560	267	10	588
Total	10,500	81,500	1,397	410	2,486
Noncommercial forestland	2,400	8,400	—	—	120
Growth (annual)	—	1,150	—	—	—
Mortality (annual)	—	380	—	—	—

[a]Total volume and potential yield include products converted to thousands of board feet.
[b]Determine yield contribution as if land were not deferred, reserved, or unregulated. Use techniques developed for RARE II to determine these volumes.
[c]From Table 4, 1979 Assessment—Forest Survey Site Productivity, based on culmination of mean annual increment of fully stocked stands.
[d]Included in available productive forestland (new terminology).
Note: Yields may be substantially higher under intensive management.
SOURCE: *Forest Service Manual* (Department of Agriculture, Forest Service, 1980).

TABLE A3   Six Rivers National Forest—Standard Component, Commercial Forestland Silvicultural Classification[a]

Silvicultural Class	Stand Age (years)	Area (acres)	Total Net Volume (thousands of board feet, Scribner rule)	Total Net Volume/Acre (board feet, Scribner rule)	Net Volume/Acre (board feet, Scribner rule)	
					Over Rotation Age	Under Rotation Age
I. Old growth/no understory		235,036	9,185,426	32,366[b]	32,366[b]	10,322[b]
II. Two-storied stands		96,610	2,266,084	25,456	13,134	—
III. Even-aged stands	180	1,708	84,570	49,514	49,514	—
	170	3,027	68,080	22,491	22,491	—
	160	—				—
	150	4,553	270,457	59,402	59,402	—
	140	1,708	88,534	51,835	—	51,835
	130	3,307	48,388	14,632	—	14,632
	120	—				—
	110	1,836	33,817	18,419	—	18,419
	100	3,155	182,050	57,702	—	57,702
	90	1,836	56,262	30,644	—	30,644
	80	9,302	317,691	34,153	—	34,153
	70	9,608	110,598	11,511	—	11,511
	60	10,130	156,681	15,467	—	15,467
	50	6,285	82,173	13,162	—	13,162
	40	—				—
	30	9,711	18,160	1,870	—	1,870
	20	10,164	15,297	1,505	—	1,505
	10	31,021	—			—
IV. Nonstocked	0	16,252	—			—
Total		455,249	12,984,268			

[a]Softwood and hardwood volume for trees, 11 or more inches d.b.h. to a utilized top.
[b]As adjusted by plot analysis.

SOURCE: Timber Management Plan, Six Rivers National Forest (Department of Agriculture, Forest Service, 1969).

A Forest Policy for Conservationists

- Withdraw as much as possible of the remaining old-growth forest to be preserved forever in its natural condition. There is no possibility of going too far with this, because so little virgin forest remains.

- Withdraw from logging all lands with unstable soils and all marginally productive lands, to be managed exclusively for recreation, scientific observation, watershed, and wildlife.

- Require that multiple-use forestry be practiced on publicly owned commercial forestland. This consists of managing the forest within the following guidelines:

  —Practice sustained yield.
  —Allow trees to mature before being cut.
  —Use some system of uneven-aged management.
  —Keep openings created by logging no larger than is necessary to meet the biological requirements of the species in that forest.
  —Maintain the habitats of all native species of plants and animals that naturally occur in the area. Possibly identify one acre out of every ten to remain forever wild, and certainly identify two or three trees per acre to live out their natural life cycles and to remain in place when dead.
  —Take extreme precautions to protect the soil.

- Require sustained-yield management of privately owned commercial forestland. This can be done by:

  —Licensing foresters.
  —Forbidding logging except under the supervision of one so licensed.
  —Requiring that a professionally developed sustained-yield plan be filed with the government and passed along with the property title.
  —Removing forestland from property taxes, but adopting a yield tax, the proceeds to be made available to the landowner for approved forest management purposes.

Glossary

Actual cut The amount of timber cut and removed from a forest during a particular period of time, in contrast with the amount planned for cutting or scheduled to be offered for sale but not actually cut or sold.

Allowable cut The amount of timber authorized to be sold from an administrative area during a specific period of time following an orderly and systematic plan, in order to achieve a sustained yield. It may be more or less than the estimated potential sustained yield.

Biosphere That part of the world in which life can exist, including the sea, the soil, and the lower atmosphere.

Biota The entire gamut of living things in a region—fauna and flora.

Commercial forestland Land capable of growing timber profitably. *Commercial timber* frequently occurs on noncommercial forestland.

Commercial timber Trees of sufficient value to be profitably logged and used in commerce.

Even-aged management Management in which trees in a given stand, covering an extensive area, are maintained at about the same age and size and are logged all at once so that a new stand may grow. Forest inventory is maintained by mapping techniques. The three basic even-aged methods are:

> *Clearcutting* The removal of an entire stand of trees in blocks, generally of 20 acres or more, followed by natural regeneration, artificial seeding, or planting of seedlings.

> *Shelterwood* The removal of marketable trees in a series of cuts to allow regeneration of a new stand under the partial shade of older trees, which are later removed. This may be accomplished in several stages, but the entire stand is removed in a fraction of the rotation, generally within 10 years.

> *Seed tree* The removal of nearly all marketable trees in one cut, except for a small number of desirable seed bearers to provide for natural regeneration.

236

Even-flow sustained yield This concept is not clearly defined. The term appears in forestry literature to distinguish between *sustained yield*, as defined herein, and management practices that provide for the mere continuous production of forest trees, in which the quantity and quality of wood decline from that of the original forest (as in tree farming).

Excellent forestry A term I composed to mean *multiple-use forestry* as I have described it, in contrast with multiple use perverted to mean its very opposite—the zoning of wild land into its various categories and the management of each for its highest and best economic use (i.e., grassland for grazing, lakes and rivers for fish and recreation, timberland for wood production, etc.). I have occasionally used the term interchangeably with multiple use to imply timber management modified sufficiently to accommodate the other uses on the same land at the same time.

Extractives Substances removed from wood chips in the process of making pulp; the components of wood other than cellulose that are removed in pulping.

Flexible cutting methods Liberty on the part of the forester to mark trees for removal individually, in small groups, or in patches, according to the forester's knowledge and judgment.

Monoculture Cultivation of a single species of trees to the exclusion of other uses of the land. It is often taken to imply cultivation of trees of the same age as well, although this is not the technical meaning of the term.

Multiple-use forestry Timber management modified to accommodate the other uses of the forest on the same land at the same time. This requires practicing sustained yield, allowing trees to mature before cutting them, keeping the logging areas as small as possible without inhibiting satisfactory growth of shade-intolerant species, maintaining the habitat for all the native species, and taking extreme precautions to protect the soil.

Only about half of the national forest property is classed as commercial forestland, and only half of that, or about 50 million acres, is suitable for sustained timber production. The national forests contain desert, grazing land, water, brush, and chaparral as well as forest. Obviously, those lands are not managed for timber production, so multiple use does not mean using all of the land for all of the uses described in the law. But it does mean management of the commercial timberland for the other uses as well as for timber.

Programmed sale quantity The amount of timber authorized for sale during a specific period of time from an administrative area. Programmed sale quantity differs from *allowable cut* in that it may be more or less than the amount available under a policy of *sustained yield* and includes timber that has nothing to do with sustained yield, as in the removal of commercial timber from noncommercial forestland.

Range Uncultivated land that supports herbaceous or shrubby vegetation. It includes vegetation, soil, associated atmosphere, water, animal life, and frequently a tree overstory.

Redd Fish eggs.

Rotation The age at which the mature timber produced by a forest property is harvested, plus the time required to achieve regeneration.

Sawlog A log of sufficient size and quality to be suitable for lumber manufacturing.

Second growth Trees that have grown up naturally following a drastic interference such as logging, fire, or insect epidemic.

Selection management or **selection system of silviculture** The annual or periodic removal of trees individually or in small groups.

Silvics The study of the life history and characteristics of forest trees, with particular reference to environmental influences.

Silviculture The establishment phase of forestry: the development, reproduction, and care of forest trees.

Standard component That part of a commercial forest that is suitable and available for the continuous production of forest products; the resource on which the sustained yield and allowable cut are calculated.

Stumpage The value of timber standing uncut, expressed in terms of an amount per cubic unit.

Sustained yield The amount of timber that may be removed from an administrative unit under a policy of sustained-yield management.

Sustained-yield management Management that involves limiting the quantity of timber removed from each administrative unit of forest to that quantity that can be removed annually in perpetuity; under sustained-yield management the quantity may increase and the quality may improve, but neither will ever decline.

Uneven-aged management Management in which trees in a given stand are maintained at all ages and all sizes to permit continuous natural regeneration. Trees may be removed singly or in groups. Inasmuch as most commercially desirable species are shade intolerant, groups must be large enough to admit overhead light for young trees.

Working circle An administrative area under a single timber management plan. In the national forests it formerly represented a ranger district, about 250,000 acres. Today it generally comprises an entire national forest and sometimes more, often exceeding 1,000,000 acres.

Young growth Young trees.

Subject Index
to Supporting Research
and Informed Opinions

(References are to entry numbers, not page numbers.)

Author Index
to Supporting Research
and Informed Opinions

(References are to entry numbers, not page numbers.)

Index

Also Available from Island Press

Land and Resource Planning in the National Forests
By Charles F. Wilkinson and H. Michael Anderson
Foreword by Arnold W. Bolle

This comprehensive, in-depth review and analysis of planning, policy, and law in the National Forest System is the standard reference source on the National Forest Management Act of 1976 (NFMA). This clearly written, nontechnical book offers an insightful analysis of the Fifty Year Plans and how to participate in and influence them.

1987. xii, 396 pp., index.
Paper, ISBN 0-933280-38-6. **$19.95**

Reforming the Forest Service
By Randal O'Toole

Reforming the Forest Service contributes a completely new view to the current debate on the management of our national forests. O'Toole argues that poor management is an institutional problem; he shows that economic inefficiencies and environmental degradation are the inevitable result of the well-intentioned but poorly designed laws that govern the Forest Service. This book proposes sweeping reforms in the structure of the agency and new budgetary incentives as the best way to improve management.

1988. xii, 256 pp., graphs, tables, notes.
Cloth, ISBN 0-933280-49-1. **$16.95**
Paper, ISBN 0-933280-45-9. **$24.95**

Last Stand of the Red Spruce
By Robert A. Mello
Published in cooperation with Natural Resources Defense Council

Acid rain—the debates rage between those who believe that the cause of the problem is clear and identifiable and those who believe that the evidence is inconclusive. In *Last Stand of the Red Spruce,* Robert A. Mello has written an ecological detective story that unravels this confusion and explains how air pollution is killing our nation's forests. Writing for a lay audience, the author traces the efforts of scientists trying to solve the mystery of the dying red spruce trees on Camels Hump in Vermont. Mello clearly and succinctly presents both sides of an issue on which even the scientific community is split and concludes that the scientific evidence uncovered on Camels Hump elevates the issues of air pollution and acid rain to new levels of national significance.

1987. xx, 156 pp., illus., references, bibliography.
Paper, ISBN 0-933280-37-8. $14.95

Weatern Water Made Simple, by the editors of **High Country News**
Edited by Ed Marston

Winner of the 1986 George Polk Award for environmental reporting, these four special issues of *High Country News* are here available for the first time in book form. Much has been written about the water crisis in the West, yet the issue remains confusing and difficult to understand. *Western Water Made Simple,* by the editors of *High Country News,* lays out in clear language the complex issues of Western water. A survey of the West's three great rivers—the Colorado, the Columbia, and the Missouri—this work includes material that reaches to the heart of the West—its ways of life, its politics, and its aspirations. *Western Water Made Simple* approaches these three river basins in terms of overarching themes combined with case studies—the Columbia in an age of reform, the Colorado in the midst of a fight for control, and the Missouri in search of its destiny.

1987. 224 pp., maps, photographs, bibliography, index.
Paper, ISBN 0-933280-39-4. $15.95

The Report of the President's Commission on Americans Outdoors: The Legacy, The Challenge
With Case Studies
Preface by William K. Reilly

"If there is an example of pulling victory from the jaws of disaster, this report is it. The Commission did more than anyone expected, especially the administration. It gave Americans something serious to think about if we are to begin saving our natural resources."—Paul C. Pritchard, President, National Parks and Conservation Association.

This report is the first comprehensive attempt to examine the impact of a changing American society and its recreation habits since the work of the Outdoor Recreation Resource Review Commission, chaired by Laurance Rockefeller in 1962. The President's Commission took more than two years to complete its study; the Report contains over sixty recommendations, such as the preservation of a nationwide network of "greenways" for recreational purposes and the establishment of an annual $1 billion trust fund to finance the protection and preservation of our recreational resources. The Island Press edition provides the full text of the report, much of the additional material compiled by the Commission, and twelve selected case studies.

1987. xvi, 426 pp., illus., appendixes, case studies.
Paper, ISBN 0-933280-36-X. $24.95

Public Opinion Polling: A Handbook for Public Interest and Citizen Advocacy Groups
By Celinda C. Lake, with Pat Callbeck Harper

"Lake has taken the complex science of polling and written a very usable 'how-to' book. I would recommend this book to both candidates and organizations interested in professional, low-budget, in-house polling."
—Stephanie Solien, Executive Director, Women's Campaign Fund.

Public Opinion Polling is the first book to provide practical information on planning, conducting, and analyzing public opinion polls as well as guidelines for interpreting polls conducted by others. It is a book for anyone—candidates, state and local officials, community organizations, church groups, labor organizations, public policy research centers, and coalitions focusing on specific economic issues—interested in measuring public opinion.

1987. x, 166 pp., tables, bibliography, appendix, index.
Paper, ISBN 0-933280-32-7. $19.95
Companion software now available.

Green Fields Forever: The Conservation Tillage Revolution in America
By Charles E. Little

"*Green Fields Forever* is a fascinating and lively account of one of the most important technological developments in American agriculture. . . . Be prepared to enjoy an exceptionally well-told tale, full of stubborn inventors, forgotten pioneers, enterprising farmers—and no small amount of controversy."—Ken Cook, World Wildlife Fund and The Conservation Foundation.

Here is the book that will change the way Americans think about agriculture. It is the story of "conservation tillage"—a new way to grow food that, for the first time, works *with*, rather than against, the soil. Farmers who are revolutionizing the course of American agriculture explain here how conservation tillage works. Some environmentalists think there are problems with the methods, however; author Charles E. Little demonstrates that on this issue both sides have a case, and the jury is still out.

1987. 189 pp., illus., appendixes, index, bibliography.
Cloth, ISBN 0-933280-35-1. $24.95
Paper, ISBN 0-933280-34-3. $14.95

Federal Lands: A Guide to Planning, Management, and State Revenues
By Sally K. Fairfax and Carolyn E. Yale

"An invaluable tool for state land managers. Here, in summary, is every-thing that one needs to know about federal resource management policies."—Rowena Rogers, President, Colorado State Board of Land Commissioners.

Federal Lands is the first book to introduce and analyze in one accessible volume the diverse programs for developing resources on federal lands. Offshore and onshore oil and gas leasing, coal and geothermal leasing, timber sales, grazing permits, and all other programs that share receipts and revenues with states and localities are considered in the context of their common historical evolution as well as in the specific context of current issues and policy debates.

1987. xx, 252 pp., charts, maps, bibliography, index.
Paper, ISBN 0-933280-33-5. $24.95

Hazardous Waste Management: Reducing the Risk
By Benjamin A. Goldman, James A. Hulme, and Cameron Johnson for the Council on Economic Priorities

Hazardous Waste Management: Reducing the Risk is a comprehensive sourcebook of facts and strategies that provides the analytic tools needed by policy makers, regulating agencies, hazardous waste generators, and host communities to compare facilities on the basis of site, management, and technology. The Council on Economic Priorities' innovative ranking system applies to real-world, site-specific evaluations, establishes a con-sistent protocol for multiple applications, assesses relative benefits and risks, and evaluates and ranks ten active facilities and eight leading commercial management corporations.

1986. xx, 316 pp., notes, tables, glossary, index.
Cloth, ISBN 0-933280-30-0. $64.95
Paper, ISBN 0-933280-31-9. $34.95

An Environmental Agenda for the Future
By Leaders of America's Foremost Environmental Organizations

". . . a substantive book addressing the most serious questions about the future of our resources."—John Chafee, U.S. Senator, Environmental and Public Works Committee. "While I am not in agreement with many of the positions the authors take, I believe this book can be the basis for constructive dialogue with industry representatives seeking solutions to environmental problems."—Louis Fernandez, Chairman of the Board, Monsanto Corporation.

The chief executive officers of the ten major environmental and conservation organizations launched a joint venture to examine goals that the environmental movement should pursue now and into the twenty-first century. This book presents policy recommendations for implementing changes needed to bring about a healthier, safer world. Topics discussed include nuclear issues, human population growth, energy strategies, toxic waste and pollution control, and urban environments.

1985. viii, 155 pp., bibliography.
Paper, ISBN 0-933280-29-7. $9.95

Water in the West
By Western Network

Water in the West is an essential reference tool for water managers, public officials, farmers, attorneys, industry officials, and students and professors attempting to understand the competing pressures on our most important natural resource: water. Here is an in-depth analysis of the effects of energy development, Indian rights, and urban growth on other water users.

1985. *Vol. III: Western Water Flows to the Cities*
v, 217 pp., maps, table of cases, documents, bibliography, index.
Paper, ISBN 0-933280-28-9. $25.00

These titles are available directly from Island Press, Box 7, Covelo, CA 95428. Please enclose $2.75 shipping and handling for the first book and $1.25 for each additional book. California and Washington, DC residents add 6% sales tax. A catalog of current and forthcoming titles is available free of charge. Prices subject to change without notice.